BANKING AND BANKING DEVELOPMENTS

COMMUNITY BANKS

ISSUES, TRENDS, AND PERFORMANCE

BANKING AND BANKING DEVELOPMENTS

Additional books in this series can be found on Nova's website under the Series tab.

Additional E-books in this series can be found on Nova's website under the E-book tab.

BANKING AND BANKING DEVELOPMENTS

COMMUNITY BANKS

ISSUES, TRENDS, AND PERFORMANCE

CHRISTOPHER B. JOSEPH
EDITOR

nova publishers
New York

Library of Congress Cataloging-in-Publication Data

ISBN: 978-1-62618-906-5

Published by Nova Science Publishers, Inc. † New York

CONTENTS

PREFACE

This book provides an overview of an FDIC Community Banking Study which identifies and explores the issues and questions relating to community banks. To study community banks, it is necessary to define them. In the past, most analysts have used a maximum asset size, often $1 billion. However, using only a size cutoff does not account for industry growth, and the attributes associated with community banks are not exclusively tied to size. The value of community banks has always been associated with the unique combination of services they provide to their customers, as well as the manner in which they do business. Community banks tend to be relationship lenders, characterized by local ownership, local control, and local decision making. By carrying out the traditional banking functions of lending and deposit gathering on a local scale, community banks foster economic growth and help to ensure that the financial resources of the local community are put to work on its behalf. Community banks have always been inextricably connected to entrepreneurship. As of 2011, they held 14 percent of banking industry assets, but 46 percent of the industry's small loans to farms and businesses.

Chapter 1 - The FDIC Community Banking Study is a data-driven effort to identify and explore issues and questions about community banks. The first chapter develops a research definition for the community bank that is used throughout the study. Subsequent chapters address, in turn, structural change, the geography of community banking, comparative financial performance, community bank balance sheet strategies, and capital formation at community banks. This study is intended to be foundational, providing a platform for future research and analysis by the FDIC and other interested parties.

Chapter 2 - A bank's efficiency ratio is defined as the ratio of a bank's non-interest expense to revenues. Higher efficiency ratios indicate less efficient banks. While there are many slightly modified definitions of the efficiency ratio, this basic ratio measures a bank's ability to generate revenues from its non-funding-related expense base.

The FDIC Community Banking Study finds that the efficiency ratios of community and noncommunity banks have diverged over time, especially since the late 1990s. The analysis in the FDIC Community Bank Study compares asset-weighted average efficiency ratios for community banks (CBs) and noncommunity banks (NCBs) over the period 1984-2011. Over this period, the banking system experienced a substantial wave of consolidation, including the formation of very large NCB institutions over the second half of the 1990s and again more recently during the financial crisis. The consolidation among NCBs has led to a high concentration of banking system assets in relatively few large institutions.

An implication of the consolidation trend is that NCB asset-weighted average efficiency ratios are heavily influenced by the efficiency ratios of the very largest NCBs, especially since the late 1990s. The largest NCBs often have very different business models compared with smaller institutions (both CBs and NCBs). These business models include wholesale banking, capital markets, and derivative market making, which are often only conducted in the largest financial institutions. These activities may give rise to a very different efficiency ratio profile compared with smaller CB and NCB institutions, making it important to control for the shift in asset concentration toward the largest NCBs when analyzing the trends in the efficiency ratios of CBs and NCBs.

In the first section of this paper, the authors control for this consolidation trend by examining the median efficiency ratios of CBs and NCBs over time. The authors' analysis shows that asset concentration in the largest NCBs does affect the efficiency performance comparison between CBs and NCBs.

Still, after correcting for the increase in asset concentration among the largest NCBs, the overall conclusions of the FDIC Community Banking Study remain; CB efficiency ratios have increased relative to NCBs over the 1984-2011 time period.

In the second section of this paper, the authors provide additional detail regarding the estimates on CB economies of scale reported in the FDIC Community Banking Study. Economies of scale are often thought to be an important factor that encourages consolidation among smaller financial institutions. There is a large literature on measuring cost economies of scale in banking, but the literature that relates to community bank-sized institutions mostly uses data from the 1980s and early 1990s. The authors revisit the important issue of cost economies of scale using more recent CB data and newer estimation techniques than are typically found in the existing literature. Still, the authors' findings are broadly consistent with historical literature that focuses on banks in the size range of modern community banks. While the authors' specific results on economies of scale depend on a CB's lending specialization, the authors' estimates provide no indication of any significant scale benefits beyond $500 million in asset size for most lending specializations. Further, the authors' estimates suggest that, in many cases, most of the cost benefits from scale appear to be achieved for CBs as small as $100 million. While economies of scale are important for community banks, historical trends in the size distribution of community banks that have survived over the last quarter century do not suggest that economies of scale require a community bank to grow or merge to asset sizes larger than $1 billion. Of the community banks that have survived the last quarter century, 60 percent remain under $200 million and many remain under $100 million in asset size.

Chapter 3 - An important measure of bank profitability is return on assets (ROA). For banks with similar business risk profiles, pretax ROA is a useful statistic for comparing the profitability of banks because it avoids distortions that are introduced by differences in financial leverage and complications in the tax laws. The authors control for the differences in economic conditions among bank markets by focusing the authors' analysis on community banks (CBs) that primarily operate in a single county. Even among this select group of CBs, ROA displays wide variation both across banks within a quarter and among banks over time.

Chapter 4 - Statement of Doreen R. Eberley (Director), Bret D. Edwards (Director), Richard A. Brown (Chief Economist), The Federal Deposit Insurance Corporation.

In: Community Banks
Editor: Christopher B. Joseph

ISBN: 978-1-62618-906-5

Chapter 1

FDIC COMMUNITY BANKING STUDY*

Federal Deposit Insurance Corporation

EXECUTIVE SUMMARY

The FDIC Community Banking Study is a data-driven effort to identify and explore issues and questions about community banks. The first chapter develops a research definition for the community bank that is used throughout the study. Subsequent chapters address, in turn, structural change, the geography of community banking, comparative financial performance, community bank balance sheet strategies, and capital formation at community banks. This study is intended to be foundational, providing a platform for future research and analysis by the FDIC and other interested parties.

Defining the Community Bank

To study community banks, it is necessary to define them. In the past, most analysts have used a maximum asset size, often $1 billion. However, using only a size cutoff does not account for industry growth, and the attributes associated with community banks are not exclusively tied to size. To overcome these problems, the study develops a new research definition of a community bank around criteria related to traditional lending and deposit gathering activities and limited geographic scope. Based on this definition, there were 7,658 FDIC-insured community banks operating within 6,914 separate banking organizations (or 94 percent of all banking organizations) as of year-end 2010. Importantly, the new definition captures 330 larger banking organizations that might have been excluded if asset size were the only criterion used.

* This is an edited, reformatted and augmented version of the Federal Deposit Insurance Corporation, dated December 2012.

Community Banks Retain a Unique Identity

Far-reaching changes in the U.S. financial sector in recent decades have made community banks a smaller part of our financial system. Of the U.S. credit market debt held by domestic financial intermediaries, the share held by U.S. chartered banks declined by almost half between 1984 and 2011, from 49 percent to 25 percent.[1] Over the same period, the share of U.S. banking assets held by community banks declined by more than half, from 38 percent to 14 percent.

Despite these changes, this study demonstrates that community banks continue to play a unique and important role in our economy. As of 2011, community banks made up 92 percent of FDIC-insured banks and 95 percent of U.S. banking organizations. The study shows that community banks hold the majority of banking deposits in U.S. rural and micropolitan counties, and that there are more than 600 counties—or almost one out of every five U.S. counties—that have no other physical banking offices except those operated by community banks.

The value of community banks has always been associated with the unique combination of services they provide to their customers, as well as the manner in which they do business. Community banks tend to be relationship lenders, characterized by local ownership, local control, and local decision making. By carrying out the traditional banking functions of lending and deposit gathering on a local scale, community banks foster economic growth and help to ensure that the financial resources of the local community are put to work on its behalf. Community banks have always been inextricably connected to entrepreneurship. As of 2011, they held 14 percent of banking industry assets, but 46 percent of the industry's small loans to farms and businesses.

The Implications of Banking Industry Consolidation

Consolidation in the U.S. banking industry is a multi-decade trend that reduced the number of federally insured banks from 17,901 in 1984 to 7,357 in 2011. Over this period, the number of banks with assets less than $25 million declined by 96 percent. The decline in the number of banks with assets less than $100 million was large enough to account for all of the net decline in total banking charters over this period. Meanwhile, the largest banks—those with assets greater than $10 billion—grew elevenfold in size over this period, raising their share of industry assets from 27 percent in 1984 to 80 percent in 2011.

These trends took place in the context of powerful historical forces that were highly conducive to consolidation, particularly in the first half of the study period. One of these forces has been bank failures. Altogether, some 2,555 banks and thrifts failed during the study period, mostly as a result of the banking crisis of the late 1980s and early 1990s and the financial crisis that began in 2007. From this experience, it is clear that the future pace of industry consolidation depends in large part on whether the coming years are marked by a period of financial stability or another wave of bank failures. The stronger the risk management practices of community banks, and the more effective the supervisory policies put in place by regulators, the less consolidation will take place as a result of failures.

Most of the consolidation that took place during the study period came about through mergers of banks belonging to different organizations and consolidation of banks within organizations. In all, some 7,583 banks exited the industry through merger during the study period, while another 4,929 exited through consolidation. In order to evaluate the implications of these trends, it is useful to consider why they occurred. One of the most important factors driving voluntary consolidation during this period was the relaxation of restrictions on intrastate branching and interstate banking that took place in the 1980s and early 1990s. Based largely in state law, these long-standing restrictions had the effect of artificially inflating the number of banking charters, and their removal was bound to result in consolidation. In the former unit banking states, for example, banking organizations that were prohibited from operating branches could instead operate separate charters within their organization. The same was true for banking organizations that crossed state lines, where interstate banking and branching were frequently restricted prior to the mid-1980s.

With the relaxation of restrictions on branching and interstate banking in the late 1980s and early 1990s, the pace of mergers and consolidations gathered steam. Between 1995 and 1998, the period immediately following the passage of the Riegle-Neal Act, an average of 5.7 percent of banks merged or consolidated each year. However, a slowing pace of mergers and consolidations suggests that the effects of these regulatory changes are beginning to wane. In the pre-crisis period between 2004 and 2007, this yearly average of mergers and consolidations fell to 3.7 percent.

It is possible that such forces as financial innovation, technology and regulatory developments could lead to additional consolidation. However, it is not clear that these forces would operate on the same scale as the past waves of consolidation that have resulted from the relaxation of branching and geographic restrictions or from failures.

The Implications of Geography

Although most banking offices operated by both community and noncommunity banks are located in metro counties, this study describes how community banks have a particular relevance in nonmetro counties—the small towns and rural areas that make up most of the country by area. Community banks are almost three times more likely than noncommunity banks to operate a banking office outside a metro area, and they hold the majority of banking deposits in both micropolitan and rural counties.

While the prevalence of community banks in nonmetro areas remains part of their unique identity, it may come at the cost of size and growth. Nonmetro areas accounted for just 16 percent of U.S. population in 2011, and just over 12 percent of U.S. economic output. Moreover, they experienced consistently slower rates of growth in population and economic output during the study period. Fifty percent of rural counties lost population between 1980 and 2010, continuing a long-term trend that has accelerated since the 2000 census.

These disparities in population and growth have not necessarily hurt the financial performance of community banks that operate in nonmetro areas. Both community and noncommunity banks headquartered in nonmetro areas outperformed their counterparts headquartered in metro areas on the basis of pretax return on assets (ROA) for the study period as a whole and for each five-year interval for which the comparison was made. Even the 1,091 community banks headquartered in depopulating rural counties in 2011 outperformed their counterparts headquartered in metro areas over the past decade. Instead, the disparities between metro and nonmetro counties are reflected in the growth rates of the institutions headquartered there. Banks headquartered in metro areas in 2011 that also operated in 1984 grew more than twice as fast over that interval as similar banks headquartered in nonmetro areas.

One of the reasons that noncommunity banks were able to accumulate an 86 percent share of industry assets during the study period was their ability to shift their activities to (and accumulate market share in) fast-growing metro areas. In the 21 fastest-growing U.S. metro areas with population of more than one million in 2011, 237 noncommunity banks were able to accumulate a 90 percent deposit share in part by directly or indirectly acquiring nearly 8,700 banks during the study period. Moreover, as described in Chapters 2 and 5, asset growth at noncommunity banks was led by mortgage and consumer lending during a period when these loan types were expanding rapidly. Between 1984 and 2011, total U.S. mortgage debt grew 7.7 times while total consumer debt grew fivefold.[2]

Most of this growth, however, predated the financial crisis that began in 2007. The crisis marked a sudden interruption of a long-term cycle of rising home prices, rising mortgage and consumer debt, and expanding residential construction activity that not only fueled balance sheet expansion at noncommunity banks, but also provided much of the impetus for economic growth in metro areas and for the U.S. as a whole. Whether metro-area growth continues to fuel the expansion of mortgage and consumer loan portfolios at noncommunity banks in the years ahead depends in no small part on the extent to which the pre-crisis pattern of growth reasserts itself in coming years.

Some signs suggest that the future pattern of U.S. economic growth may not be a replay of the past 25 years. The composition of U.S. economic output has undergone something of a shift away from some of the sectors that boomed before the financial crisis. Between 2006 and 2011, the share of U.S. economic output derived from construction, retail trade, and finance, insurance and real estate declined by 2.3 percentage points, while the share derived from mining, utilities and agriculture, forestry, and fishing expanded by 0.7 percentage points.[3] To the extent that this shift in the pattern of growth persists, it could help to mitigate the disparity in growth rates between metro and nonmetro areas that has limited the growth potential of community banks.

The Implications of Performance Gaps between Community and Noncommunity Banks

The study identifies some long-term gaps in profitability and efficiency between community and noncommunity banks. Between 1993 and 2006, noncommunity banks reported a pretax ROA that averaged 35 basis points higher than for community banks. This was a period characterized by high consumer spending and borrowing, as well as significant banking industry consolidation through which noncommunity banks increased their market share through acquisitions.

While it is true that community banks have earned a lower average pretax ROA than noncommunity banks over the past 15 years, most community banks in most periods have been profitable. Moreover, there are readily identifiable segments of the community banking sector that have posted earnings that are relatively high and stable. One such group is community banks that operated continuously from 1984 through 2011. Their weighted average pretax ROA over the study period was one basis point higher than that of continuously operating noncommunity banks.

One element of the performance gap has been a narrowing of the traditional advantage that community banks have had in generating net interest income in recent years as the net interest margin (the spread between asset yields and funding costs) has narrowed. Because of their focus on traditional lending and deposit gathering, community banks derive 80 percent of their revenue from net interest income compared with about two-thirds at noncommunity banks. Accordingly, the narrowing of net interest margins places a significant drag on the earnings of community banks.

The historically low level of interest rates in recent years has been an important factor pushing down net interest margins at community banks. The heavy reliance of community banks on deposit funding—typically an advantage during periods of higher interest rates—has been more problematic in recent years as community banks have found it difficult to pass along ultra-low interest rates to their deposit customers.

Another factor contributing to the earnings gap between community and noncommunity banks has been the ability of noncommunity banks to generate noninterest income from a wider variety of sources. These include trading, venture capital and investment banking activities that are not typically part of the community banking model. Noninterest income averaged 2.05 percent of assets at noncommunity banks over the study period compared with only 0.8 percent at community banks.

While the disparity in performance between community banks and noncommunity banks has been driven by revenue, the study also explores community bank credit losses and overhead expenses. Community banks have almost always incurred lower credit losses than noncommunity banks. This difference has been most notable in economic downturns, and is likely a result of the relationship lending approach favored by most community banks. Community banks also have traditionally incurred lower noninterest expenses than noncommunity banks, and their ratio of noninterest expenses to assets remained fairly steady over the study period. Noncommunity banks were able to lower their noninterest expenses as a percent of assets in the pre-crisis years by reducing average expenses associated with employees and premises.

One question the study tried to address was how regulatory costs have changed for community banks over time. Unfortunately, the data available through Call Reports and other regulatory filings do not provide a breakdown of regulatory versus other types of noninterest expenses. As part of this study, the FDIC conducted interviews with nine community bankers to better understand what drives the cost of regulatory compliance at their bank (see Appendix B). Most interview participants stated that while no one regulation or practice had a significant effect on their institution, the cumulative effects of regulatory requirements led them to increase staff over the past ten years. Moreover, the interviews indicated that it would be costly in itself to collect more detailed information about regulatory costs. As a result, measuring the effect of regulation remains an important question that presents substantial challenges.

The performance gap between community and noncommunity banks can also be expressed in terms of the efficiency ratio (the ratio of noninterest expense to net operating revenue). An "efficiency gap" in favor of noncommunity banks grew from 1.3 percent in 1998 to 9.7 percent in 2011. By 2011, noncommunity banks on average generated a dollar in net operating revenue for every 60 cents in noninterest expenses incurred, while community banks generated a dollar of revenue for every 70 cents in noninterest expenses. While the efficiency ratio of noncommunity banks declined (improved) through much of the study period because of lower noninterest expenses, those gains largely dissipated after the onset of the crisis that began in 2007. Instead, the efficiency gap that emerged between 1998 and 2011 was almost entirely attributable to a cumulative 8 percentage point increase (deterioration) in the efficiency ratio of community banks.

Why did community banks become so much less efficient in generating revenue after 1998? A relatively small portion (20 percent) of the net deterioration in efficiency at community banks was attributable to higher noninterest expenses, all of which came about after 2008. A much larger portion (72 percent) of the net deterioration in efficiency at community banks is attributable to a decline in net interest income (discussed above), most of which occurred in the last five years of the study period.

Whether the performance gaps of recent years might persist into the future appears to depend on three factors. One is the extent to which new community bank charters enter the industry in coming years. *De novo* institutions typically require some time to become profitable, and can also be vulnerable to problems during economic downturns. If the number of new community bank charters in the next decade were to approach the 997 de novo community banks established in the 2000s, the likely result would be to push down the aggregate financial performance of community banks over that period.

The second factor that will determine the existence and size of any performance gaps going forward is the timing, speed and magnitude of the eventual increase in interest rates to levels more in line with historical norms. The longer this normalization in rates is delayed, the longer community banks will experience a squeeze on their net interest margin and the longer the current efficiency gap is likely to persist. At the same time, a large and abrupt increase in interest rates also carries risks to institutions that have increased their holdings of long-term assets in the current low-interest-rate environment.

The third factor that appears likely to shape the competitive playing field in coming years is the ability of large noncommunity banks to generate noninterest income and cut noninterest expenses. In the years immediately preceding the crisis, the largest noncommunity banks were able to generate significant amounts of noninterest income through a variety of sources, including securitization and other capital markets activities, mortgage origination and servicing, and service charges on deposit accounts. There is reason to question whether some elements of this revenue model will regain their former importance in the wake of the financial crisis. For example, the volume of private mortgage securitization remains more than 95 percent below its pre-crisis peak, and the market share of the top five mortgage originators fell by 6 percentage points in the first half of 2012 compared with the prior year.[4]

Similarly, the large reductions in the noninterest expense ratio of noncommunity banks that took place in the pre-crisis years may not be sustainable in the post-crisis period. In the aftermath of the crisis, large noncommunity banks have incurred billions of dollars in expenses associated with problems such as process deficiencies in mortgage underwriting and servicing, insufficient controls on trading activity, and misleading disclosures to investors in capital markets instruments. Through 2011, the ratio of noninterest expenses to average assets at noncommunity banks had already risen by more than 11 percent from its 2008 low for the study period. Deficiencies that have been identified in mortgage servicing, trading, and other income-generating activities may necessitate even higher expenditures on the part of noncommunity banks in the years ahead. These developments raise the possibility that much of the large decline in noninterest expenses at noncommunity banks that occurred before the crisis will be reversed as these deficiencies are fully addressed.

Finally, the large-scale consolidation that took place during the study period naturally leads to the question of whether it is related to economies of scale among community banks that might put smaller institutions at a competitive disadvantage. As part of this study, the FDIC conducted research designed to detect the presence of economies of scale among community banks that could prompt them to try to lower their average costs through growth.[5] These results show that most of the benefit from economies of scale is realized once community banks reach $100 million to $300 million in total assets, depending on the lending specialty. These results comport well with the experience of consolidation during the study period, during which the number of banks with assets less than $25 million declined by 96 percent, but the number of banks with assets between $100 million and $10 billion increased by 19 percent. This is where 65 percent of community banks operated in 2011. In short, there does not appear to be much evidence to suggest that economies of scale are an important source of competitive disadvantage for most community banks or that they will compel significant additional consolidation in the years ahead.

The Implications of Community Bank Lending Strategies

While many community banks hold relatively diversified asset portfolios, the study categorizes community banks into seven lending specialty groups to further explore the relationship between business model and long-term performance. As of 2011, about 57 percent of community banks were categorized as mortgage specialists, consumer specialists, commercial real estate (CRE) specialists, commercial and industrial (C&I) specialists, and agricultural specialists, while the rest were categorized into a group with multiple lending specialties or a group with no lending specialty. The no specialty group was the largest group in nearly every period, and is made up of banks that are diversified lenders or that tend to have more securities and fewer loans.

Community banks in the mortgage, agricultural and no specialty groups were generally the strongest and steadiest performers over the study period, reporting lower provision expenses to assets and a lower incidence of failure than each of the other four lending specialty groups. In addition, agricultural specialists and the no specialty group reported higher average pretax ROA than any of the other five groups across the study period. At the other end of the spectrum, CRE lending specialists turned out to be the lowest-performing lending specialty group by a variety of measures. They trailed the average ROA of all community banks by one-third, and failed more than twice as often as the average community bank.

While noncommunity banks shifted their loan portfolios away from commercial lending and toward retail lending during the study period, community banks shifted their portfolios toward loans secured by commercial real estate. Among the seven lending specialty groups identified in this study, CRE specialists became the largest specialty group between 2005 and 2009, peaking at just under 30 percent of all community banks. Still, the CRE category includes a variety of loan types that performed differently in the real estate downturn of the late 2000s. More than one-third of all CRE loans held by community banks in 2011 were secured by owner-occupied nonfarm nonresidential properties, meaning that they were essentially collateralized commercial loans. This type of lending increased among community banks in every specialty group over the study period. During the recent crisis, the performance of loans secured by nonfarm nonresidential properties was roughly comparable to that of C&I loans, with both loan types performing much better than the construction and development (C&D) loans that made up 16 percent of community bank CRE portfolios in 2011.

Despite the relatively strong long-term operating results obtained by community banks in the baseline mortgage, agricultural and no specialty groups, hundreds of community banks shifted out of these groups and into other lending specialties between 2000 and 2005, mostly by accumulating larger balances of C&D and other CRE loans. The community banks most likely to undertake such a shift in lending strategy after 2000 were those organized as C corporations, those chartered since 1980, those headquartered in a metro county or in a state where home prices were rising rapidly, and those with trust preferred securities (TruPS) outstanding at the holding company level.

While these alternative strategies initially provided a small performance advantage for community banks that shifted into them after 2000, they proved to be highly problematic during the crisis period that followed. Community banks that shifted to a C&D strategy failed almost five times more frequently than the average community bank between 2006 and 2011, while more than half of those that survived after 2008 were rated 3, 4 or 5 by bank supervisors. While the results were somewhat better for community banks that shifted to a more diversified CRE strategy, they, too, failed at almost twice the rate of all community banks after 2006, and after 2008 they were rated 3, 4 or 5 more than twice as often as banks that remained in one of the baseline specialty groups.

One of the factors that appears to have contributed to the shift from the baseline groups to the C&D and CRE strategies is the search for growth. Of community banks that belonged to one of the three baseline specialty groups in 2000, those that switched to a C&D strategy grew more than 90 percent faster on average between 2000 and 2005 than those that did not, while those that switched to a CRE strategy grew more than 80 percent faster. Community banks with a growth imperative in the first half of the 2000s were able to grow faster by raising their concentrations in C&D and CRE loans than by maintaining a specialty in mortgage or agricultural loans or by holding a diversified portfolio.

Targeted research further explores the role of bank management decisions in determining the pretax ROA of community banks by estimating a model that accounts for factors such as underwriting standards, loan growth, capital base, funding mix, lending specializations, and staffing in addition to local economic conditions. The results underscore the importance of a management approach that sticks to the basics, avoiding such practices as out-of-area lending and reliance on noncore funding, and emphasizing portfolio diversification and strong practices in loan underwriting and administration. These results also suggest a trade-off between growth and financial performance that appears to define the opportunity set facing many community banks.

The high credit losses and elevated failure rates experienced by CRE and C&D lenders during the two banking crises covered by the study period point to an important policy issue for future research. This study documents the considerable costs associated with credit losses and bank failures among the CRE specialist group. Clearly, concentrations in these loan types—particularly in the C&D category—can represent a significant risk during real estate market downturns. What this study does not document are the social benefits that arise from commercial real estate financing by community banks. In many respects, CRE lending exemplifies the type of local knowledge and local decision-making at which community banks excel. Not only is construction activity essential to economic activity and the quality of life in local communities, but community banks are very important providers of credit to the construction industry. Future research should further explore the appropriate policy balance between the social benefits and social costs of CRE lending by community banks.

The Implications of Community Bank Capital Strategies

The ability of any bank to consistently meet the credit needs of its borrowers over time depends on maintaining a solid base of equity capital. By standard measures, community banks reported higher capital ratios than noncommunity banks across the study period, and they mostly maintained this level of capitalization through internally generated sources of capital. Community banks reporting positive earnings set aside 57 percent of their net income as retained earnings during the study period. Retained earnings accounted for 48 percent of all additions to equity capital from internal and external sources—percentages that were in both cases substantially higher than for noncommunity banks. Retained earnings for community banks were at their highest as a percent of prior-period equity between the early 1990s and the mid-2000s—precisely the periods when their pretax ROA was also at its highest levels. In periods where earnings have faltered, retained earnings have declined sharply or become negative, requiring more community banks to raise capital from external sources.

Relatively few community banks were found to raise capital frequently from external sources during the study period. Of community banks operating in 2011, 42 percent had never raised external capital after their first year of operation, 40 percent had done so occasionally, and 19 percent had done so frequently, or more than once in five years on average.[6] The overall frequency of external capital raising by community banks rose after 2000, as TruPS became, for a time, more common on the balance sheets of bank holding companies. With the financial crisis that began in 2007, both community and noncommunity banks initially experienced large financial losses that temporarily reduced their capital ratios and diminished their ability to generate new capital through retained earnings. As a result, both groups of institutions expanded the frequency and volume of their capital raising from external sources. However, in every year of the study period, noncommunity banks raised external capital more frequently than community banks, and also made use of TruPS and the Troubled Asset Relief Program more frequently than community banks. By 2011, however, as earnings and capital ratios recovered from the crisis, both community and noncommunity banks began to return to a more normal mix of additions to capital through internal and external sources.

While community banks were found to rely less on external capital and more on retained earnings than noncommunity banks, the study showed that many community banks were able to access external sources of capital when needed. In many cases, they did so in response to financial difficulties or a desire to grow. One-third of the capital raises carried out by community banks during the study period were undertaken by "troubled" institutions, or those that had been rated 3, 4 or 5 within the past two years. During non-crisis periods, up to half of all capital raises undertaken by community banks were found to immediately precede an acquisition or a period of significant growth.

Taken together, these trends suggest a community banking sector that can generate most of the capital it needs through retained earnings. However, two important caveats to this conclusion are in order. First, the ability to generate capital internally depends on a healthy level of earnings. In periods where earnings have faltered, retained earnings have declined sharply or become negative, requiring more community banks to raise capital from external sources. Second, retained earnings can only be a sufficient source of capital if the asset base of the institution is not growing more rapidly than its earnings. Chapter 5 demonstrates how hundreds of community banks in relatively stable, high-performing lending specialties in 2000 pursued growth-oriented strategies centered on C&D and CRE lending that ultimately underperformed for many of them. Community banks with TruPS at the holding company level were almost twice as likely to undertake such a shift in strategy as those that did not use TruPS. The experience of community banks during the study period appears to indicate that maintaining a stable balance between growth and earnings has been the surest path to long-term viability.

Topics for Future Research

The detailed analysis of banking industry data in this study provides a basis for further research of community banking issues. The study points to the considerable costs associated with credit losses and bank failures among CRE specialists. Clearly, concentrations in CRE, and especially C&D lending, can represent significant risk during real estate market downturns. However, construction activity is essential to the economic activity in local communities. Further research should explore the appropriate policy balance between the social benefits and the social costs of CRE lending by community banks. The study tried to examine how regulatory costs for community banks have changed. Measuring the effect of regulation remains an important question that presents substantial challenges. The competitive effects of chartering policies, and the benefits and risks of chartering activity during boom periods, also warrant further study. Finally, as new technology continues to transform the financial sector, more research will be needed on the future implications for the community banking sector.

1. Defining the Community Bank

To begin a study of community banking, it is necessary to define what it means to be a community bank.[7] Most people are able to articulate the characteristics of community banks, as the characteristics tend to revolve around how and where a community bank conducts business. For example, community banks focus on providing traditional banking services in their local communities. They obtain most of their core deposits locally and make many of their loans to local businesses. For this reason, they are often considered to be "relationship" bankers as opposed to "transactional" bankers.[8] This means that they have specialized knowledge of their local community and their customers. Because of this expertise, community banks tend to base credit decisions on local knowledge and nonstandard data obtained through long-term relationships and are less likely to rely on the models-based underwriting used by larger banks.

This relationship approach to lending is particularly important to small businesses that rely on community banks for loans and other services. Small businesses, particularly small start-up companies, may be unable to satisfy the requirements of the more structured approach to underwriting that larger banks use. The relationship lending approach used by community banks is often the only avenue small businesses have to obtain loans and access other financial services.

Community banks can develop these close relationships with customers because they tend to be smaller in size and only conduct business locally. The larger the institution, and the more places it does business, the more difficult it is to manage relationships at a personal level.

Community banks are also more likely to be privately owned and locally controlled than larger banks. Even when community banks have public shares, they are usually not traded on the major exchanges. This means that community banks may weigh the competing interests of shareholders, customers, employees, and the local community differently from a larger institution with stronger ties to the capital markets.[9]

While a rough consensus exists on the attributes that describe a community bank, defining one clearly proves to be more difficult in practice. The standard method used by most bank analysts has been to define community banks according to their size, as measured by their assets. Some studies rely on various asset size limits in their analysis of community banking trends without actually specifying the size that separates community banks from other institutions.[10] Others do impose a specific size limit in their definition of community banks, even while acknowledging that size alone is an imperfect criterion and that fixed size limits can be arbitrary. Many of these studies use $1 billion in total assets as a limit, which is typically applied to individual banks rather than to all banks in a banking organization; that is, at the charter level rather than the banking organization level. Some studies, however, apply the definition at the level of the banking organization.[11] More recently, a $10 billion size limit has come to be used more frequently to define community banks.[12]

One problem with defining community banks using a fixed size limit is that any dollar-based yardstick must be adjusted over time to account for factors such as inflation, economic growth, and the size of the banking industry itself. According to any of these measures, $1 billion is not what it used to be. Between 1984 and 2011, the Consumer Price Index rose 2.1 times, while the size of the U.S. economy, in terms of nominal Gross Domestic Product, rose by 3.8 times. In addition, even as more financial transactions were taking place outside of the formal banking system, the total assets of federally insured banks and savings institutions also rose by 3.8 times.

The other problem with using a fixed size limit to define community banks is that the attributes associated with community banking are only loosely correlated with size. Some smaller institutions may have business specialties that are far removed from deposit gathering and lending to local customers, while some larger institutions may continue to do just that. Therefore, a closer look at the business and office structure of the institution is necessary to determine the extent to which it is focused on traditional lending and deposit gathering activities, as well as its geographic scope of operations.

This is precisely the approach used by the FDIC to arrive at a new research definition of the community bank. The FDIC research definition makes extensive use of financial reporting data on the balance sheet and number and location of offices for each bank. It uses the data to establish standard requirements for lending and deposit gathering and to set limits on the geographic scope of operations that a banking organization must meet to be designated as a community bank. The definition remains loosely based on size, but goes beyond size alone in separating community banks from noncommunity banks. Finally, the FDIC definition of a community bank offers potential benefits over purely size-based definitions in terms of minimizing the influence of outliers that could interfere with statistical comparisons between community and noncommunity banks.

The process of designating community banks for this purpose consists of five steps, described below. A summary of the designation process appears in Table 1.1, and details are described in Appendix A.

The first step in defining a community bank is to aggregate all charter-level data reported under each holding company into a single banking organization. This aggregation applies both to balance-sheet measures and the number and location of banking offices. At year-end 2011, there were 7,357 FDIC-insured banking charters operating within 6,720 separate banking organizations. Under the FDIC definition, if the banking organization is designated as a community bank, every charter reporting under that organization is also considered a community bank when working with data at the charter level.

The second step is to *exclude* any banking organization where more than 50 percent of total assets are held in certain specialty banking charters, including: *credit card specialists, consumer nonbank banks, industrial loan companies, trust companies, bankers' banks*, and banks holding 10 percent or more of total assets in foreign offices.[13]

Table 1.1. Summary of FDIC Research Denition of Community Banking Organizations

<table>
<tr><td colspan="2">Designate community banks at the level of the banking. All charters under designated holding companies are considered community banking charters.</td></tr>
<tr><td>Exclude:
Any organization with:
• No loans or no core deposits
• Foreign Assets ≥ 10% of total assets
• More than 50% of assets in certain specialty banks, including:
  • credit card specialists
  • consumer nonbank banks[1]
  • industrial loan companies
  • trust companies
  • bankers' banks</td><td>Include:
All remaining banking organizations with:
• Total assets < indexed size threshold[2]
• Total assets ≥ indexed size threshold, where:
  • Loan to assets > 33%
  • Core deposits to assets > 50%
  • More than 1 office but no more than the indexed maximum number of ofces.[3]
  • Number of large MSAs with offices ≤ 2
  • Number of states with offices ≤ 3
  • No single offices with deposits > indexed maximum branch deposit size.[4]</td></tr>
</table>

[1] Consumer nonbank banks are financial institutions with limited charters that can make commercial loans or take deposits, but not both.

[2] Asset size threshold indexed to equal $250 million in 1985 and $1 billion in 2010.

[3] Maximum number of offices indexed to equal 40 in 1985 and 75 in 2010.

[4] Maximum branch deposit size indexed to equal $1.25 billion in 1985 and $5 billion in 2010.

Source: FDIC.

Once the specialty organizations are removed, the third step involves including organizations that engage in basic banking activities as measured by the total loans-to-assets ratio (greater than 33 percent) and the ratio of core deposits to assets (greater than 50 percent). Analysis of the underlying data shows that these thresholds establish meaningful levels of basic lending and deposit gathering while still allowing for a degree of diversity in how individual banks construct their balance sheets.

The fourth step includes organizations that operate within a limited geographic scope. This limitation of scope is used as a proxy measure for a bank's relationship approach to banking. Banks that operate within a limited market area have more ease in managing relationships at a personal level. Under this step, four criteria are applied to each banking organization. They include both a minimum and maximum number of total banking offices, a maximum level of deposits for any one office, and location-based criteria. The limits on the number of and deposits per office are gradually adjusted upward over time. For banking offices, banks must have more than one office, and the maximum number of offices starts at 40 in 1985 and reaches 75 in 2010. The maximum level of deposits for any one office is $1.25 billion in deposits in 1985 and $5 billion in deposits in 2010. The remaining geographic limitations are also based on maximums for the number of states (fixed at 3) and large metropolitan areas (fixed at 2) in which the organization maintains offices.[14]

Finally, the definition establishes an *asset-size limit*, also adjusted upward over time from $250 million in 1985 to $1 billion in 2010, below which the limits on banking activities and geographic scope are waived. This final step acknowledges the fact that most of those small banks that are not excluded as specialty banks meet the requirements for banking activities and geographic limits in any event.[15]

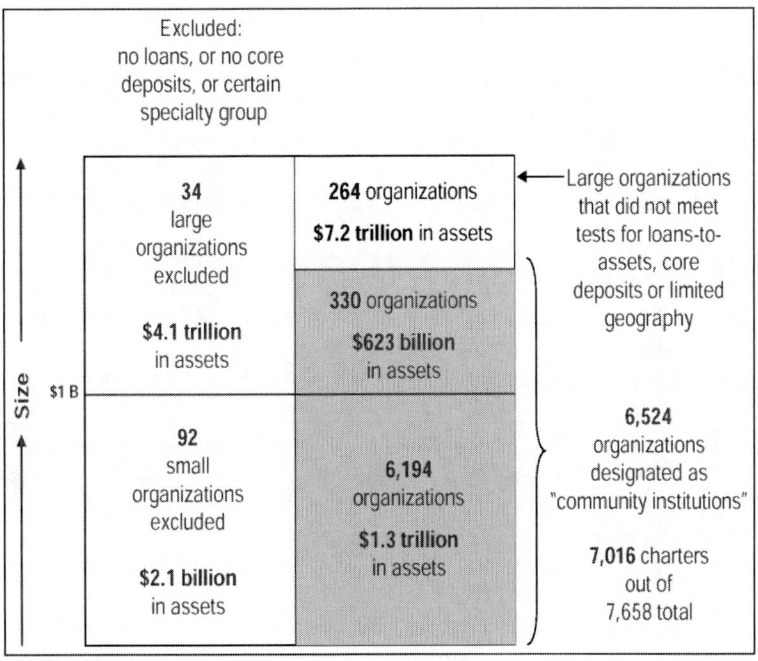

Source: FDIC.

Table 1.2. Designation of Community Banking Organizations at Year-End 2010, Using FDIC Research Criteria

WHO ARE THE NONCOMMUNITY BANKS?

While the FDIC's research focuses on refining the definition of a community bank and further analysis of that universe, it is important to review those institutions that were not identified as community banks. As of year-end 2010, there were 390 organizations that did not meet the definition of a community bank and were designated as noncommunity banks. Although noncommunity banks represent only 6 percent of all 6,914 banking organizations, they account for 63 percent of total U.S. banking offices and 85 percent of total industry assets.

Table 1.3. Composition of Noncommunity Banks Compared With Community Banks as of Year-End 2010

Noncommunity Bank Categories	Number of Organizations	%	Total Assets (in $ Billions)	%	Number of Offices	%
Four Largest Banking Organizations*	4	0%	5,989	45%	18,937	19%
Noncommunity Banks over $100 Billion	12	0%	2,172	16%	16,636	17%
Noncommunity Banks between $10 Billion and $100 Billion	76	1%	2,430	18%	15,112	15%
Noncommunity Banks between $1 Billion and $10 Billion	206	3%	764	6%	11,368	12%
Noncommunity Banks under $1 Billion	92	1%	21	0%	150	0%
Community Banks	6,524	94%	1,944	15%	36,274	37%
Industry Totals	6,914	100%	13,319	100%	98,477	100%

Source: FDIC.

* Includes 21 FDIC-insured institutions owned by the nation's four largest banking organizations by asset size: Bank of America Corporation; Citigroup Inc.; JP Morgan Chase & Company; and Wells Fargo & Company.

Note: Total asset data are based on the amounts reported by the holding company.

Total noncommunity banks were separated into the following size groups for further analysis: noncommunity banks under $1 billion, between $1 billion and $10 billion, between $10 billion and $100 billion, over $100 billion, and those institutions that are part of the four largest banking organizations (Bank of America Corporation; Citigroup Inc.; JP Morgan Chase & Company; and Wells Fargo & Company. Table 1.3 compares the number of organizations, total assets, and the number of offices for each of these noncommunity bank size groups against the corresponding totals for community banks and for the industry as of year-end 2010. The four largest banking organizations report the largest share of industry assets, with 45 percent; however, they report only 19 percent of the total number of industry offices. In comparison, community banks report 37 percent of the total number of industry offices, and 15 percent of industry assets.

While more detailed than a simple asset-size limit, the FDIC research definition of the community bank is entirely based on standard data reported by the financial institutions themselves or by federal government agencies. This ensures that the definition is as objective and transparent as possible, that it can be applied consistently across the 27-year period of the study, and that it can be replicated and used by other researchers.

Applying this research definition of the community bank shows that most banks are community banks. Of the 6,914 U.S. banking organizations reporting at year-end 2010, 94 percent were designated as community banks (Table 1.2).

Table 1.2 shows that the 390 banking organizations designated as noncommunity banks fell into three groups. The left side of the diagram shows that the 92 organizations with assets less than $1 billion, plus another 34 with assets greater than or equal to $1 billion, were excluded at the outset as specialty banks. Another 264 banking organizations (upper right of Table 1.2) failed to meet the requirements for banking activities and limited geography, and exceeded the 2010 asset-size limit of $1 billion under which those requirements could be waived.

The result was the designation of 6,524 banking organizations (holding 7,016 FDIC-insured charters) as community banks. Of these, 330 exceeded the $1 billion limit that might have identified them as noncommunity banks if a strict asset-size definition had been applied. The designation of these larger institutions as community banks is important, in that it shows that using asset-size limits alone could unnecessarily exclude relatively large banks that otherwise conduct business very much like other community institutions.

Summary

Community banks are known for their focus on traditional banking activities. Community banks mainly conduct lending and deposit gathering activities within a fairly limited market area. They are said to be relationship lenders, which rely to a significant degree on specialized knowledge gained through long-term business relationships. They are likely to be owned privately or have public shares that are not widely traded, and therefore tend to place the long-term interest of their local communities high relative to the demands of the capital markets. Since these attributes are generally—but not always—associated with smaller banking organizations, most previous studies have used asset size alone to define community banks.

Using detailed balance sheet and geographic data, this study goes further to define community banks primarily in terms of their traditional relationship banking and limited geographic scope of operations. Based on this definition, 94 percent of all U.S. banking organizations and 92 percent of FDIC-insured banking charters were community banks as of 2010. Importantly, the definition includes 330 institutions at year-end 2010 that met the criteria for community banks, but exceeded the size limit that might ordinarily have excluded them from this group. The remainder of the study employs this definition of the community bank to explore a range of structural, performance, and competitive issues.

2. Structural Change among Community and Noncommunity Banks

In the past 25 years, the number of banks has declined sharply. Between 1984 and 2011, the total number of federally insured bank and thrift charters declined by 59 percent, from 17,901 to 7,357. A confluence of new charters, failures, mergers between banking companies, and consolidation of charters within holding companies underlie this decline. Moreover, these changes and other structural changes in the industry (such as the enormous growth among the very largest banks) have taken place in distinct waves associated with banking crises and the business cycle and were influenced by regulatory changes that have generally been conducive to consolidation over time.

Community banks emerged from this period fewer in number and with a diminished share of banking industry assets. Nonetheless, they continue to represent by far the most common business model among FDIC-insured institutions.

This chapter analyzes the decline in the number of banks to determine the effects of consolidation, mergers, failures, and new charters individually. In order to gauge the stability of banks of differing asset size, rates of consolidation, merger, failure, and survivorship are calculated by asset size groups and for community and noncommunity banks. The impact of bank failures among different bank groups is captured by computing a failure index, which measures the frequency of failures within one group relative to failures for all banks during any period.

Consolidation

The banking industry experienced much consolidation during the study period from 1984 through 2011.[16] Of the 15,432 banks (as opposed to banking organizations) that exited the industry between 1984 and 2011, 17 percent failed, 49 percent merged with an unaffiliated bank, and another 32 percent consolidated with other charters within their existing bank holding company.[17] These failures, mergers, and consolidation have occurred in distinct waves. Most failures during the period (2,555 in all) occurred because of the banking and thrift crisis of the late 1980s and early 1990s and the financial crisis of 2007-2008 and its aftermath (see Chart 2.1). In contrast, only 47 institutions failed during the interval from 1996 to 2005.

Mergers peaked in the mid-1980s and mid-1990s, during periods of economic expansion (see Chart 2.2). The average number of unassisted mergers was 346 per year between 1985 and 2000 and declined to 182 per year from 2001 through 2011, with the three slowest years for merger activity occurring between 2009 and 2011. The annual number of intracompany consolidations (see Chart 2.3) also generally rose in the late 1980s and then declined after the mid-1990s. Charter consolidations averaged 234 per year between 1985 and 2000 but slowed to 107 per year from 2001 through 2011.

The relaxation of restrictions on intrastate branching and interstate banking that took place in the 1980s and early 1990s facilitated both mergers and consolidations. While only 16 states permitted unrestricted intrastate branching in 1984, by 1994 the number had risen to 40.[18] Similarly, while 42 states restricted interstate combinations of banking charters in 1984, by 1994 only Hawaii retained this restriction.[19] The Interstate Banking and Branching Efficiency (or Riegle-Neal) Act of 1994 allowed full interstate branching, which made possible the interstate consolidation of charters within banking companies.[20] While consolidation occurred throughout the 27-year period, mergers and consolidations peaked, both in number and as a percent of existing charters, in the latter half of the 1990s, soon after these restrictions were relaxed.

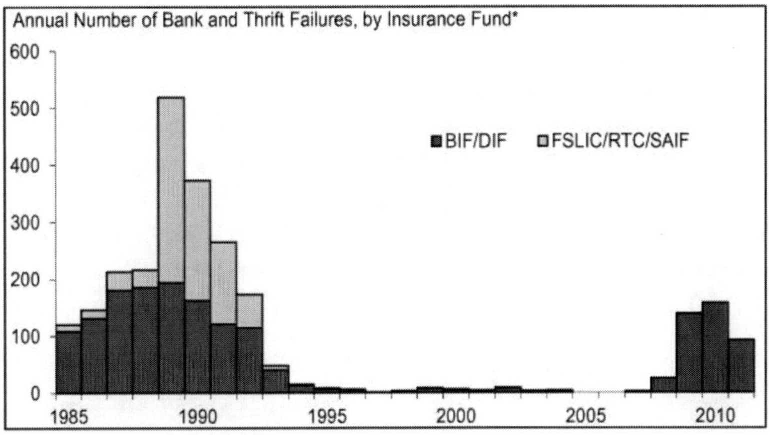

Source: FDIC.

* FSLIC/RTC/SAIF failures indicate those resolved by the Federal Savings and Loan Insurance Corporation (FSLIC), the Resolution Trust Corporation (RTC), or by the FDIC under its Savings Association Insurance Fund (SAIF). The SAIF was merged with the Bank Insurance Fund (BIF) to form the Deposit Insurance Fund (DIF) on March 31, 2006.

Chart 2.1. Bank and Thrift Failures Have Mostly Taken Place within Two Distinct Crises, Interrupted by More Than a Decade of Few Failures.

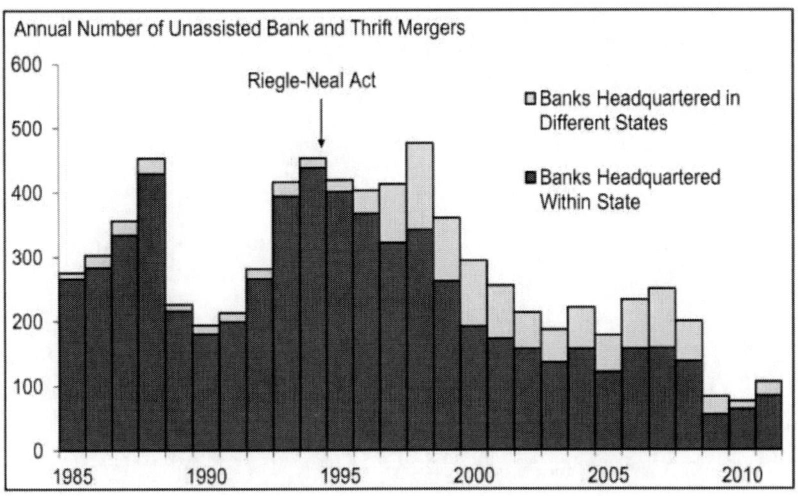

Source: FDIC.

Chart 2.2. Unassisted Mergers of Banks and Thrifts Peaked During the Economic Expansions of the 1980s and 1990s.

New Charters

Cutting against the consolidation trend since 1984, a large number of new charters were added to the industry over the study period. Some 4,888 new charters came into existence between 1984 and 2011, of which 83 percent were community banks as of their first year-end financial report. Chart 2.4 shows that these new charters arose in three distinct waves, all of which coincided with economic expansions. The first wave of new charters occurred during the mid-to-late 1980s, followed by smaller waves in the late-1990s and the mid-2000s. During these relatively prosperous years, rising loan demand created opportunities for new institutions to seek business, while generally strong bank equity share prices reflected the ready availability of capital to fund startup banks. As will be discussed later in the study, these plans were frequently put to the test within a few years as prosperity gave way to more difficult economic circumstances. Periods during and after recessions have been associated with much slower chartering activity, with the period from 2009 through 2011 marking the three slowest years of chartering activity over the 27-year study period.

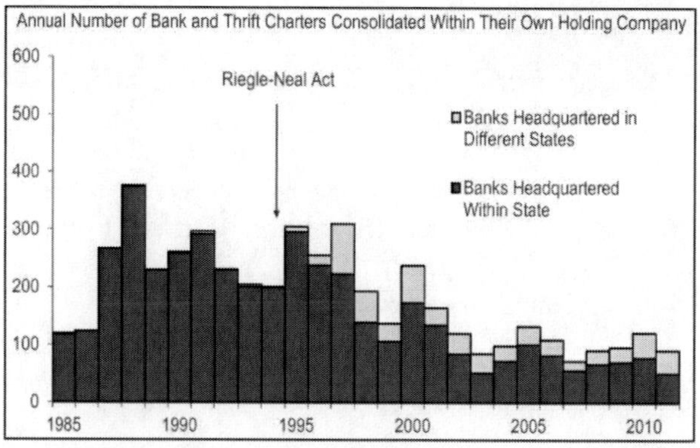

Source: FDIC.

Chart 2.3. Intracompany Consolidation of Charters Peaked between 1985 and 2000, and Has Since Leveled Off.

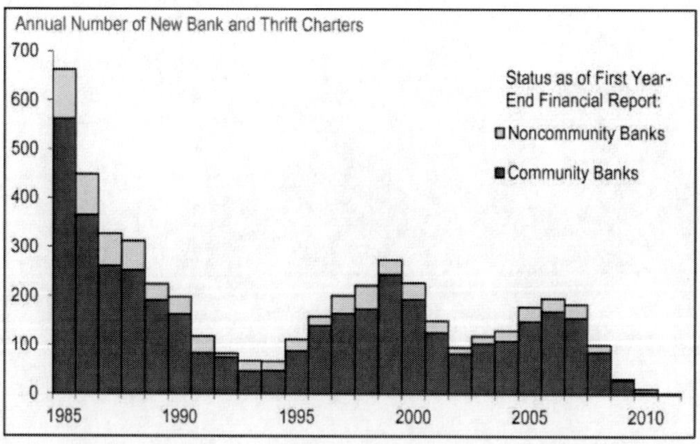

Source: FDIC.

Chart 2.4. New Bank and Thrift Charters Have Entered the Industry in Three Distinct Waves Since the Early 1980s.

The Net Effect of Structural Change

Chart 2.5 and Chart 2.6 depict the net effects of structural change in banking between 1984 and 2011 in terms of the total number and assets of banks and thrifts in five size groups. The net effect of structural change refers to the overall change in number and assets of banks and thrifts by size group without further adjustment. For example, some banks may have crossed from one size group to another during the study period. The chart reflects three important developments. The first is the net decline of 10,544 in the number of federally insured banking and thrift charters over this period. This net consolidation in total banking charters is more than fully accounted for by a gross decline of 11,392 in the number of banks in the smallest size class, with assets less than $100 million. The number of institutions in every other size class increased, on net, during this period. The second development is the enormous growth that took place among the largest banks. The number of institutions with assets greater than $10 billion grew from 32 to 107 during the period, while their assets grew from just over $1 trillion (27 percent of industry assets) in 1984 to $11.1 trillion (80 percent of industry assets) in 2011. The third development is the relative stability among institutions in the middle three size groups, with assets between $100 million and $10 billion, which grew in number by 19 percent and in assets by 24 percent over this 27-year period.

While these institutions between $100 million and $10 billion appear to have been the most stable group, in fact, their ranks were constantly being thinned over time by failures, mergers, and consolidations and replenished by new charters and growth among smaller institutions. Chart 2.7 shows that institutions starting out the period with assets between $100 million and $10 billion had *lower* survival rates and higher failure rates than both the smallest and the largest institutions. In addition, only the largest institutions, with assets greater than $10 billion, merged more often than these banks.

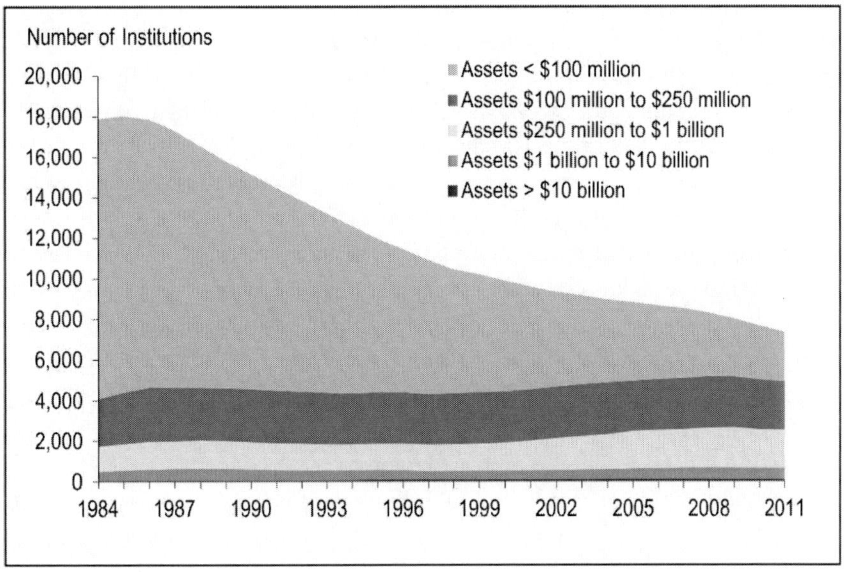

Source: FDIC.

Chart 2.5. Net Consolidation in Charters Has Occurred among the Smallest Banks and Thrifts.

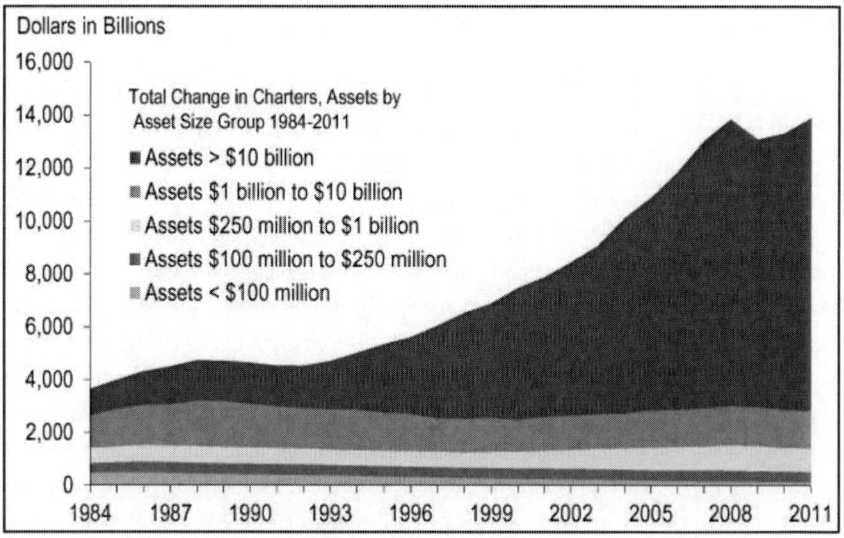

Source: FDIC.

Chart 2.6. Net Asset Consolidation Has Occurred among the Largest Banks and Thrifts.

In contrast, institutions starting out the period with assets less than $100 million—the group that would experience a net decline of 82 percent in their numbers by 2011—were in fact *more likely* than any other size group to survive the entire 27-year period. Institutions in this smallest size group were less likely to fail or merge than any other size group, while they consolidated at a rate that was similar to the other groups. Of all the institutions that started out in 1984 with total assets less than $100 million, 2,774 of them—or 20 percent of the total—not only survived until 2011 but grew into one of the larger size groups. In fact, 11 of them ended up as charters with over $10 billion in assets. Moreover, while most of the new charters that came into the industry during this period started out small, with 88 percent reporting less than $100 million in assets at their first year end, most of them tended to grow and move into larger size groups; 24 percent of the new charters that survived to 2011 continued to report assets less than $100 million at that time.

In the end, these cross-cutting trends lead to some paradoxical results. While the net number and assets of banks between $100 million and $10 billion have grown at a steady rate over time, this group has experienced more change in membership than either the smallest or the largest institutions. In addition, while the number of institutions in the smallest size group accounted for all the net decline in federally insured bank and thrift charters over this period, they were in fact the most stable group of institutions. Newly chartered institutions and other banks that started the period with assets less than $100 million were able to succeed and grow often enough to fully replenish the ranks of institutions between $100 million and $10 billion, which underwent the greatest degree of consolidation.

Structural consolidation also brought about the other main development reflected in Chart 2.6, the elevenfold increase in banking industry assets at charters with assets greater than $10 billion, giving these 107 institutions control of 80 percent of industry assets by 2011. About one-half of the increase in assets at these banks over the study period came directly from the acquisition and consolidation of other charters. In total, the 107 largest institutions directly acquired or consolidated 1,258 charters with $5.6 trillion in total assets.[21] In turn, these 1,258 acquisition targets had already directly or indirectly acquired or consolidated 7,515 other charters since the beginning of the study period in 1984. In this way, banks that closed the study period with assets greater than $10 billion directly or indirectly absorbed 57 percent of the charters that exited the industry between 1984 and 2011.

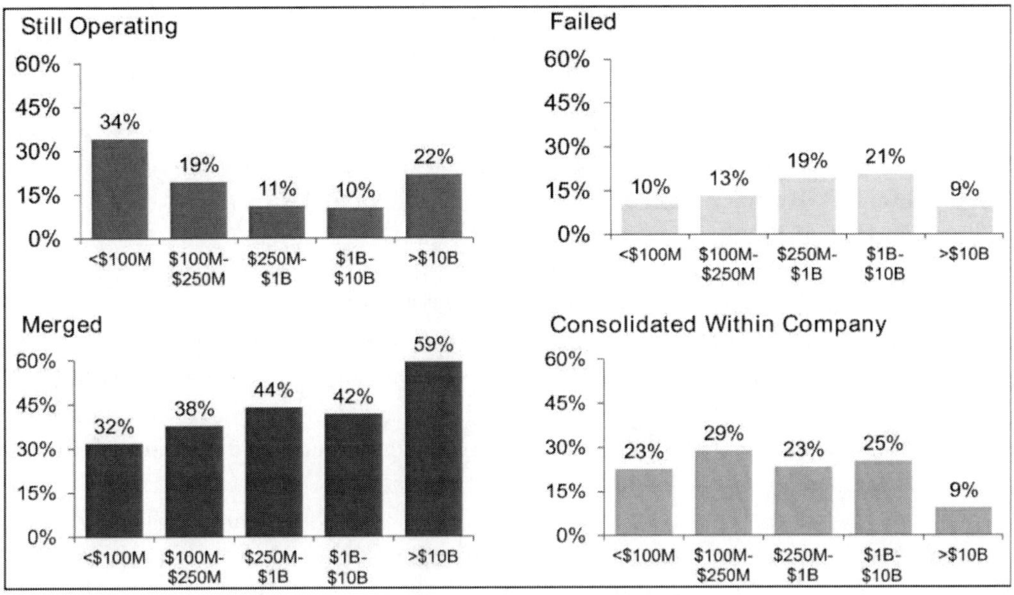

Source: FDIC.

Chart 2.7. Banks With Assets Less Than $100 Million in 1984 Experienced Less Structural Change Than Any Other Group, While Midsize Banks Experienced the Most.

INCREASED CONCENTRATION OF BANKING ASSETS IN THE VERY LARGEST INSTITUTIONS

Between 1984 and 2011, as the number of federally insured banks and thrift institutions was declining by 59 percent, total industry assets grew almost fourfold, from $3.7 trillion to $13.9 trillion. Banks with assets over $10 billion had almost all of this growth (see Chart 2.6). If this group is stratified further, however, growth within this group of banks was actually concentrated at the very largest banks, most notably in the four largest banking organizations as of year-end 2011: JP Morgan Chase & Co., Bank of America Corporation, Citigroup Inc., and Wells Fargo & Company. Total assets held by banks in just these four organizations increased from $228 billion in 1984 (6.2 percent of industry assets in 1984) to $6.1 trillion (44.2 percent of industry assets in 2011).

Assets held by other charters with assets over $10 billion also grew during this period, but their share of industry assets did not grow nearly as dramatically as the share held by the four largest banking organizations. At year-end 1984, the 29 banks with assets over $10 billion that were not part of today's four largest banking organizations held 22 percent of industry assets. Twenty-seven years later, 94 banks outside these four largest banking organizations held assets greater than $10 billion, and their share of industry assets had risen to 35 percent.

Between 1984 and 2011, the four largest banking organizations directly acquired 353 insured institutions with total assets of $2.5 trillion. These direct acquisition targets included many large institutions, with 24 reporting assets greater than $10 billion when they were acquired. In addition, the direct acquisition targets of the four largest banking organizations had previously acquired another 1,841 federally insured banks and thrifts, which we refer to as indirect acquisition targets.

Chart 2.8 depicts the share of industry assets held by banks in the four largest banking organizations in every quarter from year-end 1984 to year-end 2011, along with the total assets of institutions they would eventually acquire directly or indirectly. In 1984, the four largest banking organizations held just 6.2 percent of industry assets, but charters they would eventually acquire held another 31.4 percent of industry assets at that time. Summed together, the assets of the four largest banking organizations and their eventual acquisition targets represented 37.7 percent of industry asset in 1984, close to the industry share the four largest banking organizations would hold in 2011.

As these four banking organizations rapidly grew over time, the composition of their loan portfolios shifted toward retail lending. In 1984, one-to-four family mortgages represented just over 9 percent of their total loans, and loans to individuals made up another 17 percent. By 2011, one-to-four family mortgages made up 37 percent of total loan balances and loans to individuals almost 22 percent.

Retail loans have always represented a large share of banking industry loan portfolios, and that share increased from 45 percent in 1984 to 51 percent in 2011. A far more significant development over the period was the enormous increase in the share of total retail loans held by the top four banking organizations. The share of total one-to-four family mortgages held by these organizations rose from 2 percent in 1984 to 45 percent in 2011, while their share of loans to individuals rose from 8 percent to 51 percent.

As retail lending became much more concentrated at the largest banking organizations, community banks not only held a smaller share of total industry assets, but also loan portfolios that were more heavily concentrated in the various types of commercial loans.[1]

Acquisitions by these large banking organizations significantly expanded not just their balance sheets, but also their branch networks. The number of total banking offices operated by the top four banking organizations more than tripled to 18,743 between 1994 and 2011. During this period, these four banking organizations acquired institutions with 12,859 banking offices. Just under one-fifth of all U.S. branches in 2011 belonged to one of the top four banking organizations, compared with approximately 5 percent in 1994 (see Table 2.1). In 2011, the top four banking organizations operated at least one office in 43 percent of all U.S. counties.

These four banking organizations have greatly expanded their branch networks and share of total banking offices in the largest U.S. cities. In metropolitan statistical areas ranked in the top 25 percent by population, the top four banking organizations operated 26 percent of all banking offices in 2011 compared with just 6 percent in 1994.[2] For comparison, in all other U.S. metropolitan areas, the top four banking organizations held a 14 percent share of all branches in 2011 (Chart 2.9).

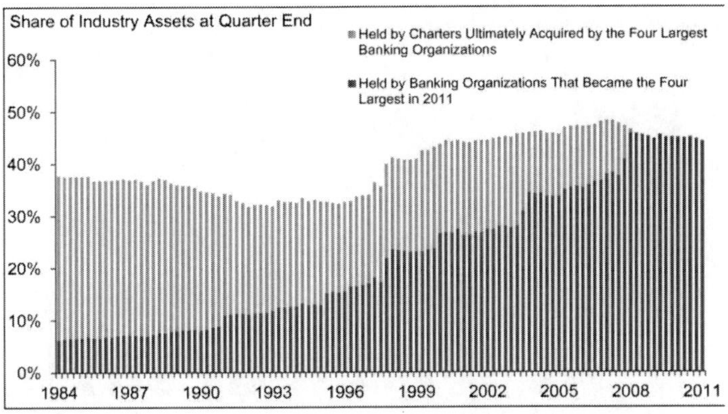

Source: FDIC.

Chart 2.8. Share of Industry Assets, 1984-2011, Held by Banking Organizations That Became the Four Largest by 2011.

Table 2.1. Total Offices of Banking Organizations That Became the Four Largest as of 2011

	Number of Banking Offices	Percent of Total U.S. Banking Offices
Total Banking Offices of the Four BHCs in 1994	3,904	4.8%
Offices Added Through Acquisition, 1994-2011	12,859	--
Total Banking Offices of the Four BHCs in 2011	18,743	19.1%

Source: FDIC.

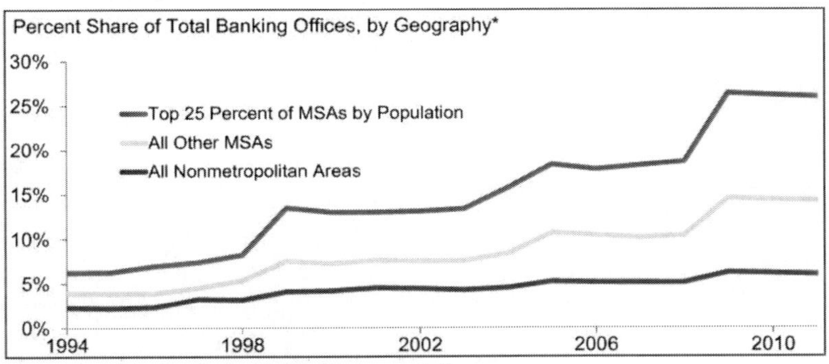

Sources: FDIC, Moody's Analytics, U.S. Bureau of Census.

Note: The four largest banking organizations as of year-end 2011 were: Bank of America Corporation, Citigroup Inc., JP Morgan Chase & Co., and Wells Fargo & Company.

*Calculated as the weighted average share of banking offices operated by organizations that became the four largest as of 2011. Metropolitan Statistical Areas (MSAs) are ranked in size according to 2011 total population.

Chart 2.9. The Four Largest Banking Organizations Have Greatly Expanded Their Branch Networks and Office Share in the Largest U.S. Cities.

[1] Changes in the composition of community bank loan portfolios are discussed in more detail in Chapter 5, Comparative Performance of Community Bank Lending Specialty Groups.

[2] The population ranking is based on Moody's data as of June 2011.

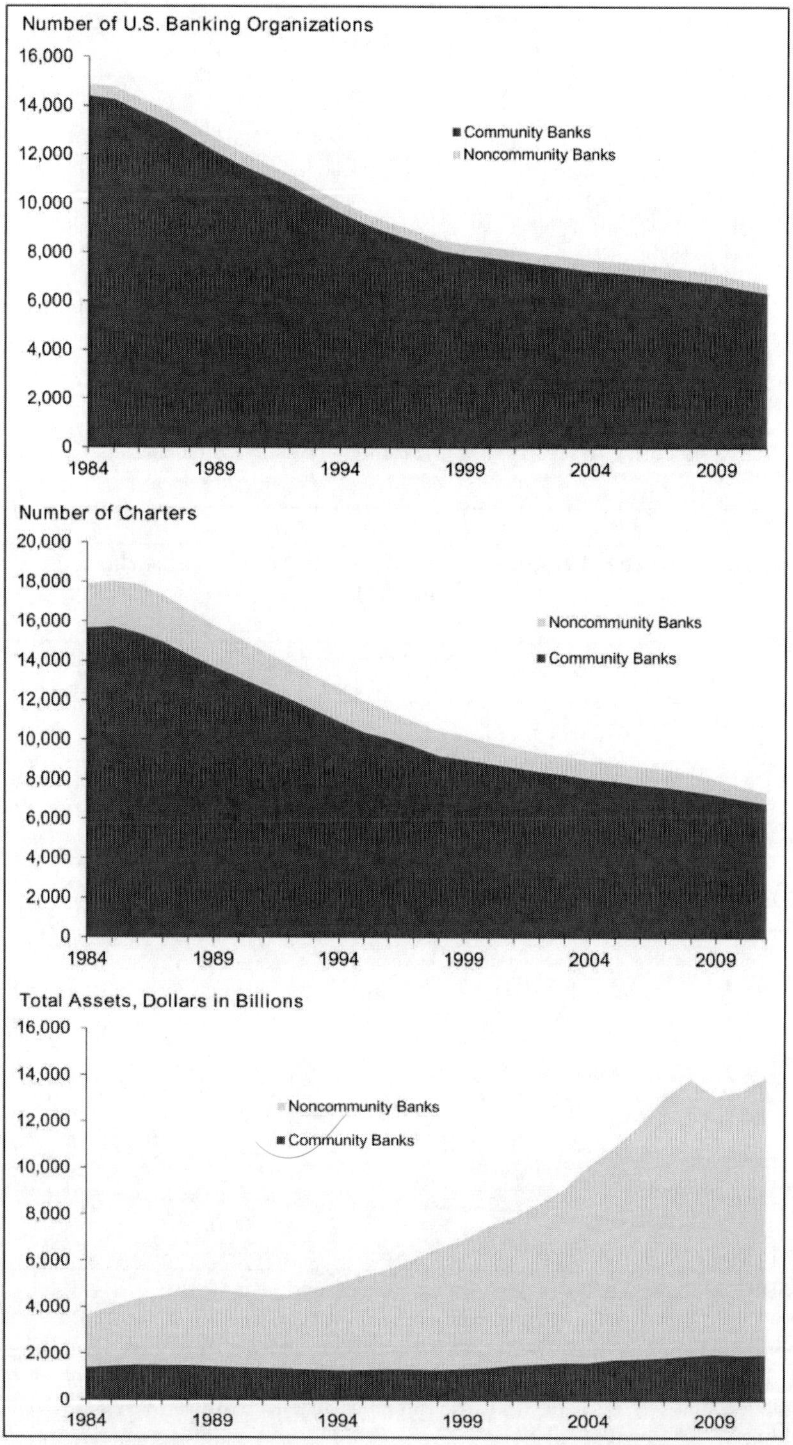

Source: FDIC.

Chart 2.10. Long-Term Consolidation of Charters and Assets at Community and Noncommunity Banks.

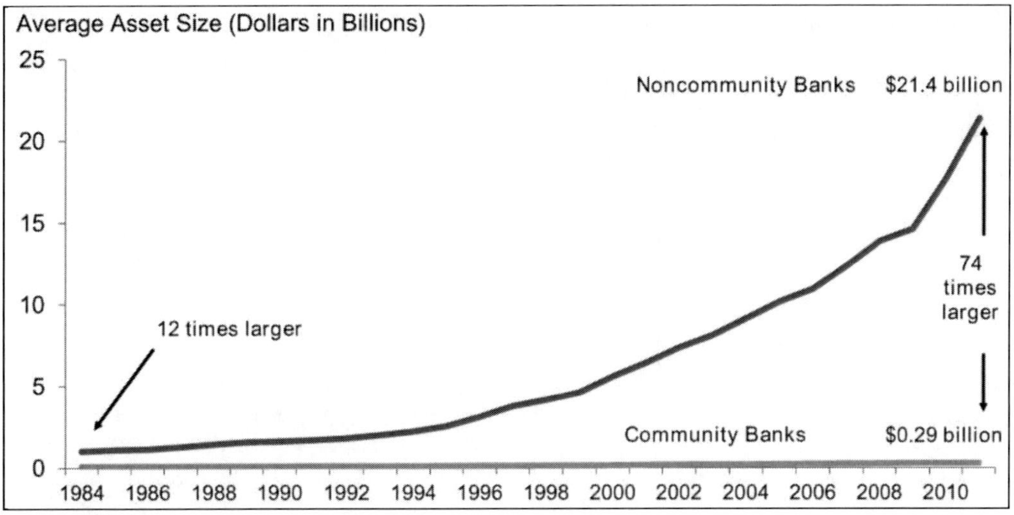

Source: FDIC.

Chart 2.11. The Disparity in Average Size Between Community and Noncommunity Banks Has Risen More Than Sixfold Since 1984.

Structural Change among Community and Noncommunity Banks

The effects of structural change are also evident when viewed through the lens of the FDIC's research definition for community banks. Table 2.2, Table 2.3, and Chart 2.10 depict long-term net structural change among FDIC-insured community and noncommunity banks in terms of the number of banking organizations, the number of charters, and total assets. These tables show that both community and noncommunity banking organizations have experienced substantial declines in their numbers since 1984. Over this period, the number of community banks declined by 56 percent while the number of noncommunity banks declined by 23 percent. The faster rate of consolidation, however, has not appreciably diminished the community bank share of U.S. banking organizations. While community banks made up 97 percent of all U.S. banking organizations in 1984, their share had fallen only slightly to 95 percent by 2011.

In addition, when measured in terms of the number of individual banks, community banks have risen as a proportion of all federally insured banks and thrifts, from 87 percent to 92 percent. Noncommunity banks consolidated much faster over the period when measured in terms of charters, which declined by 72 percent, than when measured in terms of banking organizations, which declined by 23 percent. This disparity is entirely attributable to a very high rate of charter consolidation within noncommunity banking organizations during the period, as discussed further below.

Noncommunity banks have accumulated an overwhelming share of industry assets over the past 27 years. While noncommunity banking organizations held $2.3 trillion in assets in 1984 (62 percent of industry assets at that time), by 2011 they held $11.9 trillion in assets, or 86 percent of industry assets. The increased concentration of industry assets at noncommunity banks has resulted in a rising disparity in the average size of institutions in these two groups.

Chart 2.11 shows that while noncommunity banks were, on average, 12 times larger than community institutions in 1984, by 2011 they had become 74 times as large.

Table 2.2. Number of Community and Noncommunity Banking Organizations, Charters and Assets, 1984-2011

Year	Banking Organizations		Bank and Thrift Charters		Total Assets ($ Billion)	
	Community	Noncommunity	Community	Noncommunity	Community	Noncommunity
1984	14,408	478	15,663	2,238	$1,379.8	$2,273.3
1985	14,265	508	15,728	2,305	$1,461.6	$2,531.8
1986	13,790	523	15,426	2,450	$1,512.2	$2,815.3
1987	13,314	558	14,967	2,358	$1,499.3	$3,002.8
1988	12,715	570	14,323	2,237	$1,496.2	$3,240.3
1989	12,109	553	13,707	2,089	$1,445.4	$3,281.5
1990	11,582	540	13,150	2,008	$1,396.6	$3,252.0
1991	11,133	514	12,615	1,867	$1,374.5	$3,169.2
1992	10,692	475	12,081	1,772	$1,343.0	$3,193.3
1993	10,162	438	11,524	1,697	$1,310.8	$3,397.1
1994	9,612	438	10,925	1,679	$1,280.8	$3,739.9
1995	9,156	429	10,381	1,590	$1,288.2	$4,052.8
1996	8,794	414	10,078	1,376	$1,316.3	$4,294.9
1997	8,475	418	9,674	1,249	$1,322.6	$4,722.1
1998	8,098	426	9,206	1,258	$1,303.7	$5,227.4
1999	7,920	436	9,018	1,204	$1,343.8	$5,539.8
2000	7,799	450	8,817	1,087	$1,390.2	$6,072.7
2001	7,663	442	8,622	992	$1,499.1	$6,369.9
2002	7,518	450	8,416	938	$1,550.5	$6,885.4
2003	7,397	448	8,260	921	$1,612.2	$7,463.4
2004	7,246	461	8,045	931	$1,611.1	$8,496.3
2005	7,183	459	7,933	900	$1,746.1	$9,133.1
2006	7,073	454	7,758	922	$1,794.4	$10,067.4
2007	6,952	456	7,626	908	$1,840.3	$11,193.6
2008	6,835	449	7,446	859	$1,924.9	$11,916.3
2009	6,719	402	7,252	760	$1,992.8	$11,094.0
2010	6,524	390	7,016	642	$1,944.0	$11,375.0
2011	6,356	364	6,799	558	$1,972.7	$11,919.5

Source: FDIC.

Despite Declining Numbers, Community Banks Have Proved Resilient

Notwithstanding the sharp decline in the number of banks with assets less than $100 million and the accumulation of industry assets at noncommunity banks, the community banking sector continued to represent the vast majority of banking organizations (95 percent) and charters (92 percent) as of 2011. Moreover, as was the case when discussing charters with assets less than $100 million, community banks in some ways experienced less structural change than noncommunity banks over the period of this study.

Table 2.3. Community and Noncommunity Banking Organizations, Charters and Assets, as Percent of Total, 1984-2011

Year	Banking Organizations		Bank and Thrift Charters		Total Assets	
	Community	Noncommunity	Community	Noncommunity	Community	Noncommunity
1984	97%	3%	87%	13%	38%	62%
1985	97%	3%	87%	13%	37%	63%
1986	96%	4%	86%	14%	35%	65%
1987	96%	4%	86%	14%	33%	67%
1988	96%	4%	86%	14%	32%	68%
1989	96%	4%	87%	13%	31%	69%
1990	96%	4%	87%	13%	30%	70%
1991	96%	4%	87%	13%	30%	70%
1992	96%	4%	87%	13%	30%	70%
1993	96%	4%	87%	13%	28%	72%
1994	96%	4%	87%	13%	26%	74%
1995	96%	4%	87%	13%	24%	76%
1996	96%	4%	88%	12%	23%	77%
1997	95%	5%	89%	11%	22%	78%
1998	95%	5%	88%	12%	20%	80%
1999	95%	5%	88%	12%	20%	80%
2000	95%	5%	89%	11%	19%	81%
2001	95%	5%	90%	10%	19%	81%
2002	94%	6%	90%	10%	18%	82%
2003	94%	6%	90%	10%	18%	82%
2004	94%	6%	90%	10%	16%	84%
2005	94%	6%	90%	10%	16%	84%
2006	94%	6%	89%	11%	15%	85%
2007	94%	6%	89%	11%	14%	86%
2008	94%	6%	90%	10%	14%	86%
2009	94%	6%	91%	9%	15%	85%
2010	94%	6%	92%	8%	15%	85%
2011	95%	5%	92%	8%	14%	86%

Source: FDIC.

Table 2.4 is a *transition matrix* that highlights the various sources of structural change among community and noncommunity banks. Of the 17,901 charters that reported at year-end 1984, 5,372 reported continuously through 2011, for an overall survival rate of 30 percent. Among institutions that started out in 1984 as community banks, however, the survival rate was 33 percent, compared with only 6 percent for those that began as noncommunity banks. Thus, community banks were more than five times more likely than noncommunity banks to remain in operation for the entire 27-year period.

Of the 2,238 charters that started out in 1984 as noncommunity banks, only 134 survived through 2011. Of those that survived, 37 percent had become community banks by the end of the period. In contrast, of the 5,237 institutions that started out in 1984 as community banks and survived through 2011, 96 percent continued to report as community banks. Nonetheless, given that the vast majority of institutions at any given time are community banks, switching even a small percentage of them to noncommunity banks will result in a large increase in that category. Some 41 percent of institutions reporting as noncommunity banks in 2011 had originally reported as community banks in 1984.

Table 2.4. Transition Matrix: Structural Change among Community and Noncommunity Banks, 1984-2011

Group of Origin		Institutions That Closed: 1985-2011					Institutions Reporting in 2011		
		Failed	Consolidated	Merged	Other Closing	Total	Community Banks	Noncommunity Banks	Total
Number of Institutions									
Community Banks in 1984	15,663	1,902	2,893	5,459	172	10,426	5,004	233	5,237
Noncommunity Banks in 1984	2,238	179	1,321	566	38	2,104	50	84	134
Total Banks in 1984	17,901	2,081	4,214	6,025	210	12,530	5,054	317	5,371
New Charters, 1985-2011	4,888	474	715	1,558	155	2,902	1,740	246	1,986
Total, Banks in 1984 Plus New Charters	22,789	2,555	4,929	7,583	365	15,432	6,794	563	7,357
Percent of Institutions in Group of Origin									
Community Banks in 1984	100%	12%	18%	35%	1%	67%	32%	1%	33%
Noncommunity Banks in 1984	100%	8%	59%	25%	2%	94%	2%	4%	6%
Total Banks in 1984	100%	12%	24%	34%	1%	70%	28%	2%	30%
New Charters, 1985-2011	100%	10%	15%	32%	3%	59%	36%	5%	41%
Total, Banks in 1984 Plus New Charters	100%	11%	22%	33%	2%	68%	30%	2%	32%

Source: FDIC.

Most of the consolidation among both community and noncommunity charters during the period was the product of voluntary mergers and consolidations within banking holding companies, as opposed to failures. Table 2.4 shows that of all institutions reporting in 1984 or newly chartered before 2011, 55 percent had exited the industry by 2011 through merger or consolidation, while another 11 percent had failed. Among institutions that started in 1984 as community banks, 35 percent exited through merger, while 18 percent consolidated and 12 percent failed. Among those that started out in 1984 as noncommunity banks, 25 percent exited through merger, while 59 percent consolidated and 8 percent failed. Of the 4,888 institutions that were newly chartered during the period, 59 percent had exited by 2011, with the majority exiting via merger. New entrants that survived to 2011 were more likely than the general population to be noncommunity banks, with 14 percent of them reporting as such in 2011.

Another way to view the resiliency of community banks is to examine their failure rates. Community banks and noncommunity banks have failed in roughly the same proportions since 1984. Overall, just over 89 percent of all institutions that have failed since 1984 have been community banks, roughly in line with their prevalence among all banks, which varied between 86 percent and 92 percent during the study period. A more comprehensive measure of relative failure rates between community and noncommunity banks is a *failure index* that measures the frequency of failures within each group relative to their prevalence among all banks for any period, expressed as:

$$\text{Failure Index} = \frac{\dfrac{\text{Failures in group}}{\text{All failures}}}{\dfrac{\text{Banks in group}}{\text{All banks}}}$$

Table 2.5 calculates the failure index for community and noncommunity banks for the entire period 1985 through 2011, as well as for five-year intervals between 1986 and 2010. For the period as a whole, community banks failed at a rate slightly above their prevalence in the population, while noncommunity banks failed slightly less often. Among the five-year intervals between 1986 and 2010, however, community banks had a higher propensity to fail than noncommunity banks only during the 1986-1990 period, when more than half the failures occurred. In every other five-year period since 1990, noncommunity banks have had a higher propensity to fail.

Table 2.5. Failure Index*

Community and Noncommunity Banks 1985-2011 and by Five-Year Interval						
Group	**1986-1990**	**1991-1995**	**1996-2000**	**2001-2005**	**2006-2010**	**1985-2011**
Community Banks	1.05	1.00	0.95	0.95	0.93	1.01
Noncommunity Banks	0.71	1.03	1.37	1.45	1.60	0.92
Total Number of Failures	1,467	509	24	20	323	2,435

Source: FDIC.

* The failure index for each group is calculated as failures within that group as a ratio to all failures divided by institutions in that group as a ratio to all institutions in that period. Index values above 1 indicate that institutions in the group failed more often than their prevalence in the population, while index values less than 1 indicate that they failed less often.

Another measure of the relative stability of community banks is found in the age distribution of charters. As of 2011, 69 percent of community bank charters were more than 50 years old, compared with 58 percent of noncommunity banks. This distinction is important because charters older than 50 years have historically been underrepresented among bank failures. In fact, the failure index of institutions older than 50 years was 0.63 for the entire period between 1984 and 2011, compared with an index value of 1.65 for all banks less than 50 years old, indicating that the younger banks failed about two-and-a-half times more often than the older banks over the 27-year period. Moreover, noncommunity banks have been overrepresented among new charters.

Of the 4,888 new charters established during the period, 17 percent were, by definition, noncommunity banks at their first year-end financial report. This exceeds the proportion of noncommunity banks in the industry as a whole, which was just 8 percent in 2011. Of the 563 noncommunity banks reporting at year-end 2011, 246 (almost 44 percent) had been chartered since 1984. In contrast, institutions chartered since 1984 made up just 26 percent of community banks as of 2011.

Sources of Asset Growth

The dramatic shift in industry assets from community to noncommunity banks over this period naturally leads to the question about the sources of asset growth. Table 2.6 compares the total assets of community and noncommunity banks reporting in 2011 to the assets of institutions they have directly acquired or consolidated since 1984.

As with the previous discussion of banks with assets greater than $10 billion, growth in the assets of noncommunity banks came about largely on the strength of charter acquisition. The 558 noncommunity banks operating at year-end 2011 directly acquired or consolidated 2,401 charters during the period with assets of $6 trillion, an amount equal to just over one-half of the assets held by noncommunity bank in 2011. Moreover, the 2,401 institutions directly acquired by noncommunity banks had already acquired or consolidated 8,490 other charters since the beginning of the period in 1984. In this way, institutions reporting as noncommunity banks in 2011 directly or indirectly absorbed 71 percent of the charters that exited the industry between 1984 and 2011.

By contrast, acquisition appears to represent a far less important source of asset growth for community institutions over this period. Relative to their numbers, community banks reporting in 2011 accounted for far fewer direct and, especially, indirect acquisitions than did noncommunity banks. Moreover, the assets of institutions directly acquired by community banks during the period totaled to only around 15 percent of the assets held by community banks in 2011, indicating that acquisition and consolidation were far less important to charter growth among community institutions.

Summary

Large-scale structural change in the banking industry since 1984 has reduced the number of federally insured banking and thrift charters by over half, and has resulted in the largest institutions holding well over one-half of industry assets. Amid the waves of new charters, failures, mergers, and intracompany consolidations that reshaped the industry over this period, community banks declined in number and, in particular, in terms of their share of banking industry assets. Nonetheless, they also showed signs of resilience, remaining by far the most prevalent form of FDIC-insured institution. Community banks reporting in 1984 were five times more likely than noncommunity banks to report continuously through 2011, and those that did nearly always continued to meet the FDIC research definition of a community bank. By contrast, noncommunity banks were much more likely to consolidate, be acquired, or undertake acquisitions themselves than were the more stable community banks, leading these banks to accumulate an 86 percent share of banking industry assets by year-end 2011. Chapter 3 explores the implications of industry consolidation on the geography of U.S. community banking.

Table 2.6. Acquisitions Were Instrumental in the Rapid Growth of Assets at Noncommunity Banks between 1984 and 2011

Group		As of Year-End 2011		Between 1984 and 2011			
		Number of Charters	Total Assets ($ Million)	Number of Charters Acquired		Assets of Charters Directly Acquired ($ Million)	Assets Acquired as Percent of 2011 Total Assets
				Directly	Indirectly		
Community Banks	Reported at Year-End 1984	5,057	$1,436,786	2,573	567	$217,204	15.1%
	New Charter After 1984	1,742	$535,952	454	103	$65,641	12.3%
	Total	6,799	$1,972,737	3,027	670	$282,844	14.3%
Noncommunity Banks	Reported at Year-End 1984	314	$10,129,136	2,111	8,147	$5,494,491	54.2%
	New Charter After 1984	244	$1,790,372	290	343	$514,868	28.8%
	Total	558	$11,919,507	2,401	8,490	$6,009,360	50.4%
Total		**7,357**	**$13,892,245**	**5,428**	**9,160**	**$6,292,204**	**45.3%**

Source: FDIC.

3. The Geography of Community Banks

Community banking in the United States is inextricably linked with geography. Community banks are defined, in part, by the fact that they operate within limited geographic areas. There are also significant differences between community and noncommunity banks in the degree to which they locate their operations outside of major metropolitan areas and in how they have been able to expand their geographic footprint—the areas in which they do business—over time. This chapter explores these differences in the geography of community and noncommunity banks and discusses the implications for relative rates of growth between these two sectors of the banking industry.

Location of Bank Headquarters and Other Banking Offices

Federally insured banks report to the FDIC the headquarters location of the bank and the location of individual banking branch offices.[22] Maps 3.1 and 3.2 depict the headquarters locations of U.S. community and noncommunity banks, respectively, as of 2011. The maps show that community bank headquarters locations far outnumber those of noncommunity banks, and are particularly concentrated in the upper Midwest and the Northeast corridor between coastal New England and the mid-Atlantic states. Headquarters offices of both community and noncommunity banks are less frequently located in the sparsely populated regions of the Western states.

A much different picture emerges, however, when looking at the geographic distribution of total banking offices in 2011. The offices of noncommunity banks outnumber those of community banks by around 75 percent, demonstrating a physical presence far beyond their headquarters locations. Moreover, Map 3.2 shows particularly dense concentrations of noncommunity bank offices in the urban areas of not only the Northeast corridor, but also other major metropolitan areas of the upper Midwest as well as the Southern and Western states. While community bank offices are also mostly located in metropolitan areas, they also exist in large numbers outside the metropolitan areas, as discussed further below.

While Banks Have Consolidated, Banking Offices Have Increased

Despite the large, long-term decline in the number of banks since the mid-1980s (see Chapter 2), the total number of U.S. banking offices increased from 84,202 in 1987 to 98,180 in 2011 (Chart 3.1). This growth, however, did not occur in a straight line. Total banking offices declined by nearly 5,000 between 1987 and 1993 as the number of banks declined by more than 4,100. After 1993, as industry consolidation continued, the number of banking offices began to increase, peaking at just under 100,000 in 2009 before settling at 98,180 in 2011.

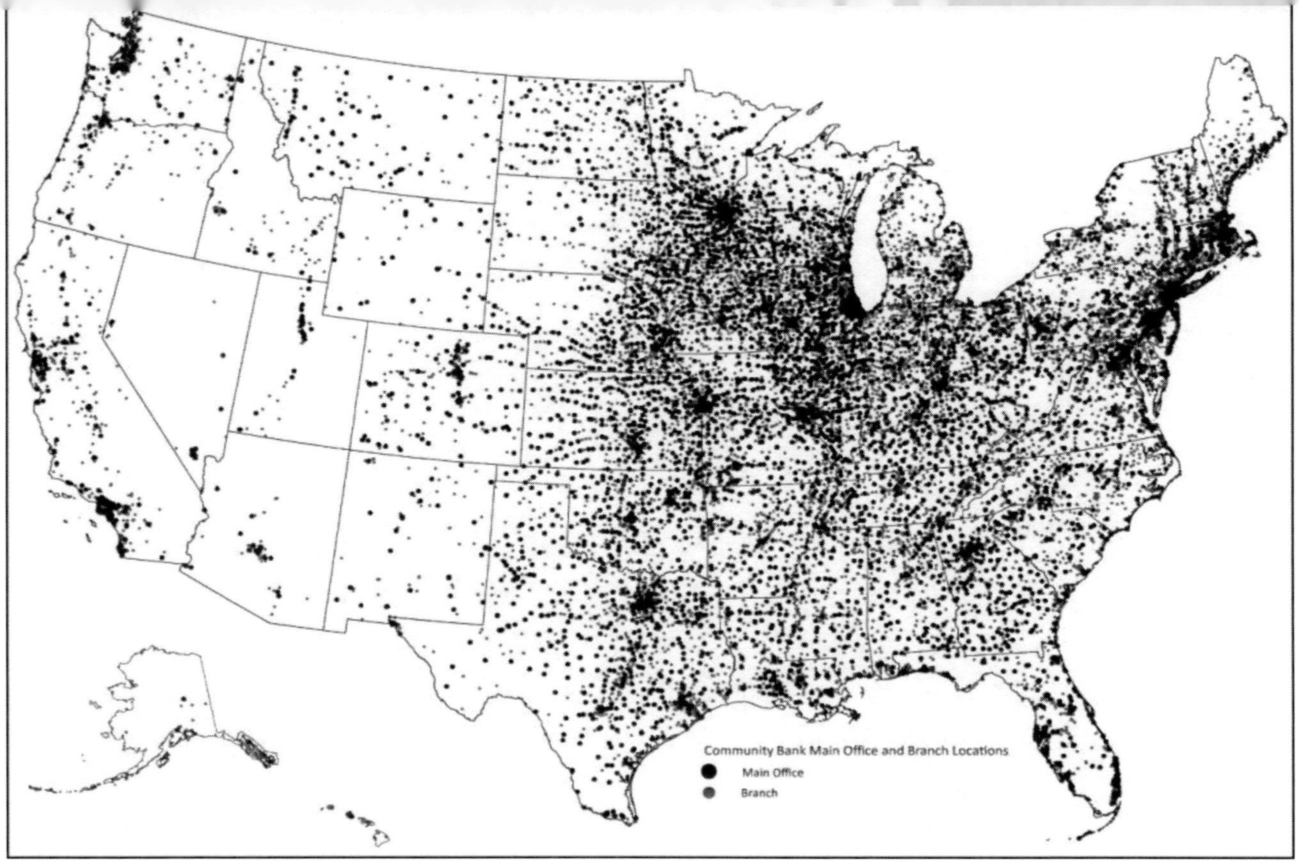

Source: FDIC.
Note: Merger-adjusted to reflect community bank designations as of year-end 2011.

Map 3.1. Community Bank Headquarters and Branch Locations, Year-End 2011.

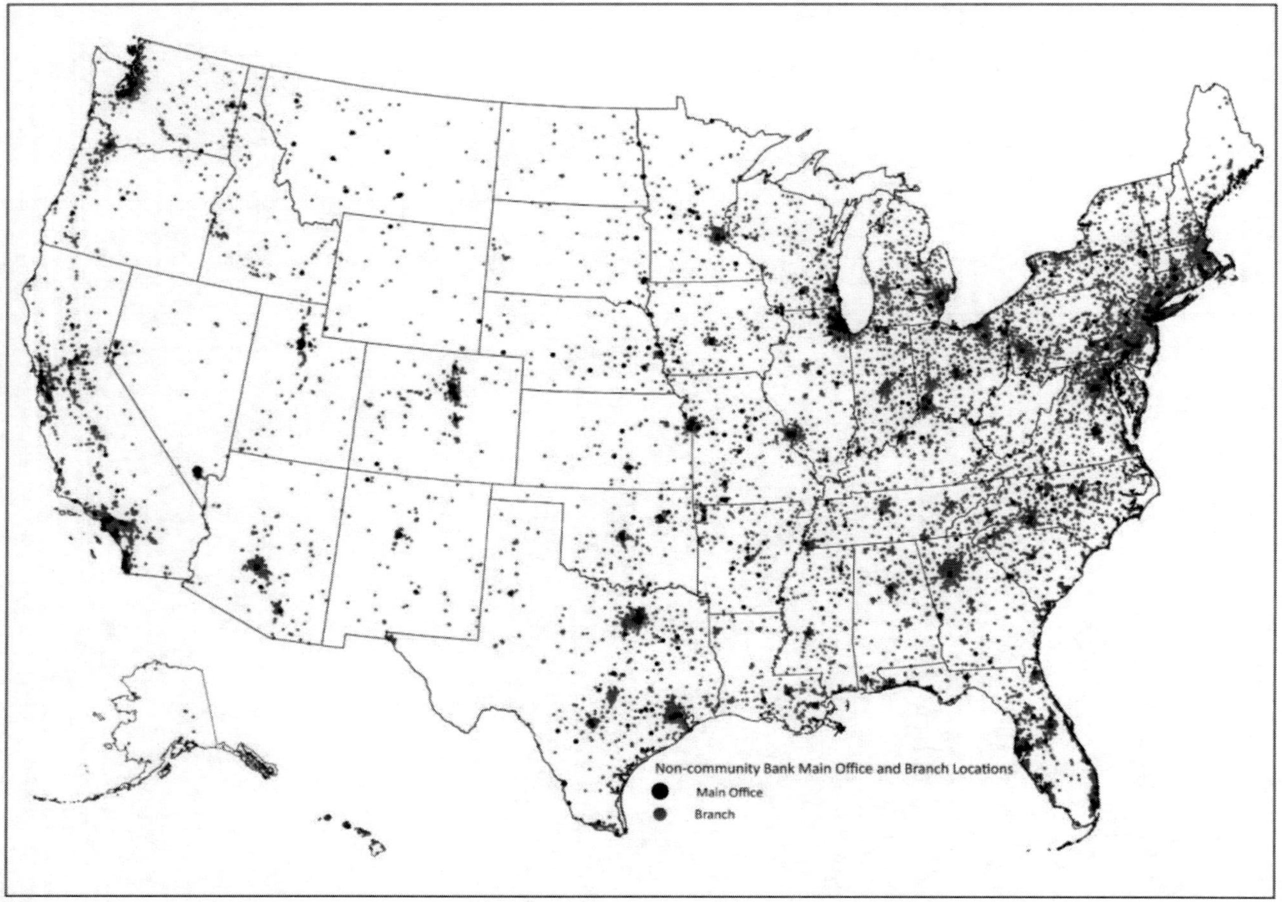

Source: FDIC.
Note: Merger-adjusted to reflect community bank designations as of year-end 2011.

Map 3.2. Noncommunity Bank Headquarters and Branch Locations, Year-End 2011.

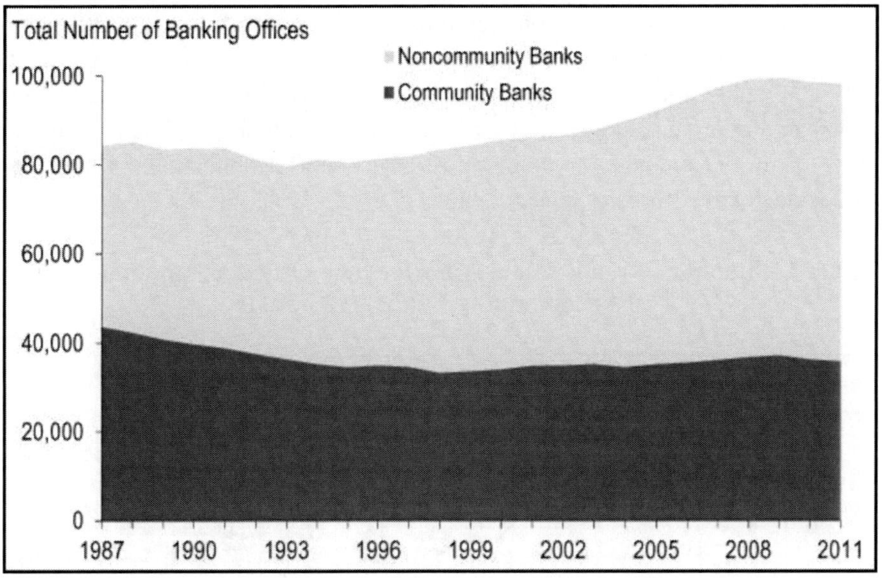

Source: FDIC.

Chart 3.1. Total Offices Operated by Noncommunity Banks Have Risen Steadily Since 1987, While Community Bank Offices Declined Overall.

Just as banking industry assets have shifted over time away from community banks and toward noncommunity banks, there has also been a shift toward noncommunity banks in their share of total banking offices (Chart 3.1). Overall, the number of community banking offices declined by 18 percent between 1987 and 2011, while the number of noncommunity banking offices increased by 53 percent.

The Geographic Footprint of Community Banks

Community banks average fewer banking offices per organization and tend to have a smaller average geographic footprint than noncommunity banks (Table 3.1). As of 2011, the average noncommunity banking organization operated more than 30 times more banking offices than the average community bank. Nonetheless, the average geographic footprint of both community and noncommunity banks has expanded over time as the industry has consolidated. The average number of banking offices per community banking organization increased by about two-thirds, from 3.3 in 1987 to 5.6 by 2010. Over the same period, the average number of banking offices per noncommunity banking organization more than doubled from 73 to 171.

Another way to express the relative size of the geographic footprint of community banks is in terms of the number of counties in which each community banking organization maintains banking offices. In 1987, 77 percent of all community banking organizations located all of their banking offices within a single county, while another 17 percent located all of their offices within a three-county area (Table 3.2). In contrast, noncommunity banks exhibited a substantially wider geographic scope, with just 26 percent locating all of their offices within a single county and another 10 percent locating their offices within two or three counties. Community institutions continued to have a narrower geographic scope than noncommunity institutions through 2011, although the disparity narrowed somewhat due to the wider geographic footprint of community banks. By 2011, fewer than one-half of community banking organizations operated in a single county, although 82 percent operated within three or fewer counties. In contrast, just 37 percent of noncommunity banking organizations operated within three or fewer counties in 2011.

Table 3.1. Banking Organizations, Charters and Offices of Community and Noncommunity Banks, 1987-2011

Year	Community Banks					Noncommunity Banks				
	Number of Banking Organizations	Number of Bank and Thrift Charters	Number of Banking Offices	Offices per Organization	Offices per Charter	Number of Banking Organizations	Number of Bank and Thrift Charters	Number of Banking Offices	Offices per Organization	Offices per Charter
1987	13,314	14,967	43,680	3.3	2.9	558	2,358	40,658	72.9	17.2
1988	12,715	14,323	42,387	3.3	3.0	570	2,237	42,724	75.0	19.1
1989	12,109	13,707	40,842	3.4	3.0	553	2,089	42,689	77.2	20.4
1990	11,582	13,150	39,745	3.4	3.0	540	2,008	44,004	81.5	21.9
1991	11,133	12,615	38,866	3.5	3.1	514	1,867	44,849	87.3	24.0
1992	10,692	12,081	37,560	3.5	3.1	475	1,772	43,537	91.7	24.6
1993	10,162	11,524	36,370	3.6	3.2	438	1,697	43,248	98.7	25.5
1994	9,612	10,925	35,291	3.7	3.2	438	1,679	45,904	104.8	27.3
1995	9,156	10,381	34,561	3.8	3.3	429	1,590	45,866	106.9	28.8
1996	8,794	10,078	34,978	4.0	3.5	414	1,376	46,388	112.0	33.7
1997	8,475	9,674	34,633	4.1	3.6	418	1,249	47,255	113.1	37.8
1998	8,098	9,206	33,281	4.1	3.6	426	1,258	50,092	117.6	39.8
1999	7,920	9,018	33,638	4.2	3.7	436	1,204	50,686	116.3	42.1
2000	7,799	8,817	34,072	4.4	3.9	450	1,087	51,489	114.4	47.4
2001	7,663	8,622	34,874	4.6	4.0	442	992	51,224	115.9	51.6
2002	7,518	8,416	34,934	4.6	4.2	450	938	51,646	114.8	55.1
2003	7,397	8,260	35,244	4.8	4.3	448	921	52,592	117.4	57.1
2004	7,246	8,045	34,548	4.8	4.3	461	931	55,301	120.0	59.4
2005	7,183	7,933	35,218	4.9	4.4	459	900	56,896	124.0	63.2
2006	7,073	7,758	35,559	5.0	4.6	454	922	59,273	130.6	64.3
2007	6,952	7,626	36,142	5.2	4.7	456	908	61,225	134.3	67.4
2008	6,835	7,446	36,785	5.4	4.9	449	859	62,400	139.0	72.6
2009	6,719	7,252	37,199	5.5	5.1	402	760	62,334	155.1	82.0
2010	6,524	7,016	36,275	5.6	5.2	390	642	62,290	159.7	97.0
2011	6,356	6,799	35,851	5.6	5.3	364	558	62,329	171.2	111.7

Source: FDIC.

Most Banking Offices Are Located in Metropolitan Areas

This study adopts the convention of dividing the 3,238 U.S. counties into two main categories: *metropolitan* (or metro) and *nonmetropolitan* (or nonmetro).[23] Metro counties, which numbered 1,168 as of 2010, are defined by being economically linked to one of the 374 U.S. *Metropolitan Statistical Areas* (MSAs), each of which encompasses an urban core with population of at least 50,000 people. Nonmetro counties can be divided into two subcategories: *micropolitan* (or micro) and *rural*. The 694 U.S. micropolitan counties are also centered on an urban core, but one with population between 10,000 and 50,000 people, while the 1,376 rural counties are defined by populations with fewer than 10,000 people. This study employs metro, micro and rural county definitions as of 2010 and applies them retroactively to prior years.

As of 2011, over 55 percent of bank headquarters and nearly 78 percent of all banking offices were located in metro counties (Table 3.3). As large as they are, these concentrations of banking activity in metro counties still fall short of the metro share of U.S. population and economic output. Almost 84 percent of the U.S. population resided within metropolitan statistical areas in 2011, and an estimated 88 percent of U.S. Gross Domestic Product (GDP) also originated there.

Table 3.2. Geographic Scope of Community and Noncommunity Banking Organizations' Percent of Banking Offices Within 1 to 3 Counties, 1987-2011

Year	Percent of Community Banking Organizations With		Percent of Noncommunity Banking Organizations With	
	All Banking Offices in 1 County	All Banking Offices in 2 or 3 Counties	All Banking Offices in 1 County	All Banking Offices in 2 or 3 Counties
1987	77%	17%	26%	10%
1988	76%	18%	28%	9%
1989	75%	19%	29%	9%
1990	74%	20%	30%	11%
1991	73%	21%	32%	11%
1992	72%	22%	33%	11%
1993	71%	22%	32%	13%
1994	70%	23%	33%	12%
1995	68%	24%	34%	11%
1996	66%	26%	37%	11%
1997	64%	27%	37%	11%
1998	62%	29%	36%	9%
1999	61%	29%	37%	9%
2000	59%	30%	37%	10%
2001	57%	31%	38%	9%
2002	56%	32%	37%	8%
2003	54%	33%	32%	8%
2004	54%	33%	31%	9%
2005	52%	34%	32%	8%
2006	51%	34%	31%	8%
2007	50%	35%	30%	9%
2008	49%	35%	28%	9%
2009	48%	35%	28%	7%
2010	47%	35%	27%	8%
2011	46%	36%	28%	8%

Source: FDIC.

Note: The community and noncommunity bank share of offices are merger-adjusted to each year-end.

In Relative Terms, Community Banks Are More Likely to be Located in Nonmetro Areas

Despite this overall tilt in the location of banking offices toward metro areas, community banks are more likely to locate their headquarters and banking offices in nonmetro areas than are noncommunity banks (see Table 3.4). As of 2011, 53 percent of community banks were headquartered within metro counties, compared with 85 percent of noncommunity banks. Some 62 percent of the banking offices operated by community banks in 2011 were located within metro counties, compared with 87 percent of noncommunity banking offices. In all, community banks were almost three times more likely than noncommunity institutions to locate their offices in a nonmetro area in 2011, and were four times more likely to operate offices in rural counties. These percentages have remained remarkably constant over time, reflecting longstanding differences in office location between community and noncommunity banks.

While noncommunity banks have adeptly located in metropolitan areas that have the greatest concentrations of population and economic activity, community banks are prevalent in both metro and nonmetro areas. As a result, while most metro areas tend to be well-served by institutions with a variety of business models, many nonmetro (and a surprising number of metro) areas tend to rely much more heavily on community banks as their lifeline to mainstream financial services. In 2011, there were 629 U.S. counties, with just over 6 million in population, where community banks operated offices, but where no noncommunity banking offices were present. Three-quarters of these counties were rural, but 14 percent were part of metropolitan areas. There were another 639 counties where community banks operated offices but where fewer than three noncommunity banking offices were present. Some 71 percent of these counties were rural, and another 16 percent were metro counties. Taken together, these data point to more than 1,200 U.S. counties (out of a total of 3,238), encompassing 16.3 million people, who would have limited physical access to mainstream banking services without the presence of community banks.

Table 3.3. 2011 Share of Economic Output, Resident Population, Bank Headquarters and Total Banking Offices in U.S. Metro, Micro and Rural Counties

	Share of 2011 Total:			
	Real Economic Output	**Resident Population**	**Bank Headquarters**	**Banking Offices**
Metropolitan Counties	87.6%	83.8%	55.2%	77.5%
Micropolitan Counties	7.9%	10.0%	18.9%	11.9%
Rural Counties	4.4%	6.2%	26.0%	8.7%

Sources: FDIC, U.S. Census Bureau, U.S. Bureau of Economic Analysis, Moody's Analytics.

Deposit Market Shares Are Declining for Community Institutions

Consistent with their declining share of banking industry assets, Table 3.5 depicts a parallel long-term decline in the community bank shares of banking offices and total deposits. In 1987, the first year for which data are available at this level of detail, community banks operated 52 percent of U.S. banking offices and held 41 percent of industry deposits. By 2011, the community bank share of offices had declined by more than one-quarter, while their share of industry deposits had fallen by more than one-half. The decline was particularly evident in the metro counties, whereby 2011 community banks operated just 29 percent of banking offices and held 15 percent of deposits. In contrast, the community bank shares were more stable in micro and rural counties (Chart 3.2), where community banks still held a larger share of offices and deposits than noncommunity banks in 2011. The nation's rural areas continue to be dominated by community banks, where community banks have more than 70 percent of both offices and deposits. While this analysis does not necessarily capture banking transactions that may be conducted remotely with community or noncommunity banks, it does show that community banks continue to maintain an important physical presence in nonmetro areas.

Table 3.4. Percent Share of Community and Noncommunity Bank Headquarters and Total Banking Offices Located in Metro and Nonmetro Counties, 1987-2011

Year	Community Banks				Noncommunity Banks			
	Headquarters		Total Banking Offices		Headquarters		Total Banking Offices	
	Metro	Nonmetro	Metro	Nonmetro	Metro	Nonmetro	Metro	Nonmetro
1987	54%	46%	66%	34%	80%	20%	87%	13%
1988	54%	46%	66%	34%	77%	23%	87%	13%
1989	54%	46%	66%	34%	77%	23%	87%	13%
1990	53%	47%	65%	35%	78%	22%	87%	13%
1991	53%	47%	64%	36%	78%	22%	87%	13%
1992	53%	47%	64%	36%	78%	22%	86%	14%
1993	53%	47%	63%	37%	75%	25%	86%	14%
1994	52%	48%	63%	37%	74%	26%	85%	15%
1995	52%	48%	62%	38%	76%	24%	85%	15%
1996	51%	49%	62%	38%	77%	23%	86%	14%
1997	51%	49%	61%	39%	79%	21%	85%	15%
1998	51%	49%	60%	40%	77%	23%	85%	15%
1999	51%	49%	60%	40%	80%	20%	85%	15%
2000	52%	48%	61%	39%	81%	19%	85%	15%
2001	52%	48%	61%	39%	85%	15%	85%	15%
2002	52%	48%	61%	39%	85%	15%	85%	15%
2003	52%	48%	61%	39%	85%	15%	86%	14%
2004	52%	48%	60%	40%	84%	16%	86%	14%
2005	52%	48%	61%	39%	86%	14%	86%	14%
2006	52%	48%	61%	39%	85%	15%	87%	13%
2007	53%	47%	61%	39%	85%	15%	87%	13%
2008	53%	47%	62%	38%	85%	15%	87%	13%
2009	53%	47%	62%	38%	86%	14%	87%	13%
2010	53%	47%	62%	38%	84%	16%	87%	13%
2011	53%	47%	62%	38%	83%	17%	87%	13%

Source: FDIC.

Note: The community and noncommunity bank share of headquarters and offices are merger-adjusted to each year-end.

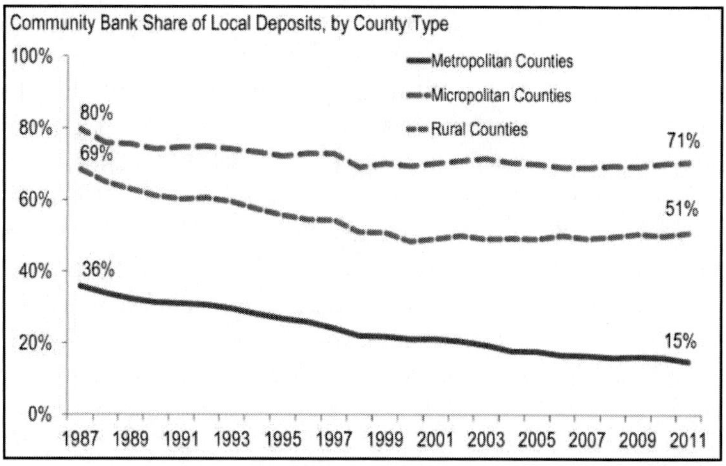

Source: FDIC.

Chart 3.2. The Deposit Market Share of Community Banks Has Declined by Two-Thirds Since 1987 in Metro Counties, but Has Remained More Stable in Nonmetro Counties.

Table 3.5. Community Bank Share of Banking Offices and Total Deposits Located in Metro, Micro and Rural Counties, 1987-2011

Year	Community Bank Share of Banking Offices, by County Type (Percent)				Community Bank Share of Total Deposits, by County Type (Percent)			
	Metro	Micro	Rural	Total Share	Metro	Micro	Rural	Total Share
1987	44.9%	68.1%	81.0%	51.8%	35.9%	68.5%	79.7%	40.9%
1988	43.1%	66.3%	78.8%	49.9%	33.9%	65.0%	75.9%	38.7%
1989	42.3%	65.5%	78.7%	49.2%	32.4%	63.0%	75.5%	37.2%
1990	40.7%	64.3%	77.6%	47.8%	31.4%	61.2%	74.1%	36.2%
1991	39.7%	63.7%	77.9%	46.9%	31.1%	60.2%	74.7%	36.0%
1992	38.8%	63.6%	77.5%	46.3%	30.7%	60.5%	74.8%	35.8%
1993	38.3%	62.1%	76.1%	45.8%	29.7%	59.5%	74.1%	35.0%
1994	36.1%	59.7%	74.7%	43.6%	28.1%	57.4%	73.3%	33.4%
1995	35.3%	58.9%	74.2%	42.9%	26.8%	55.7%	72.1%	32.2%
1996	35.2%	59.5%	75.2%	42.9%	25.9%	54.5%	72.9%	31.3%
1997	34.3%	59.1%	74.4%	42.2%	24.2%	54.3%	72.8%	29.8%
1998	32.0%	56.5%	72.1%	39.8%	22.1%	51.0%	69.0%	27.4%
1999	31.9%	56.6%	72.2%	39.8%	21.9%	50.9%	70.1%	27.3%
2000	32.1%	56.4%	71.3%	39.8%	21.2%	48.4%	69.5%	26.3%
2001	32.8%	57.5%	71.6%	40.5%	21.2%	49.2%	70.2%	26.3%
2002	32.5%	58.0%	72.2%	40.3%	20.6%	50.1%	70.9%	25.7%
2003	32.1%	58.2%	72.7%	40.1%	19.4%	49.1%	71.5%	24.4%
2004	30.4%	57.2%	71.9%	38.4%	17.8%	49.3%	70.4%	22.7%
2005	30.3%	57.3%	71.7%	38.2%	17.7%	49.2%	70.0%	22.3%
2006	29.7%	56.7%	71.6%	37.4%	16.7%	50.1%	69.1%	21.3%
2007	29.4%	56.6%	71.6%	37.1%	16.6%	49.3%	69.0%	21.2%
2008	29.5%	56.4%	71.8%	37.1%	16.0%	49.8%	69.5%	20.7%
2009	29.9%	56.5%	71.4%	37.4%	16.2%	50.5%	69.3%	20.7%
2010	29.4%	55.8%	70.7%	36.8%	16.0%	50.0%	70.1%	20.6%
2011	29.0%	55.8%	70.5%	36.5%	14.9%	50.8%	70.5%	19.4%

Source: FDIC. Based on 2010 county designations made by the U.S. Office of Management and Budget.

Note: The community bank share of deposits and offices are merger-adjusted to each year-end.

Noncommunity Banks Have Gravitated toward the Fastest-Growing Metro Areas

Metro counties have experienced significantly faster rates of growth in population and economic output compared with nonmetro counties over the past 27 years (Table 3.6). In terms of economic output, U.S. metro counties have grown at a compound annual rate of 2.6 percent over this period, compared with 2.4 percent for micropolitan counties and 2.2 percent for rural counties. While these differences in annualized growth rates may not seem large, they add up to a difference of 11 percentage points in total growth between metro and rural economies over the entire 27-year period. Although total population grew slower than the economy in all three county types, metro counties grew in population twice as fast as micropolitan counties and six times faster than rural counties over this period. The highly disparate rate of population growth between metro and rural counties added up to a difference of 33 percentage points in the total population growth between these two groups over the 27-year period.

Table 3.6. Compound Annual Rates of Growth in Economic Output and Resident Population, 1984-2011 U.S. Metro, Micro and Rural Counties

	Compound Annual Rate of Growth, 1984-2011:	
	Economic Output	**Resident Population**
Metropolitan Counties	2.6%	1.2%
Micropolitan Counties	2.4%	0.6%
Rural Counties	2.2%	0.2%

Sources: FDIC, U.S. Census Bureau, U.S. Bureau of Economic Analysis, Moody's Analytics.

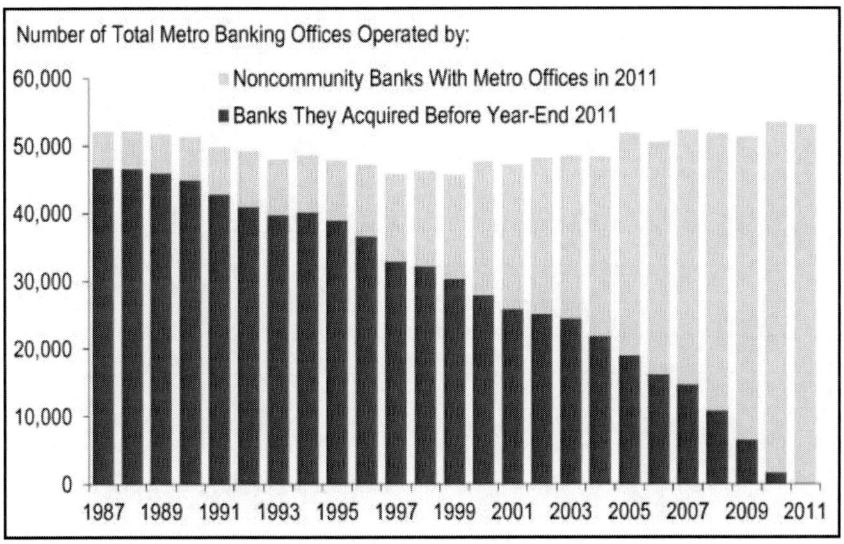

Source: FDIC.

Chart 3.3. Metro-County Banking Offices Operated by 2011 Noncommunity Banks With Their Metro Banking Offices, and Those of Banks They Eventually Acquired, 1987-2011.

These disparities in long-term growth rates between metro and nonmetro areas point to greater opportunities for growth on the part of banks that do business in metro areas. In fact, banks headquartered in metro areas in 2011 that also operated in 1984 grew more than twice as fast over that interval as similar banks headquartered in nonmetro areas. The ability of noncommunity banks to expand their presence in metro areas through new charters and by acquisition appears to have significantly enhanced their ability to grow over the long term. Almost 95 percent of the new noncommunity charters that entered the industry during the study period were headquartered in metro areas, compared with 84 percent of new community bank charters. Meanwhile, the vast majority of metro offices operated by noncommunity banks in 2011 had been acquired by those banks through a previous merger. Chart 3.3 shows the total metro-area banking offices operated by noncommunity banks in 2011, as well as the metro banking offices operated in prior periods by these same banks and by banks they would acquire by 2011. While the total number of metro banking offices operated by these noncommunity banks grew nearly tenfold between 1987 and 2011, virtually all of this growth came about through acquisition.

Table 3.7. Fastest Growing U.S. Metropolitan Areas, 1985-2011 with 2011 Population Over 1 Million

Metroplitan Area	Total Population Growth 1985-2011	Total Resident Population 2011 (thou.)
Las Vegas-Paradise, NV	251%	1,970.0
Raleigh-Cary, NC	149%	1,163.5
Austin-Round Rock, TX	135%	1,783.5
Riverside-San Bernardino-Ontario, CA	127%	4,305.0
Phoenix-Mesa-Scottsdale, AZ	121%	4,263.2
Orlando, FL	118%	2,171.4
Atlanta-Sandy Springs-Marietta, GA	100%	5,359.2
Charlotte-Gastonia-Concord, NC-SC	93%	1,795.5
Dallas-Fort Worth-Arlington, TX	81%	6,526.5
Sacramento--Arden-Arcade--Roseville, CA	74%	2,176.2
Houston-Baytown-Sugar Land, TX	67%	6,086.5
Nashville-Davidson--Murfreesboro, TN	67%	1,617.1
San Antonio, TX	67%	2,194.9
Jacksonville, FL	64%	1,360.3
Portland-Vancouver-Beaverton, OR-WA	63%	2,262.6
Denver-Aurora, CO	60%	2,599.5
Salt Lake City, UT	56%	1,145.9
Miami-Fort Lauderdale-Miami Beach, FL	56%	5,670.1
Seattle-Tacoma-Bellevue, WA	55%	3,500.0
Washingtn-Arlingtn-Alexandria, DC-VA-MD-WV	53%	5,703.9
Tampa-St. Petersburg-Clearwater, FL	50%	2,824.7

Source: FDIC.

Note: Calculations based on Census data.

Rural Depopulation Continues to Limit the Growth Potential for Some Community Banks

The 2010 Census data made it possible to update the FDIC's 2004 analysis of rural population trends and the implications for banks headquartered in rural areas. Based on the 30-year comparisons made in the 2004 study, the new Census data show that 50 percent of U.S. rural counties lost population between 1980 and 2010, compared with 38 percent between 1970 and 2000.[1] In addition, there has been a marked increase in the number of rural counties labeled as "accelerated declining" because of the quickening pace of their population decline. As of 2010, there were 272 "accelerated declining" rural counties, or nearly double the 2000 total of 142 counties (see Map 3.3).

As Map 3.3 shows, the Great Plains has the largest share of rural counties reporting declining population and those with accelerating population declines. Over 86 percent of the rural counties in the Great Plains faced such declines, by far the most rapidly depopulating of the four depopulating regions in the country. At the same time, the Delta-South and Corn Belt areas also saw decline in population trends over the last decade, as previously growing counties began to lose population or previously declining counties experienced acceleration in population loss. In the four depopulating areas, only a small minority of counties showed a substantial increase in population trends over the decade.

Depopulation continues to have a pronounced effect on the age distribution in many rural counties. Compared with growing U.S. counties, depopulating rural counties tend to experience a "pinched" age distribution among those aged 20-45, reflecting out-migration among young adults seeking better opportunities in other places. The departure of people entering their prime working years can place fiscal pressure on local governments coping with an aging population, and the absence of recent college graduates may deprive local businesses and governments of the skilled, young workforce necessary to grow. To the extent that these trends reduce the vitality of the area over time, the dynamics of out-migration and depopulation can become self-reinforcing.

Besides the effects on overall economic growth in these regions, these demographic trends pose a direct challenge to the ability of community banks to attract and retain qualified staff, management, and officers.

Nonetheless, it appears that many banks are successfully dealing with the problem of succession planning. A 2012 supervisory review of banks in the FDIC's Kansas City Region found that an officer who was 55 years of age or younger led nearly one-half of the community banks in rural depopulating areas reviewed, while just one in five banks was led by an officer who was 65 or older. While two-thirds of banks reviewed maintained a satisfactory succession plan, a majority also had an ownership structure that was closely tied to current senior management. These situations pose the greatest risk that the retirement of current executives could necessitate the sale of the bank, if a qualified successor cannot be found.

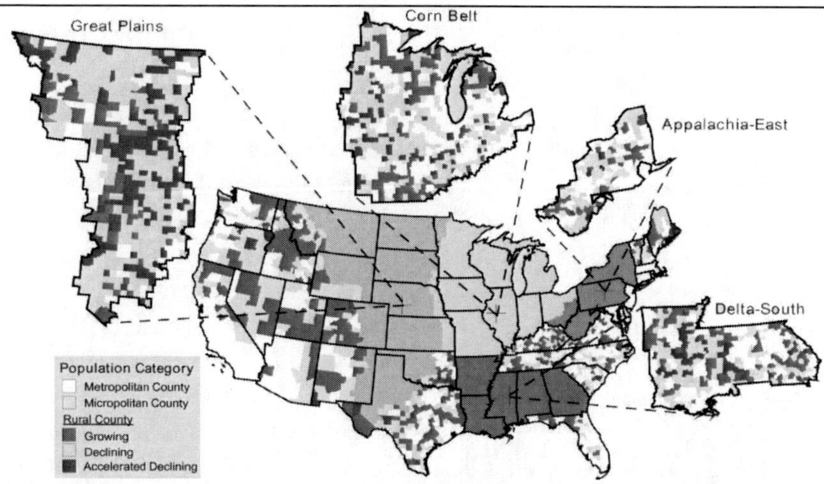

Source: U.S. Census Bureau.

Notes: The 2010 U.S. Census Population compared with the 1980 U.S. Census Population and the 2010 U.S. Office of Management and Budget Metropolitan and Micropolitan Statistical Area county classifications. Rural is FDIC-defined as those counties not designated by the U.S. Office of Management and Budget as part of a Metropolitan or Micropolitan Statistical Area. Rural county classifications for the 2012 study: *Growing*—the population increased between 1980 and 2010, *Declining*—population declined between 1980 and 2010; *Accelerated declining*—population declined between 1980 and 2010, and the rate of decline between 2000 and 2010 worsened from the previous two decades.

Map 3.3. Depopulation Continues to Affect Rural Counties in Four Distinct U.S. Regions.

Despite these demographic challenges, FDIC-insured institutions in depopulating regions continued to perform relatively well. There were 1,091 community banks headquartered in U.S. depopulating rural counties at the end of 2011. While these banks tend to be small, they represent about 16 percent of all community banks. The 2004 study focused on the Great Plains and found that earnings ratios and rates of long-term consolidation were similar between community banks in the rural Great Plains and other rural areas, while Great Plains banks reported comparatively lower rates of growth in total assets, loans and deposits than their metro-based counterparts. The update of this analysis, covering the decade from 2001 through 2011, encompasses depopulating rural areas across the entire Unted States. As in the 2004 study, growth rates for assets, loans and deposits were lower among depopulating rural institutions than their metro counterparts from 2001 through 2007. From 2007 through 2011, however, metro bank growth rates dropped below those of depopulating rural banks. Growth rates for community banks in depopulating rural counties were similar to those of community banks located in growing rural counties; by contrast, the 2004 study found that institutions in growing rural counties had an advantage. As in the 2004 study, consolidation patterns among rural banks in depopulating rural counties were similar to those in metro and micro counties.

Updated analysis shows that community banks located in depopulating rural counties reported lower pretax returns than community banks located in growing rural areas from 2001 through 2007 but reported higher earnings over the past four years. Earnings at community banks located in depopulating rural areas exceeded those in metro-based community banks across all time periods. Asset quality at community banks located in depopulating rural areas was not as strong as metro-based community banks from 2001 through 2007, but those institutions again fared better from 2008 through 2011.

The recent performance success of depopulating rural banks relative to other institutions owes much to their dependence on agriculture. Some 47 percent of community banks in depopulating rural counties are agricultural lending specialists, compared with 11 percent in growing rural counties and only 4 percent in metro counties. The agricultural sector has been strong in recent years, even while the nation entered and slowly exited a serious recession. In inflation-adjusted dollars, five of the best years for U.S. net farm income in the past half century have occurred since 2004.

In addition, the adoption of new technologies for extracting oil and gas led to a new energy boom and even in-migration to a number of depopulating rural counties, most notably in western North Dakota, where previous depopulation trends had been severe.

On the whole, however, the demographic forces that have contributed to rural depopulation and slow growth for rural community banks do not appear likely to reverse in the near term. Community banks doing business in depopulating areas continue to find ways to cope with these challenges and serve the needs of local businesses and households for which they may be the only link to mainstream financial services. While rural depopulation does not immediately threaten the survival of rural community banks, it does place limits on their long run growth potential.

[1] These figures refer to rural counties as defined by the U.S. Office of Management and Budget as of 2010, a definition that this study applies retroactively to previous years.

The migration of noncommunity banks toward areas of rapid economic growth is particularly evident in some of the fastest-growing U.S. metropolitan areas. Table 3.7 lists 21 large U.S. metropolitan areas, encompassing around 21 percent of 2011 U.S. population, that experienced the fastest population growth between 1985 and 2011. Between 1987 and 2011, these metro areas accounted for 36 percent of the net increase in U.S. banking offices. What was most remarkable about the changes in the banking structure of these metro areas was the extent to which noncommunity banks increased their share of both the banking offices and deposits located there. In 1987, noncommunity banks operated just 62 percent of total banking offices in these markets (with 69 percent of total deposits), and by 2011 their share of offices had grown to 80 percent and their share of total deposits had risen to 90 percent.

New charters and acquisitions have been very important in reshaping the mix of community and noncommunity banks in these fast-growing markets. Of all institutions headquartered in these fast-growing markets at year-end 2011, fully two-thirds of both the community and noncommunity banks were chartered sometime after 1984. The 111 noncommunity banks headquartered in these markets in 2011 made up 16 percent of the fast-growing market banks, but they held $2.8 trillion in assets, or 93 percent of the assets of all banks headquartered in these fast-growing markets. As described previously, acquisition was a critical factor in the growth of noncommunity banks in these markets. Since 1984, noncommunity banks headquartered in these fast-growing markets had directly acquired 375 institutions with $1.5 trillion in assets and had indirectly acquired another 1,558 charters.

This example illustrates the process by which noncommunity banks have been able to alter their geographic footprint over time and come to dominate many of the fastest-growing metro areas. While new community banks have continued to be chartered in these same metro markets (more than 1,000 new community banks were chartered after 1984 in these 21 fastest-growing large metro areas alone), as a group they have lost market share as total assets and deposits have risen much faster at noncommunity banks.

Community Banks Predominate in Nonmetro Areas Where Growth Is Slow or Negative

In contrast to noncommunity banks' dominance in metro areas, community banks hold a much stronger competitive position in nonmetro counties. Table 3.4 shows that community banks not only hold a majority share of offices and deposits in micro and rural counties, but that their share has been very stable over the past decade. The downside of this trend is that growth in population and economic output has been slower in these nonmetro areas than in the metro areas where noncommunity banks and offices have proliferated. This slower rate of growth in nonmetro counties tends to limit the growth opportunities available to community banks.

The disparity in growth between metro and nonmetro counties is most pronounced among rural counties. A 2004 FDIC study examined rural depopulation at the county level between 1970 and 2000, identifying 662 rural counties as "declining" or "accelerating declining" in terms of long-term population trends.[24] Over 90 percent of these declining rural counties were located in four distinct geographic regions—the Great Plains, the Corn Belt, the Delta-South, and Appalachia-East—where a heavy reliance on agriculture or mining had contributed to significant declines in total employment over time. Despite these challenges and the lack of opportunity for growth, the 2004 study found that banks headquartered in depopulating rural areas performed comparably to other rural banks in terms of their rate of charter consolidation and most indicators of financial performance.

New Census data showed that the long-term trend of rural depopulation in these regions continued and, in certain respects, intensified between 2000 and 2010. (See the inset box). At the same time, high commodity prices and strong export demand boosted the fortunes of agricultural producers and other commodity-based businesses, helping to offset the effects of declining rural populations. Some of the economic and demographic challenges faced by depopulating regions appear likely to continue in the future. While community banks located in rural areas appear to still perform well, their long-term growth potential will likely remain lower than for banks located in metropolitan markets.

Summary

Community banking is defined to a substantial degree by geography. Community banks have fewer banking offices on average and occupy a smaller geographic area than noncommunity banks, but their geographic reach has expanded somewhat over time. While most banking offices are located in metro areas, community banks are more likely than noncommunity banks to operate offices in nonmetro areas, where, in many cases, they continue to hold a dominant share of total deposits. Community banks are especially important to rural and other nonmetro counties and conduct business in more than 1,200 counties—more than a third of all U.S. counties—where few, if any, noncommunity banks choose to operate.

Overall, deposit market shares have risen over time for noncommunity banks, particularly in the nation's metropolitan areas. Noncommunity banks have been able to dramatically increase their presence in fast-growing metro counties through new charters and especially, in many cases, the acquisition of existing banks. Growth and consolidation in these markets have also created opportunities for community banks, but to a lesser extent. In contrast, the nonmetro areas where community banks generally retain a larger market share have grown more slowly or even declined in population. While these economic and demographic challenges do not appear to be adversely affecting financial performance or leading to higher rates of consolidation among nonmetro community banks, they do appear to limit growth opportunities.

4. Comparative Financial Performance: Community versus Noncommunity Banks

Any meaningful comparison between community and noncommunity banks must address the issue of financial performance, and one common measure for comparing the financial performance of banks of different sizes is return on assets (ROA) or, more precisely, pretax ROA.[25] A comparison of pretax ROA reveals that during most of the study period, noncommunity banks have outperformed community banks. The weighted average pretax ROA for noncommunity banks was 1.31 percent over the study period, compared with 1.02 percent for community banks. This earnings gap was most notable during the period 1993 through 2006, when the profitability advantage for noncommunity institutions averaged 35 basis points, as seen in Chart 4.1.

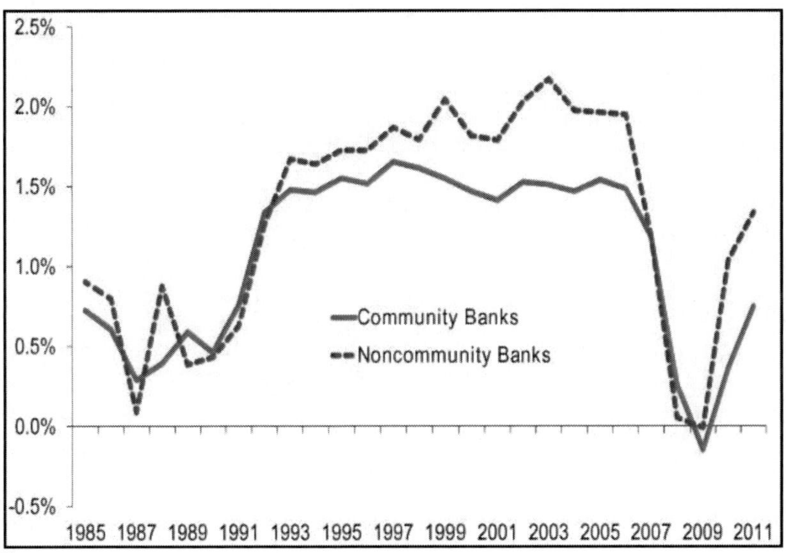

Source: FDIC.

Chart 4.1. Pretax Return on Assets, 1985-2011.

Table 4.1 shows how particular subgroups of community banks have performed compared with their noncommunity bank counterparts. Noncommunity banks outperformed community banks in both metropolitan and nonmetropolitan areas. Older community banks generally performed more favorably compared with noncommunity banks, but among younger banks, noncommunity banks generally had much stronger earnings.

Table 4.1. Weighted Average Pretax ROA by Structural Subgroups

	1986-1990	1991-1995	1996-2000	2001-2005	2006-2010	Aggregate 1985-2011
All Banks	**0.50%**	**1.38%**	**1.79%**	**1.90%**	**0.77%**	**1.26%**
Community Banks	0.47%	1.31%	1.56%	1.49%	0.60%	1.05%
Noncommunity Banks	0.51%	1.41%	1.85%	1.99%	0.80%	1.31%
Headquartered in a Metropolitan Area						
Community Banks	0.38%	1.20%	1.53%	1.49%	0.45%	0.94%
Noncommunity Banks	0.50%	1.40%	1.83%	1.98%	0.79%	1.30%
Not Headquartered in a Metropolitan Area						
Community Banks	0.78%	1.60%	1.63%	1.50%	0.95%	1.25%
Noncommunity Banks	1.10%	1.87%	2.91%	2.39%	1.34%	1.88%
Continuously Operating 1985-2011						
Community Banks	1.20%	1.60%	1.66%	1.56%	0.84%	1.27%
Noncommunity Banks	0.78%	1.55%	1.79%	1.85%	0.84%	1.26%
Not Continuously Operating 1985-2011						
Community Banks	0.20%	1.13%	1.45%	1.38%	0.03%	0.76%
Noncommunity Banks	0.44%	1.35%	1.90%	2.17%	0.68%	1.37%
Less Than 5 Years Old						
Community Banks	-1.12%	0.71%	0.04%	0.26%	-0.74%	-0.29%
Noncommunity Banks	0.63%	1.56%	2.30%	1.68%	0.34%	1.16%
5-10 Years Old						
Community Banks	-0.11%	1.00%	1.44%	1.32%	0.20%	0.64%
Noncommunity Banks	1.55%	1.82%	2.43%	2.07%	0.59%	1.56%
10-25 Years Old						
Community Banks	-0.05%	1.17%	1.66%	1.74%	0.47%	1.01%
Noncommunity Banks	0.46%	2.11%	2.24%	2.74%	0.91%	1.80%
25-50 Years Old						
Community Banks	0.02%	1.30%	1.62%	1.64%	0.46%	0.93%
Noncommunity Banks	-0.14%	1.03%	1.76%	1.97%	1.03%	1.21%
More Than 50 Years Old						
Community Banks	0.73%	1.38%	1.58%	1.50%	0.78%	1.14%
Noncommunity Banks	0.53%	1.36%	1.76%	1.82%	0.79%	1.23%

Source: FDIC.

The factors behind the earnings advantage for noncommunity banks over community banks can be found by breaking down pretax ROA into its major components—net interest income, noninterest income, noninterest expense, and provisions for loan losses. Noncommunity banks have had greater success in generating noninterest income from a variety of sources, explaining much of the gap in earnings. The erosion in recent years of the advantage that community banks have typically enjoyed in generating net interest income from traditional lending activities also contributes to the gap in earnings. Because of their heavy dependence on lending as a source of income, community banks have been disproportionately affected by the long-term trend toward lower net interest margins.

Nonetheless, community banks have almost always incurred lower credit losses than noncommunity banks—a difference that has been most notable during economic downturns—which has helped to narrow the overall earnings gap in recent years. Still, while community banks enjoyed a significant advantage prior to 2000 in terms of lower noninterest expenses, noncommunity banks have since managed to substantially reduce their noninterest expenses to a level that is comparable to community banks when expressed as a percentage of assets.

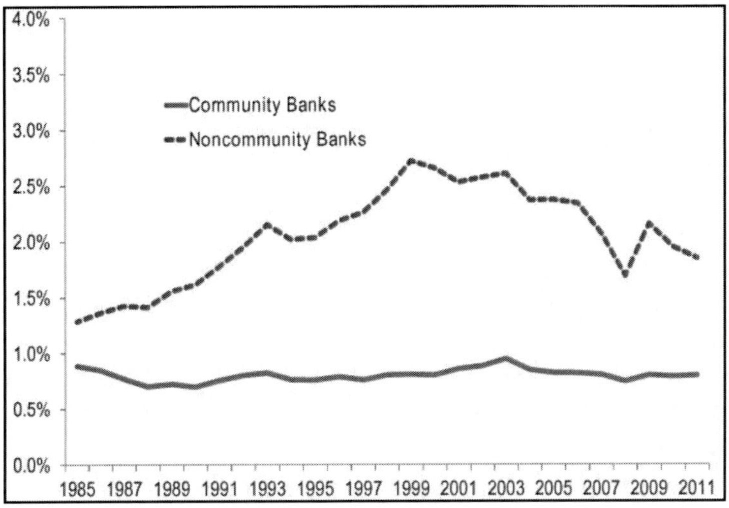

Source: FDIC.

Chart 4.2. Noninterest Income to Average Assets, 1985-2011.

Table 4.2. Noninterest Income at Community and Noncommunity Banks (Call Report Filers Only)

Category of Noninterest Income	As a Percentage of Noninterest Income		As a Percentage of Average Assets	
	Community Banks	Noncommunity Banks	Community Banks	Noncommunity Banks
Service Charges on Deposit Accounts	40%	16%	0.34%	0.35%
Fiduciary Income	8%	12%	0.07%	0.28%
Gains on Asset Sales	10%	3%	0.09%	0.08%
Market Sensitive Revenue*	3%	13%	0.03%	0.29%
Securitization Income	0%	8%	0.02%	0.18%
Servicing Income	3%	8%	0.02%	0.17%
Insurance Income	3%	2%	0.03%	0.04%
All Other Noninterest Income	33%	38%	0.28%	0.86%
Total Noninterest Income	100%	100%	0.85%	2.25%

Source: FDIC. Weighted averages of Call Report data from 2001-2011.

* Includes trading, venture capital, and investment banking income.

Note: Beginning in 2011, FDIC-insured institutions that file Call Reports began reporting more detailed data on noninterest income components. Similar data are not available for Thrift Financial Report filers.

Noninterest Income Explains Much of the Earnings Gap

The largest and most apparent advantage in profitability for noncommunity banks compared with community banks is their ability to generate much higher volumes of noninterest income. Over the study period, noninterest income averaged 2.05 percent of average assets at noncommunity banks, compared with only 0.8 percent for community banks. As illustrated in Chart 4.2, throughout the late 1980s and the 1990s, noncommunity banks steadily increased the level of their noninterest income relative to their assets (from 1.21 percent in 1985 to 2.6 percent in 1999), while noninterest income levels remained essentially unchanged at community banks.

The ability of noncommunity banks to generate such high levels of noninterest income relative to community banks is closely connected to their ability to earn noninterest income from a wider range of sources. Table 4.2 illustrates the primary sources of noninterest income for community banks and noncommunity banks that filed Call Reports over the last 11 years of the study period.[26] For example, almost 13 percent of the noninterest income earned by these noncommunity banks came from market-sensitive revenues, which include income from trading, venture capital, and investment banking activities. This compares to only 3.4 percent of the noninterest income earned by community banks from such sources. Noncommunity banks also generate much higher levels of income from asset servicing and fiduciary (trust) activities. By comparison, community banks obtained about 40 percent of their noninterest income from service charges on deposit accounts and about 10 percent from asset sales.

Table 4.2 illustrates the categories of noninterest income that are reported in every Call Report. Other categories of noninterest income (which are included in all other noninterest income) are reported by banks only if they exceed minimum levels.[27] Based upon the incomplete information available on the "all other" category, interchange fees appear to be the single most important component of "other noninterest income" for both community and noncommunity bank Call Report filers in 2011. Amounts reported for 2011 by banks that itemized these fees indicate that they may be significantly more important for noncommunity banks (14.6 percent of total noninterest income) than for community banks (8.8 percent).

Narrower Margins Pose a Challenge for Community Banks

Historically, community banks have been more successful than noncommunity banks in generating net interest income (see Chart 4.3). Over the entire study period, the ratio of net interest income to total assets has been higher at community banks in all but one year.

A similar pattern can be seen in the net interest margin, which measures the spread between asset yields and funding costs for earning assets. Peak levels for net interest margins were reached by both groups in 1993 and 1994 (Chart 4.4). The subsequent decline in the net interest margin has had more significant competitive implications for community banks, as net interest income accounts for more than 80 percent of community bank net operating revenue, compared with about two-thirds of revenue at noncommunity banks. In addition, the long-term advantage in net interest income for community banks has narrowed in recent years, as the net interest margin for noncommunity banks rose sharply from 2008 through 2010.

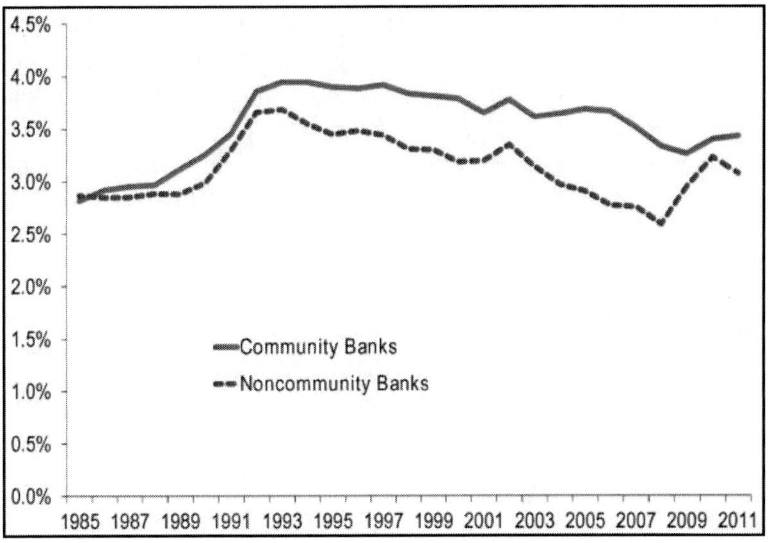

Source: FDIC.

Chart 4.3. Net Interest Income to Average Assets, 1985-2011.

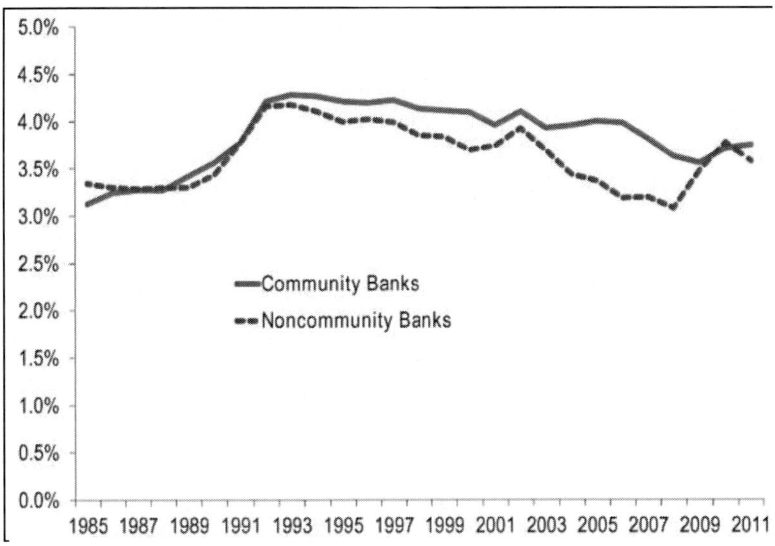

Source: FDIC.

Chart 4.4. Net Interest Margin, 1985-2011.

Community Banks Generally Have Higher Yields on Earning Assets

One key to the traditional advantage of community banks in generating net interest income is a generally higher yield on earning assets. The ratio of interest income to earning assets at community banks has exceeded that of noncommunity banks in 17 of the past 27 years (see Chart 4.7), including every year since 2001. Over the entire study period, total interest income as a percent of earning assets averaged 7.6 percent at community banks, compared with just 6.7 percent for noncommunity banks. One factor that may contribute to a higher yield on earning assets for community banks is the nature of their loan portfolios. Loans held by community banks tend to be less homogeneous in structure and terms than loans made by noncommunity banks, which are more likely to be large-scale, transactional lenders. Interest-earning assets represent a larger share of total assets at community banks. Over the study period, earning assets averaged 91.8 percent of total assets at community banks, compared with 86 percent at noncommunity banks.

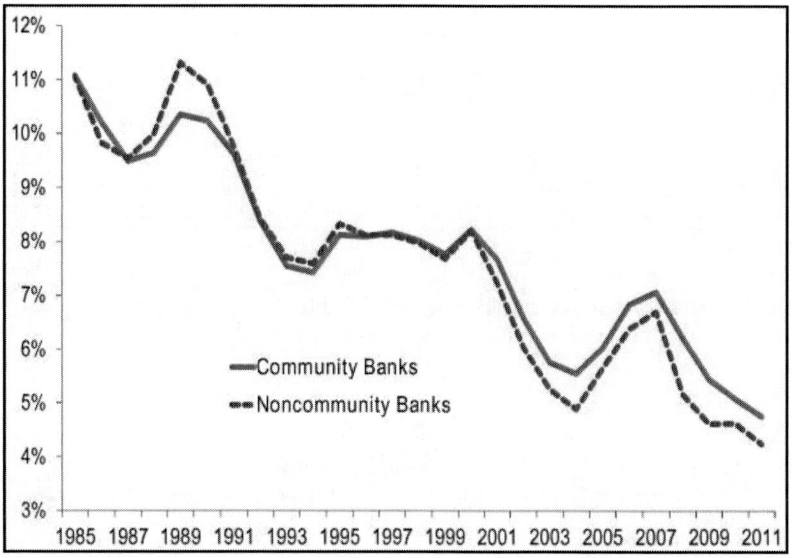

Source: FDIC.

Chart 4.5. Average Yield on Earning Assets, 1985-2011.

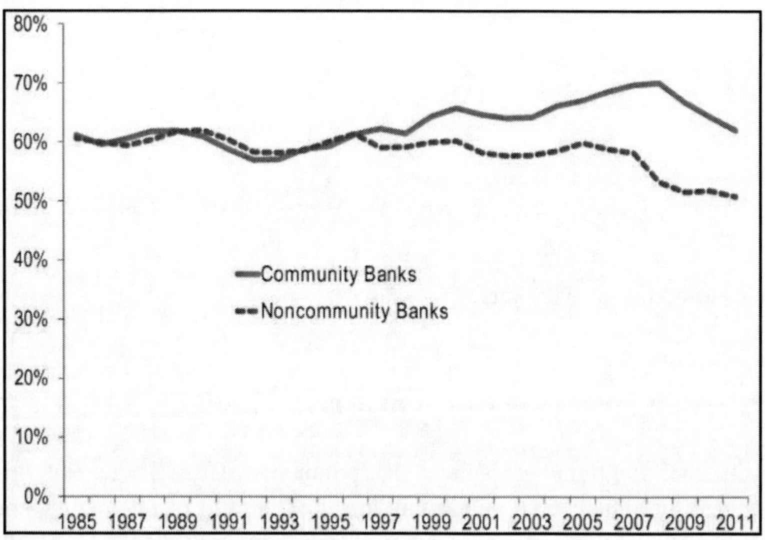

Source: FDIC.

Chart 4.6. Net Loans and Leases to Average Assets, 1985-2011.

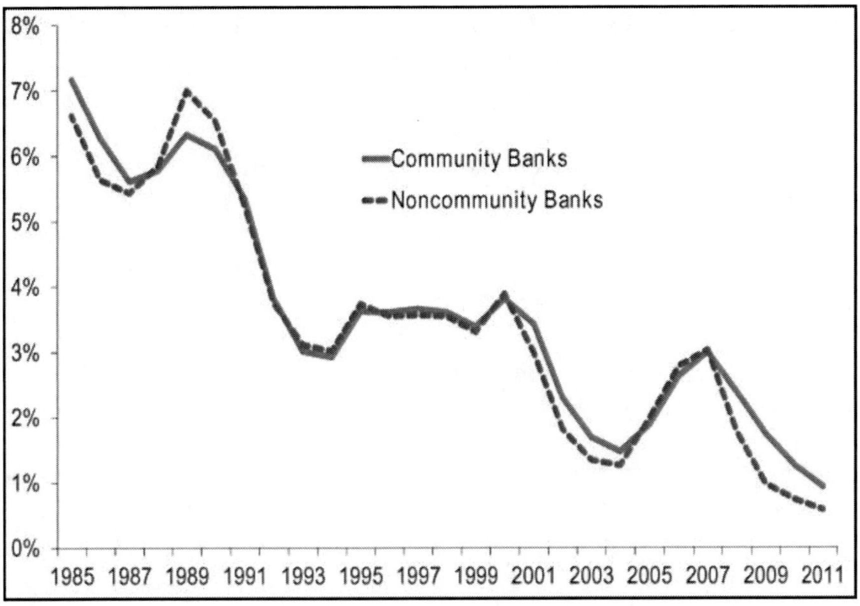

Source: FDIC.

Chart 4.7. Total Interest Expense to Average Assets, 1985-2011.

Table 4.3. Asset Composition Trends

	Total Loans / Total Assets			CRE Loans / Total Assets*			Long-Term Assets / Total Assets**		
	1990	2000	2011	1990	2000	2011	1990	2000	2011
Community Banks	60.9%	65.8%	62.0%	14.5%	19.6%	26.7%	14.9%	22.3%	27.4%
Noncommunity Banks	62.0%	60.2%	50.8%	12.1%	9.9%	8.8%	14.6%	19.5%	22.6%

Source: FDIC.

* Includes real estate construction and development loans, loans secured by nonfarm nonresidential and multifamily residential real estate properties, and loans to finance construction and commercial real estate not secured by real estate properties.

** Call Report filers only.

Another possibility, however, is that community banks have maintained higher yields in part by changing the composition of their loan portfolios, as shown by the three measures in Table 4.3. First, community banks have increased the share of loans on their balance sheets. Loan balances rose as a share of total assets at community banks from a low of 56.9 percent at the end of 1992 to a peak level of 70.1 percent at the end of 2008 (see Chart 4.6). While the loans-to-assets ratio declined for community banks in each of the next three years, it remained at 62 percent at the end of 2011, compared with only 50.8 percent at noncommunity banks. Second, community banks also have increased their holdings of longer-maturity loans and securities. The share of community bank assets with remaining maturities of five years or more rose from 19 percent at the end of 2006 to 27 percent at the end of 2011. During this interval, the share of long-term assets at noncommunity banks declined slightly, from 24 percent to 23 percent. Finally, community banks have evolved over the study period from being predominantly retail lenders to commercial lenders, with a particular focus on lending secured by commercial real estate. This shift will be discussed in greater detail in Chapter 5 of the study, which discusses bank lending specialty groups.

Noncommunity Banks Generally Have Lower Borrowing Costs

In contrast to the traditionally higher asset yields found at community banks, noncommunity banks have typically had an advantage in funding costs (see Chart 4.5). Interest expenses averaged 3.4 percent of total assets for community banks over the study period, compared with 2.7 percent for noncommunity banks. Community banks did report lower average funding costs in ten of the past 27 years, but noncommunity banks have usually fared better when interest rates have been low or falling, as has been the case during most of the past decade.

Several factors explain the higher cost of funds for community banks in recent years. First, community banks rely much more on time deposits for funding compared with noncommunity banks. Time deposits tend to be costlier and reprice more slowly than other liabilities. From 1985 through 2011, time deposits funded an average of 41 percent of community bank assets, more than twice the average for noncommunity banks. Also, when short-term interest rates fall to especially low levels, competitive pressures may result in an effective floor for interest-bearing deposits, pricing them above other forms of short-term funding. This helps to explain why community bank funding costs have compared favorably with noncommunity banks when interest rates were stable or rising, but have not compared as well when rates fell to very low levels (see Chart 4.8). More recently, the cost of funds at noncommunity banks has benefited from guarantees or additional insurance above the normal FDIC insurance limit for noninterest-bearing deposits, as the bulk of these noninterest-bearing deposits have flowed into noncommunity banks.[28]

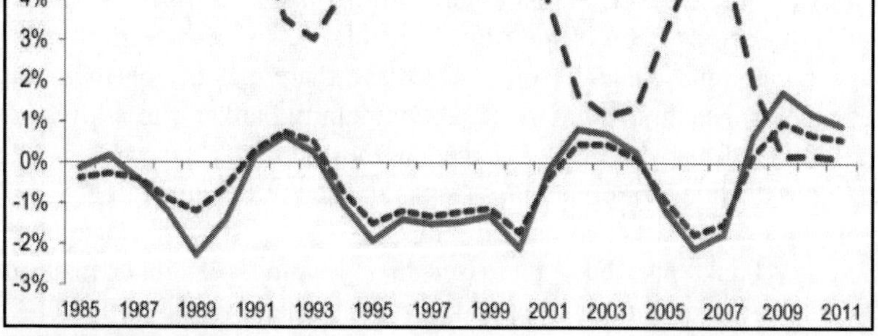

Sources: FDIC, Federal Reserve.

Chart 4.8. Spread Between Average Funding Cost and Fed Funds Rate, 1985-2011.

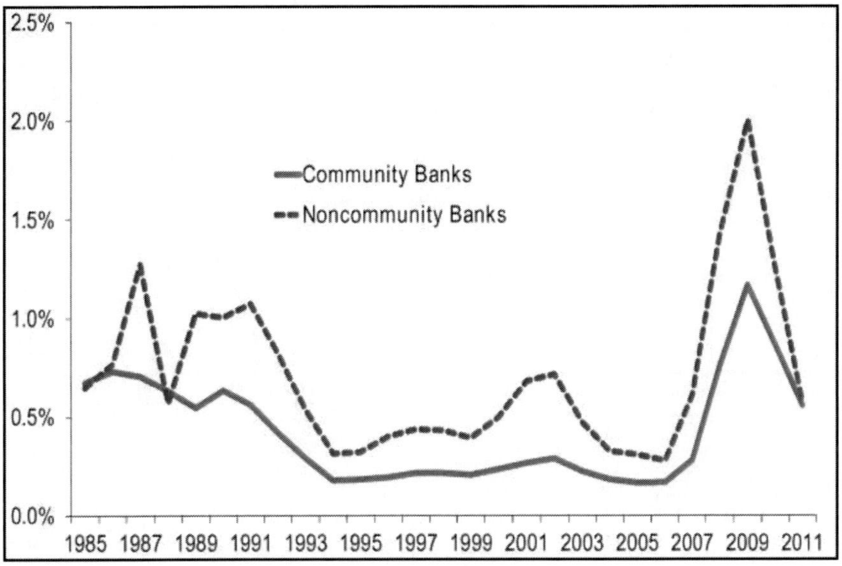

Source: FDIC.

* Does not include Thrift Financial Report filers prior to 1987.

Chart 4.9. Loss Provision to Average Assets, 1985-2011.*

Community Banks Have Lower Expenses for Credit Losses

Community banks have generally had a sizable advantage over noncommunity banks with respect to expenses for credit losses. This difference is reflected in the loan-loss provisions of the two groups, shown in Chart 4.9, and mirrors the relative loss rates in their loan portfolios. Noncommunity banks generally had higher loan-loss rates both in the early years of the study period, when their loan portfolios were more heavily weighted toward commercial loans, as well as in more recent years, after their portfolios shifted more to consumer lending. Loan-loss rates at community banks have remained lower throughout the study period even as their loan mix shifted in the opposite direction, from retail to commercial loans.

One reason that the shift in loan mix and the overall increase in the risk of community bank portfolios has not led to a convergence in credit loss rates is that most problem loans at community banks are secured loans, while a higher share of problem loans at noncommunity banks are unsecured. Between 1991 through 2011, credit card lines alone account for more than one-third of net loan charge-offs at noncommunity banks. Moreover, a comparison of loss rates on individual loan categories suggests that community banks may also do a better job of underwriting loans than noncommunity institutions (see Table 4.4). In two retail loan categories—residential real estate loans and loans to individuals—community banks consistently reported lower average loss rates from 1991 through 2011, the period for which these data are available. While average loss rates on commercial real estate loans have been comparable for community and noncommunity banks in noncrisis years when losses were low, loan loss rates were much higher at noncommunity banks than at community banks during real estate downturns, when loss rates rose. Similarly, while noncommunity banks have generally reported lower average loss rates on commercial and industrial (C&I) loans during economic expansions, their C&I loan losses spiked well above those at community banks during economic downturns.

In the end, the relative advantage that community banks have enjoyed in terms of lower loan-loss expenses has served only to mitigate, not reverse, their overall earnings gap with noncommunity banks. Despite generally higher loan-loss rates, noncommunity banks have been able to consistently generate higher returns on assets.

Table 4.4. Average Net Charge-Off Rates by Loan Type

Loan Type	Bank Type	1991-1995	1996-2000	2001-2005	2006-2010	Aggregate 1991-2011
Nonfarm, nonresidential CRE	Community	0.55%	0.07%	0.09%	0.35%	0.29%
	Noncommunity	1.21%	0.04%	0.11%	0.61%	0.49%
Construction and development	Community	0.87%	0.08%	0.09%	2.04%	1.25%
	Noncommunity	2.56%	0.04%	0.09%	2.86%	1.82%
1-4 family residential	Community	0.13%	0.06%	0.06%	0.35%	0.18%
	Noncommunity	0.24%	0.12%	0.11%	1.16%	0.65%
C&I	Community	1.30%	0.63%	0.67%	1.06%	0.89%
	Noncommunity	0.83%	0.48%	1.13%	1.24%	0.91%
Credit card	Community	2.41%	3.61%	4.02%	7.76%	3.73%
	Noncommunity	3.80%	4.70%	5.30%	6.91%	5.58%
Other consumer	Community	0.59%	0.70%	0.81%	0.90%	0.74%
	Noncommunity	0.82%	1.12%	1.46%	2.11%	1.54%
Agricultural*	Community	0.17%	0.15%	0.14%	0.15%	0.15%
	Noncommunity	0.26%	0.20%	0.33%	0.44%	0.34%

Source: FDIC.

* Includes agricultural production loans and real estate loans secured by farmland. Detailed data on loss rates by loan type were not reported prior to 1991.

Community Banks Have Historically Had Lower Noninterest Expenses

Over the course of the study, average noninterest expenses have almost always been lower at community banks than at noncommunity banks (see Chart 4.10). Total noninterest expense averaged 2.9 percent of assets for community banks from 1985 through 2011 compared with an average of 3.1 percent for noncommunity banks. Despite a long-term advantage of 22 basis points, the gap in expense ratios between the two groups has been gradually narrowing for more than a decade. Noncommunity banks have reduced their expenses, so that the gap is now almost nonexistent.

In the early years of the study period, noncommunity banks reported higher expense ratios for both salaries and employee benefits and for expenses associated with premises and fixed assets (see Chart 4.11 and Chart 4.12). During the latter half of the period, however, noncommunity banks were able to reduce these costs below community bank levels. Community banks have not been able to reduce these costs in a similar fashion, and in fact have increased their overall payroll costs over time, although community banks do continue to report lower average payroll expenses per employee than noncommunity banks. Because community banks maintain more employees per dollar of assets, their payroll expenses are higher than those of noncommunity banks when measured as a percentage of assets. Over time, institutions of all sizes have been able to reduce their numbers of employees per dollar of assets. Noncommunity banks, however, have been particularly successful in this regard, raising the ratio of assets per employee from $2.6 million in 1984 to $7.2 million by 2011. Despite the significant expansion in the number of total banking offices since 2000, noncommunity banks have managed to steadily reduce their premises and fixed asset expense levels, while these expenses have remained largely unchanged at community banks (see Chart 4.12).

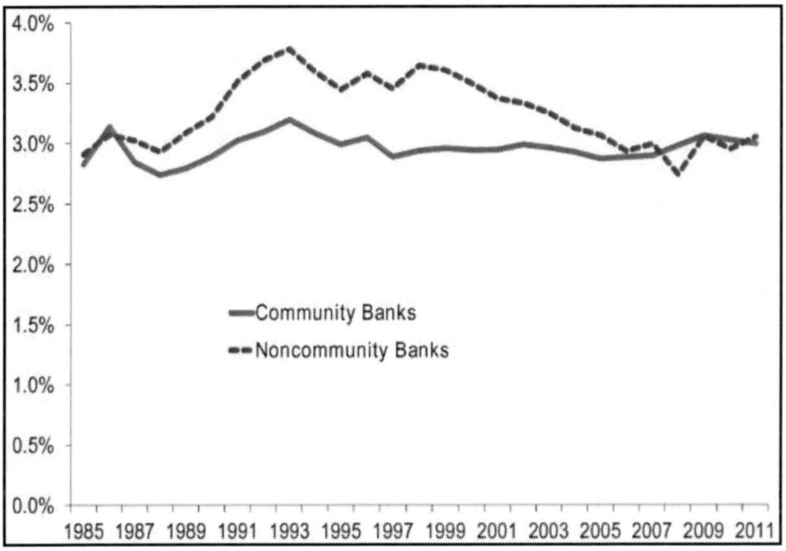

Source: FDIC.

Chart 4.10. Noninterest Expense to Average Assets, 1985-2011.

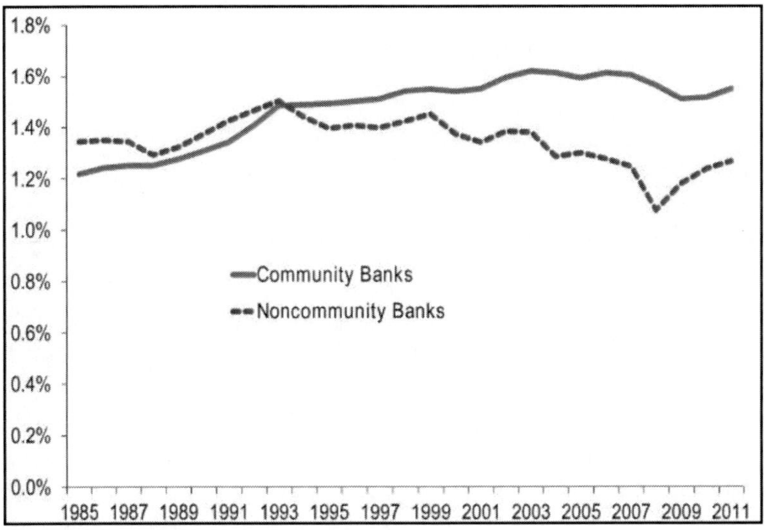

Source: FDIC.

Chart 4.11. Salaries and Employee Benefits Expense to Average Assets, 1985-2011.

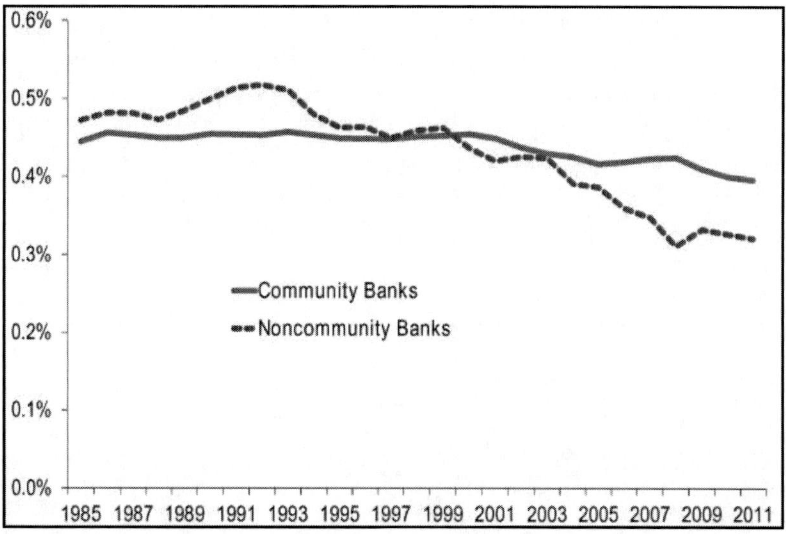

Source: FDIC.

Chart 4.12. Premises and Fixed Asset Expense to Average Assets, 1985-2011.

The "Efficiency Gap" Between Community and Noncommunity Institutions

The individual income and expense components that make up pretax ROA reveal a more detailed picture of how the performance of community and noncommunity banks differ. Taken together, they indicate that community banks have typically not generated the same level of earnings as noncommunity banks over the long term.

Three of these earnings components—noninterest expense, noninterest income and net interest income—can be rearranged into what is commonly referred to as the efficiency ratio:

$$\text{Efficiency Ratio} = \frac{\text{Noninterest Expense}}{\text{Net Operating Revenue}}$$

$$\text{Net Operating Revenue} = \text{Net Interest Income} + \text{Noninterest Income}$$

The efficiency ratio is a simple expression of the underlying operational performance of banks apart from differences in performance caused by asset quality factors. It compares the level of overhead costs (total noninterest expense) to net operating revenues (the sum of net interest income and total noninterest income). A higher efficiency ratio actually suggests inefficiency, as it indicates that the bank is less productive in terms of converting expenditures into revenue.

Comparing the efficiency ratio of community and noncommunity banks over time (see Chart 4.13) shows that community banks have traditionally been less efficient than noncommunity banks—that is, they have incurred more expenses per dollar revenue. This "efficiency gap" has widened considerably since the late 1990s. The average annual gap between community and noncommunity banks was 3.5 percent between 1985 and 1998, but widened to an average level of 9.2 percent between 1999 and 2011. This widening of the efficiency gap mirrors the gap that has emerged in terms of profitability as measured by pretax ROA.

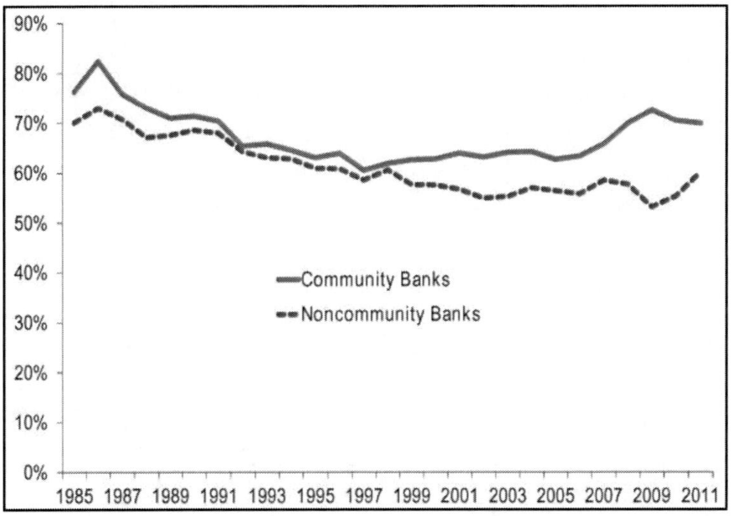

Source: FDIC.

Chart 4.13. Efficiency Ratio, 1985-2011.

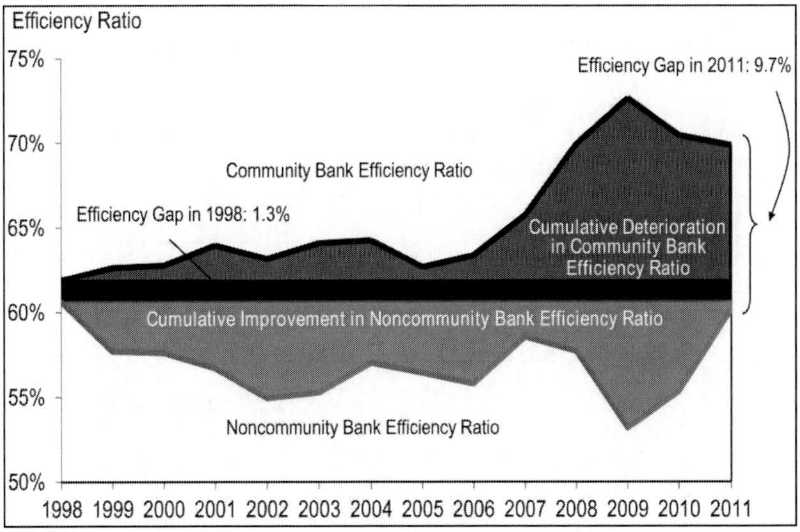

Source: FDIC.

Chart 4.14. A Sizable Efficiency Gap Has Developed Between Community and Noncommunity Banks Since 1998.

Chart 4.14 takes a closer look at the widening of the efficiency gap over time. The last time the efficiency gap was less than 2 percent was in 1998, when it narrowed to just 1.3 percent. Since 1998, the efficiency gap has widened considerably, reaching a peak of 19.5 percent in 2009 before narrowing to a still wide 9.7 percent in 2011. Almost all of the cumulative widening of the gap that took place over this 13-year period occurred as a result of a deterioration in the efficiency ratio of community banks. While the community bank efficiency ratio increased from 61.9 percent to 69.9 percent over this period, the efficiency ratio of noncommunity banks improved slightly, from 60.6 percent to 60.2 percent. Chart 4.14 also shows that the 9.7 percent efficiency gap reported in 2011 was actually a sizable improvement from a gap of 19.5 percent in 2009. The efficiency gap as of 2009 reflected cumulative deterioration in the efficiency ratio of community banks since 1998 from 61.9 percent to 72.7 percent, improvement in the efficiency ratio of noncommunity banks from 60.6 percent as of 1998 to 53.2 percent as of 2009, plus a relatively small 1.3 percent efficiency gap that existed as of 1998.

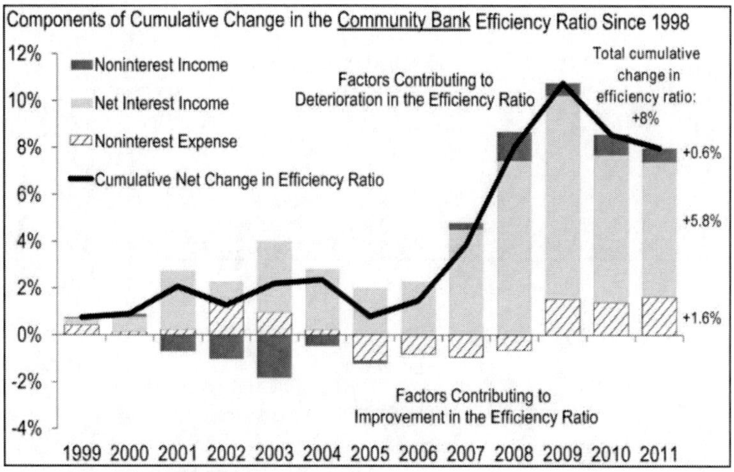

Source: FDIC.

Chart 4.15. Declining Net Interest Income to Assets Explains More Than 70 Percent of the Increase in the Community Bank Efficiency Ratio Since 1998.

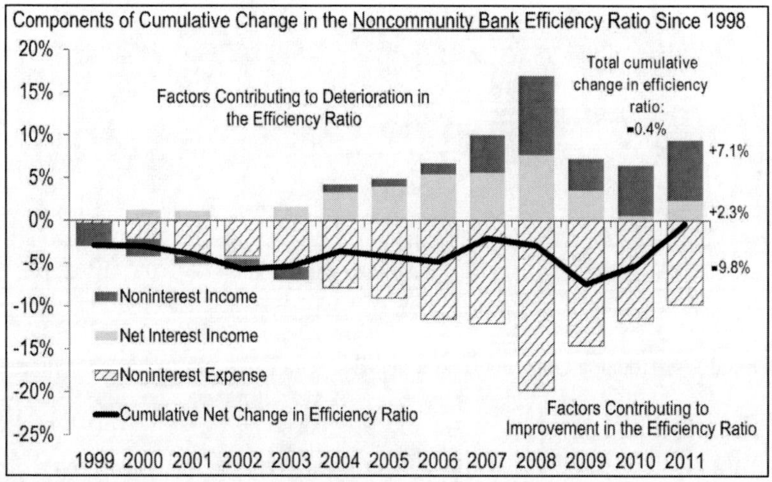

Source: FDIC.

Chart 4.16. Long-Term Deterioration in Income Ratios for Noncommunity Banks Has Been Offset by Better Expense Ratios, Leaving Efficiency Nearly Unchanged.

The factors that account for the widening of the efficiency gap since 1998 can be identified and measured with considerable precision by differentiating the efficiency ratio with respect to each of the income and expense ratios that constitute it. Performing these calculations, substituting in the appropriate ratios for each year, and accumulating the total changes attributable to each component since 1998, yields the results in Charts 4.15 and 4.16.

Chart 4.15 depicts the components of cumulative change in the community bank efficiency ratio since 1998. By far the most important factor explaining the rise in the community bank efficiency ratio since 1998 was the compression of net interest margins. Between 1998 and 2011, the ratio of net interest income to average assets declined by 41 basis points, resulting in a 5.8 percentage point increase in the community bank efficiency ratio. This factor alone explained more than 70 percent of the total increase in the community bank efficiency ratio since 1998. While noninterest income and noninterest expense helped to lower the efficiency ratio slightly in the years leading up to the financial crisis, these factors turned into small net negatives in the years after the financial crisis. In fact, a net increase of just 6 basis points in the ratio of noninterest expense to total assets between 1998 and 2011 resulted in over one-fifth of the total increase in the community bank efficiency ratio during that interval.

Chart 4.16 depicts the same breakdown in terms of changes in the noncommunity bank efficiency ratio. While the efficiency ratio for this group underwent only a very small 0.4 percentage point decline between 1998 and 2011, this net change belies more substantial—and largely offsetting—changes to the components of the ratio. Noncommunity banks experienced a net improvement in the ratio of noninterest expense to average assets of almost 8 basis points between 1998 and 2011. With a multiplier that averaged 19 during the period, this relatively small improvement in noninterest expenses was enough to fully cancel out the deterioration in income ratios for noncommunity banks.

Charts 4.15 and 4.16 also show how many of these same income and expense trends contributed to the development of the even larger 19.5 percent efficiency gap in 2009.

That year marked the highest efficiency ratio for community banks since the late 1980s and the lowest efficiency ratio for noncommunity banks since at least 1984. Since 2009, noncommunity banks have experienced a net increase in noninterest expenses and declines in both income categories. Meanwhile, community banks have seen a small improvement in their ratio of net interest income to average assets, while noninterest income and noninterest expense ratios are little changed. It remains to be seen whether the efficiency gap between community and noncommunity banks will continue to narrow in coming years as interest rates normalize, lending activity continues to recover, and regulatory reforms are fully enacted. There is at least the possibility that the pre-crisis and crisis years that marked the emergence of this efficiency gap represent an anomaly that will not be repeated once banking activity returns to normal.

A recent research paper by FDIC economists further explores the causes of the widening efficiency ratio gap between community banks and noncommunity banks.[29] The analysis presented in the paper decomposes the efficiency ratio to examine additional factors that may have contributed to changes in the ratio over time. The paper also extends the discussion of average costs to explore the importance of economies of scale at community banks and finds that most of the divergence in the efficiency ratio between community and noncommunity banks can be attributed to a decline in the spread between community bank yields on loans and the cost of deposits. Additionally, the analysis presented in the paper shows that the decline in the spread has been magnified by the increased reliance of community banks on revenues derived from loans.

Summary

The most important factor in the earnings difference between community and noncommunity banks is the ability of noncommunity banks to generate noninterest income. Looking at the earnings gap through the lens of the efficiency ratio, the relationship between noninterest expense and net operating revenue shows a similar advantage for noncommunity banks. Another major element in bank earnings is the trade-off between net interest income and credit losses. Community banks generally have an advantage over noncommunity banks in each of those areas, reporting both higher average yields and lower loan losses than noncommunity banks. Nonetheless, gradual erosion in the net interest income ratio of community banks in recent years has pushed their efficiency ratio higher, even as community banks have added risk to their balance sheets in search of additional yield. Chapter 5 examines the shift in community bank balance sheets and the prevalence and performance of different bank lending specialties.

5. Comparative Performance of Community Bank Lending Specialty Groups

Introduction

Community banks are defined in large part by their focus on traditional lending and deposit gathering activities. However, over the study period, the composition of their loan portfolios has changed. This chapter begins with discussion of overall lending trends in the banking industry and documents how community banks have shifted their focus away from retail and toward commercial lending, with a particular emphasis on loans secured by commercial real estate. Next, community banks are characterized by their lending specialty to observe how their business strategy has changed over time and to measure the relative performance of different business models. The chapter concludes with a discussion of commercial real estate lending trends and the implications of this lending strategy on the financial performance of community banks.

The Changing Composition of Community Bank Asset Portfolios

Chapter 4 described the gradual increase in the riskiness of community bank asset portfolios over the study period, driven by increases in loans as a percent of total assets and holdings of longer-maturity loans and securities. Another important trend that altered community bank loan portfolios over this period was the shift away from a retail focus and toward a commercial focus. This occurred as noncommunity banks were shifting their portfolios in the opposite direction, from a commercial to a retail lending focus, and generally reducing the share of loans on their balance sheets. Chart 5.1 shows that retail loans (1-4 family residential real estate loans and loans to individuals) represented over 61 percent of all loans at community banks in 1984, compared with 35 percent of all loans at noncommunity banks. By the end of 2011, these ratios had virtually reversed, as retail loans made up 36 percent of community bank loans and 54 percent of noncommunity bank loans.

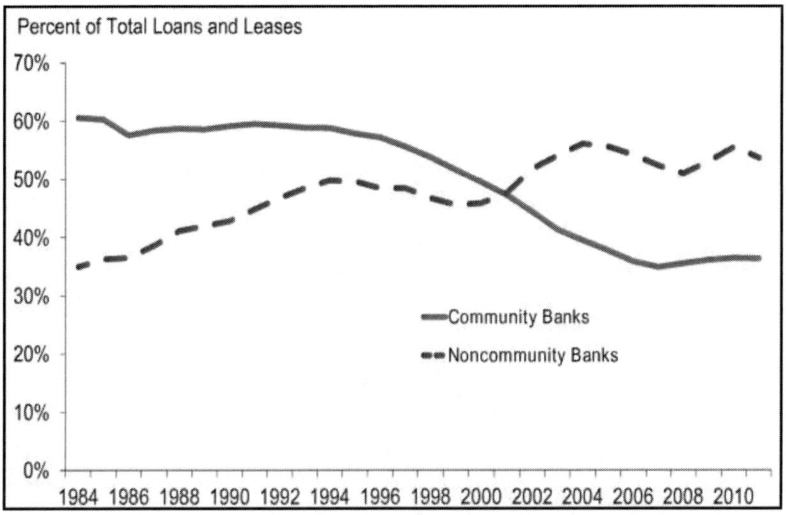

Source: FDIC.

Note: Retail loans include loans secured by 1-4 family residential real estate properties plus loans to individuals.

Chart 5.1. Retail Loans as a Percent of Total Loans and Leases, 1984-2011.

While this shift was taking place, community banks remained focused on loans secured by real estate. At the end of 1984, 70 percent of all community bank loans were secured by real estate, a share that rose to 78 percent by 2011. Over time, community banks shifted the primary emphasis of their real estate lending from residential real estate loans to commercial real estate loans, including construction loans. Between 1984 and 2011, residential real estate loans fell from 47 percent of community bank total loans to 32 percent, while commercial real estate loans rose from 21 percent of loans to 42 percent. By comparison, total real estate loans held by noncommunity banks increased from 36 percent of all loans in 1984 to 51 percent at the end of 2011. All of the increase in real estate lending by noncommunity banks during this period can be accounted for by a rise in their holdings of residential mortgages.

Table 5.1 depicts the overall changes in the portfolio composition of community and noncommunity banks over the period of the study. It shows the shift in community bank assets from securities to loans, led by increases in construction loans and other commercial real estate loans, as well as agricultural loans. Meanwhile, community bank holdings of consumer loans and residential mortgages declined as a percent of assets, while commercial and industrial (C&I) loans remained steady at just over 8 percent of total assets. Community banks continued to represent a significant source of credit to local farms and businesses. As of 2011, community banks held 14 percent of banking industry assets, but 46 percent of the industry's small loans to farms and businesses.[30] Noncommunity banks had sizable increases in their percentage holdings of securities, residential mortgages and consumer loans, which were offset by declines in percentage holdings of C&I loans, construction loans and other commercial real estate loans, and other loans and leases. Agricultural loans continued to make up less than 1 percent of total assets at noncommunity banks. Total assets at noncommunity banks increased more than fivefold over the study period, while their holdings of consumer loans increased more than sixfold, and their holdings of mortgage loans increased almost sevenfold.

Lending Specialty Groups

Beyond analyzing the changes in the aggregate lending mix at both community and noncommunity banks, it is valuable to examine those community banks that have chosen to specialize in particular types of lending. The majority of community bank loans fall into one of five major loan categories: mortgage loans, consumer loans, CRE loans, agricultural loans, and C&I loans. Table 5.2 lists these five major loan categories along with C&D loans, which represent an important subcomponent of CRE loans. Summary statistics show that the most widely held loan types include mortgage loans, consumer loans, CRE loans and C&I loans, with 95 percent or more of all community banks reporting positive balances of these loan types at year-end 2011. A slightly smaller share also reported holdings of C&D loans (90.2 percent) and agricultural loans (77 percent). However, whether measured in terms of total, mean or median holdings, loans secured by commercial and residential real estate are the two largest loan types held by community banks.

While many community banks hold relatively diversified loan portfolios, a small majority can be considered as having a lending specialty in one of five broad groups. Table 5.3 shows the lending specialty groups used in this study. Banks meeting more than one of these five single-specialty definitions are categorized as *multi-specialists,* while banks meeting none of the specialty definitions are grouped into the *no specialty* category.[31] These categories are helpful in understanding the various lending strategies employed by community banks, how these strategies have evolved, and how the relative performance of these groups compares over time.

Table 5.4 shows the number and percent of community banks that met the criteria for each lending specialty group between 1984 and 2011. About 57 percent of community banks had a single lending specialty by these definitions in 2011, while the rest are either multi-specialists or had no specialty.

The number of CRE lending specialists increased over the study period, from 2 percent of community banks in 1984 to 24 percent in 2011. Mortgage specialists and agricultural specialists each made up a substantial share of community banks over the study period, although the number and share of mortgage specialists declined after 2000. The share of consumer specialists declined sharply during the study period, from 9 percent of community banks in 1984 to 1 percent (or just 46 banks) in 2011, as noncommunity banks increasingly migrated toward this line of business. Although the total share of C&I loans held by community banks as a percent of assets in 2011 remained unchanged from 1984 (at 8 percent), fewer community banks (in both number and percent) were C&I specialists by the end of the study. Over 11 percent of community banks qualified as C&I specialists in 1984, but only 2 percent (153 banks) met that definition in 2011. Community banks with no lending specialty represented a significant share of community banks each year, and were the largest group of community banks in 2011 (31 percent). Multi-specialists increased slightly during the study period, from 8 percent of community banks in 1984 to 12 percent in 2011.

Table 5.1. Changes in the Portfolio Composition of Community and Noncommunity Banks, 1984-2011

Loan or Asset Category	Community Banks			
	Year-End 1984		Year-End 2011	
	Dollars in Billions	Percent of Total Assets	Dollars in Billions	Percent of Total Assets
Mortgage Loans*	$399.7	29.0%	$400.3	20.3%
Consumer Loans	$114.3	8.3%	$53.0	2.7%
Commercial Real Estate (CRE) Loans**	$182.1	13.2%	$523.8	26.6%
Construction and Development (C&D) Loans	$34.0	2.5%	$83.8	4.3%
Commercial and Industrial (C&I) Loans	$115.1	8.3%	$163.5	8.3%
Agricultural Loans***	$35.4	2.6%	$85.5	4.3%
Other Loans and Leases	$1.6	0.1%	$21.4	1.1%
Less: Loan Loss Provisions and Unearned Income	$14.3	1.0%	$23.5	1.2%
Net Loans and Leases	$834.0	60.4%	$1,224.0	62.0%
Securities	$350.9	25.4%	$450.1	22.8%
Other Assets	$194.9	14.1%	$298.6	15.1%
Total Assets	$1,379.8	100.0%	$1,972.7	100.0%
	Noncommunity Banks			
Mortgage Loans*	$299.8	13.2%	$2,088.3	17.5%
Consumer Loans	$196.7	8.7%	$1,254.6	10.5%
Commercial Real Estate (CRE) Loans*	$203.6	9.0%	$994.9	8.3%
Construction and Development (C&D) Loans	$67.3	3.0%	$156.2	1.3%
Commercial and Industrial (C&I) Loans	$466.9	20.5%	$1,183.1	9.9%
Agricultural Loans***	$15.2	0.7%	$44.5	0.4%
Other Loans and Leases	$235.7	10.4%	$663.0	5.6%
Less: Loan Loss Provisions and Unearned Income	$27.5	1.2%	$169.4	1.4%
Net Loans and Leases	$1,390.4	61.2%	$6,059.1	50.8%
Securities	$322.8	14.2%	$2,400.2	20.1%
Other Assets	$560.1	24.6%	$3,460.2	29.0%
Total Assets	$2,273.3	100.0%	$11,919.5	100.0%

Source: FDIC.

* Mortgage loans include home equity lines of credit, junior liens and other loans secured by residential real estate.

** CRE loans include construction and development (C&D) loans, loans secured by multifamily properties, and loans secured by nonfarm, nonresidential real estate.

*** Agricultural loans include production loans and loans secured by farm real estate.

Table 5.2. Holdings of Major Loan Types by FDIC-Insured Community Banks, Year-End 2011

Loan Type	Percent of Community Banks With Positive Holdings	Loan Type as Percent of Total Assets							
		Mean	Percentiles						
			5th	10th	25th	50th (Median)	75th	90th	95th
Commercial Real Estate (CRE) Loans	99.3%	21.4%	1.9%	3.6%	8.9%	19.4%	31.4%	41.9%	48.3%
Construction and Development (C&D) Loans (Subset of CRE)	90.2%	3.5%	0.0%	0.0%	0.7%	2.4%	5.2%	8.3%	10.7%
Mortgage Loans	99.4%	19.8%	2.6%	4.8%	9.4%	16.4%	26.0%	40.8%	50.6%
Agricultural Loans	77.0%	8.1%	0.0%	0.0%	0.0%	2.3%	11.5%	25.7%	34.6%
Commercial and Industrial (C&I) Loans	96.8%	7.7%	0.3%	1.4%	3.5%	6.4%	10.4%	15.4%	19.5%
Consumer Loans	99.1%	3.3%	0.1%	0.3%	0.9%	2.2%	4.2%	7.1%	9.4%

Source: FDIC. Based on 6,799 community banks reporting at year-end 2011.

Table 5.3. Lending Specialty Groups Defined for Analysis of FDIC-Insured Community Banks

Lending Specialty Group	Definition
Mortgage Specialists	Holds residential mortgage loans greater than 30 percent of total assets
Consumer Specialists	Holds credit card lines and other loans to individuals greater than 20 percent of total assets
Commercial Real Estate (CRE) Specialists	Holds construction and development (C&D) loans greater than 10 percent of assets OR total CRE loans (C&D, multifamily, and secured by other commercial properties) greater than 30 percent of total assets
C&I Specialists	Holds commercial and industrial (C&I) loans greater than 20 percent of total assets
Agricultural Specialists	Holds agricultural production loans plus loans secured by farm real estate greater than 20 percent of total assets
Multi-Specialists	Meets more than one of the single-specialty definitions above OR holds either retail loans or commercial loans greater than 40 percent of total assets
No Specialty	All other institutions

Source: FDIC.

Note: All specialty groups require the institution to hold loans greater than 33 percent of total assets.

Table 5.4. Number of Community Banks by Lending Specialty Group, 1984-2011

Lending Specialty Group		Year-End							
		1984	1985	1990	1995	2000	2005	2010	2011
Commercial Real Estate (CRE) Specialists	Number of Institutions	347	447	477	541	940	2,052	1,841	1,620
	Percent of Community Banks	2%	3%	4%	5%	11%	26%	26%	24%
Mortgage Specialists	Number of Institutions	2,820	2,864	2,702	2,248	1,942	1,249	1,131	1,105
	Percent of Community Banks	18%	18%	21%	22%	22%	16%	16%	16%
Agricultural Specialists	Number of Institutions	2,071	1,704	1,519	1,574	1,327	1,112	1,026	972
	Percent of Community Banks	13%	11%	12%	15%	15%	14%	15%	14%
C&I Specialists	Number of Institutions	1,738	1,656	874	471	510	258	157	153
	Percent of Community Banks	11%	11%	7%	5%	6%	3%	2%	2%
Consumer Specialists	Number of Institutions	1,387	1,332	693	395	280	86	44	46
	Percent of Community Banks	9%	8%	5%	4%	3%	1%	1%	1%
No Specialty	Number of Institutions	5,982	6,332	5,838	4,286	2,697	1,986	1,858	2,080
	Percent of Community Banks	38%	40%	44%	41%	31%	25%	26%	31%
Multi-Specialists	Number of Institutions	1,318	1,393	1,047	866	1,121	1,190	959	823
	Percent of Community Banks	8%	9%	8%	8%	13%	15%	14%	12%
Number of Community Banks		15,663	15,728	13,150	10,381	8,817	7,933	7,016	6,799

Source: FDIC.

Table 5.5 shows the aggregate total assets of each lending specialty group and its share of total community bank assets as of year-end 2011. CRE specialists were the largest lending specialty in terms of total assets and had the greatest disparity between their share of total community banks (24 percent) and their share of total community bank assets (33 percent), indicating that the CRE specialists tend to be about one-third larger than the average community bank. Mortgage specialists made up 16 percent of community banks both in number and in total assets. Agricultural specialists tend to be less than half the size of the average community bank, making up 14 percent of all community banks but holding only 6 percent of total community bank assets. C&I specialists comprised 2 percent of the number of community banks, but 3 percent of total community bank assets, indicating that they were larger than the average community bank. Consumer specialists comprised 1 percent of both the number and total assets of community banks. Those community banks with no lending specialty or that are multi-specialists reported 26 percent and 14 percent of total community bank assets, respectively. This indicates that community banks with no lending specialty tend to be smaller than the average community bank, while multi-specialists tend to be slightly larger.

Table 5.5. Assets and Number of Community Banks by Lending Specialty Group, 2011

Lending Specialty Group		Year-End 2011	
Commercial Real Estate (CRE) Specialists	Number of Institutions / Percent of Community Banks	1,620	24%
	Total Assets ($ Billions) / Percent of Community Bank Assets	$659.6	33%
Mortgage Specialists	Number of Institutions / Percent of Community Banks	1,108	16%
	Total Assets ($ Billions) / Percent of Community Bank Assets	$323.8	16%
Agricultural Specialists	Number of Institutions / Percent of Community Banks	972	14%
	Total Assets ($ Billions) / Percent of Community Bank Assets	$121.3	6%
C&I Specialists	Number of Institutions / Percent of Community Banks	153	2%
	Total Assets ($ Billions) / Percent of Community Bank Assets	$62.1	3%
Consumer Specialists	Number of Institutions / Percent of Community Banks	46	1%
	Total Assets ($ Billions) / Percent of Community Bank Assets	$18.3	1%
No Specialty	Number of Institutions / Percent of Community Banks	2,080	31%
	Total Assets ($ Billions) / Percent of Community Bank Assets	$507.0	26%
Multi-Specialists	Number of Institutions / Percent of Community Banks	823	12%
	Total Assets ($ Billions) / Percent of Community Bank Assets	$280.5	14%

Source: FDIC.

As might be expected, community banks with the same lending specialty tend to have relatively similar geographic characteristics. Maps 5.1 through 5.6 show the headquarters of community banks with CRE, mortgage, and agriculture specialties, as well as the headquarters of multi-specialists, banks with no lending specialty, and those with at least 10 percent of total assets in C&D loans. Each map shades the ten states that had the highest proportion of community banks with that particular lending specialty, and differentiates between metro and nonmetro headquarters locations.[32]

How Do Noncommunity Banks Break Down by Lending Specialty Group?

A comparison at year-end 2011 shows that the CRE specialists were as prevalent among noncommunity banks as they were among community banks (see Chart 5.2). Just under 25 percent of noncommunity banks met the definition of CRE specialist in 2011, compared with 24 percent of community banks. C&I specialists and consumer specialists were more prevalent among noncommunity banks, with about 7 percent meeting the definition for each group in 2011. Not surprisingly, agricultural lending specialists made up just 2 percent of noncommunity banks (or just 12 institutions). Mortgage lenders were also less prevalent among noncommunity banks, making up just 8 percent of the total due in part to the degree of concentration in the mortgage lending business. In 2011, just five institutions (none of which were community banks) made up almost 60 percent of total mortgage originations. This concentration shows the scale-driven approach that large lenders have taken in the mortgage business.

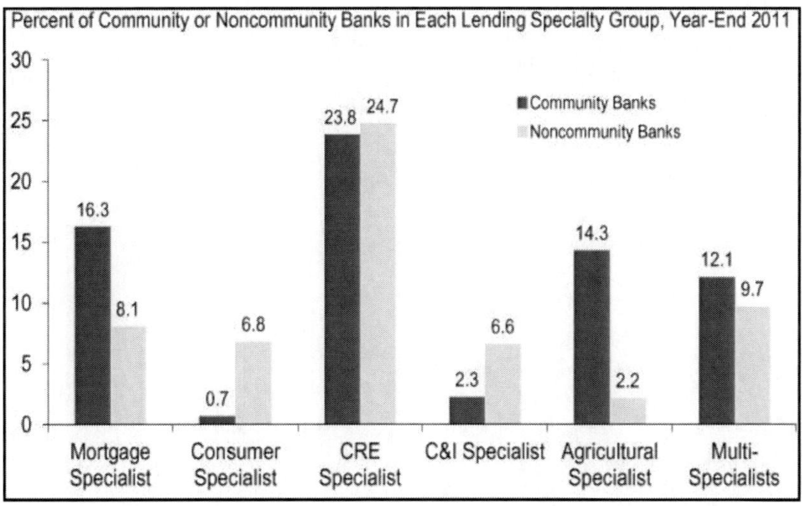

Source: FDIC.

Note: The remaining banks in each group are categorized as "No Specialty."

Chart 5.2. Percent of Community and Noncommunity Banks by Lending Specialty Group, 2011.

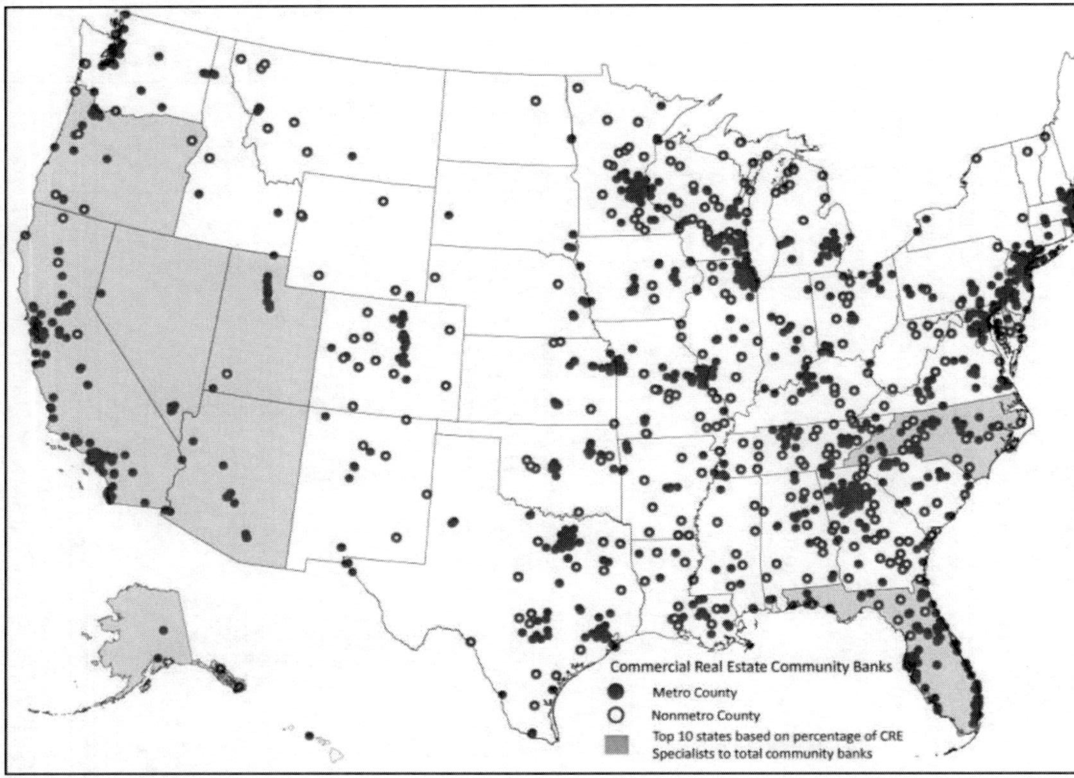

State	CRE Specialists %
DE	89%
CA	70%
AK	67%
OR	67%
FL	64%
DC	60%
AZ	58%
UT	55%
NV	54%
NC	53%

Source: FDIC.

Map 5.1. Headquarters Locations of CRE Specialists, Year-End 2011.

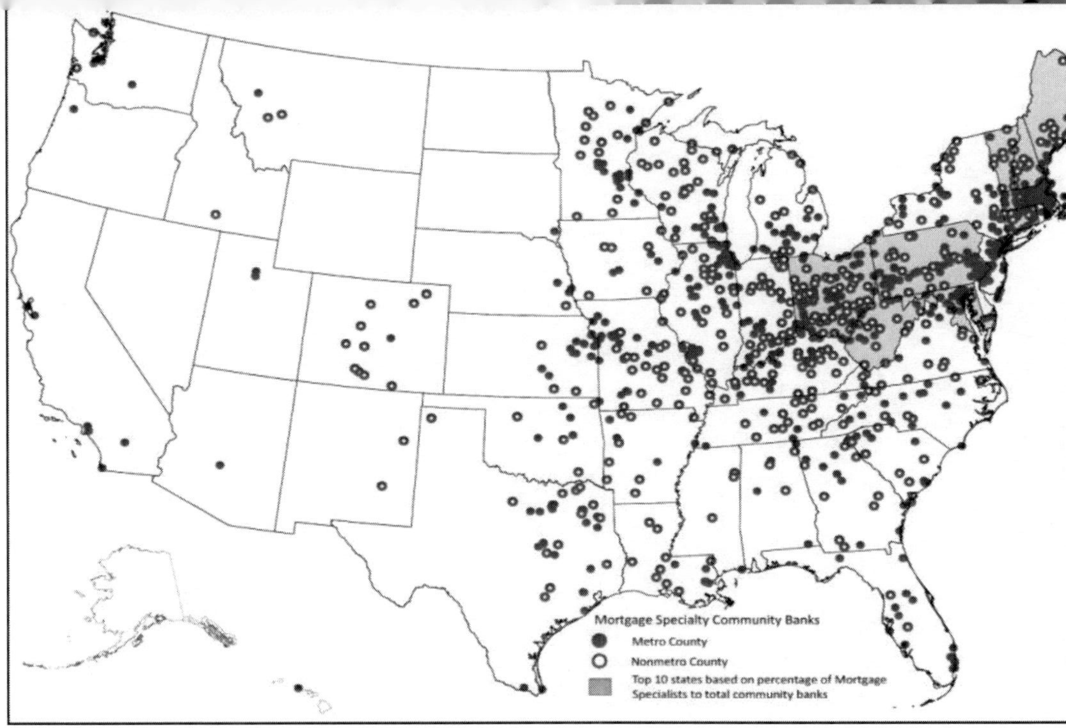

State	Mortgage Specialists %
ME	81%
VT	71%
NH	70%
MA	68%
CT	61%
PA	46%
OH	45%
WV	44%
MD	41%
DC	40%

Source: FDIC.

Map 5.2. Headquarters Locations of Mortgage Specialists, Year-End 2011.

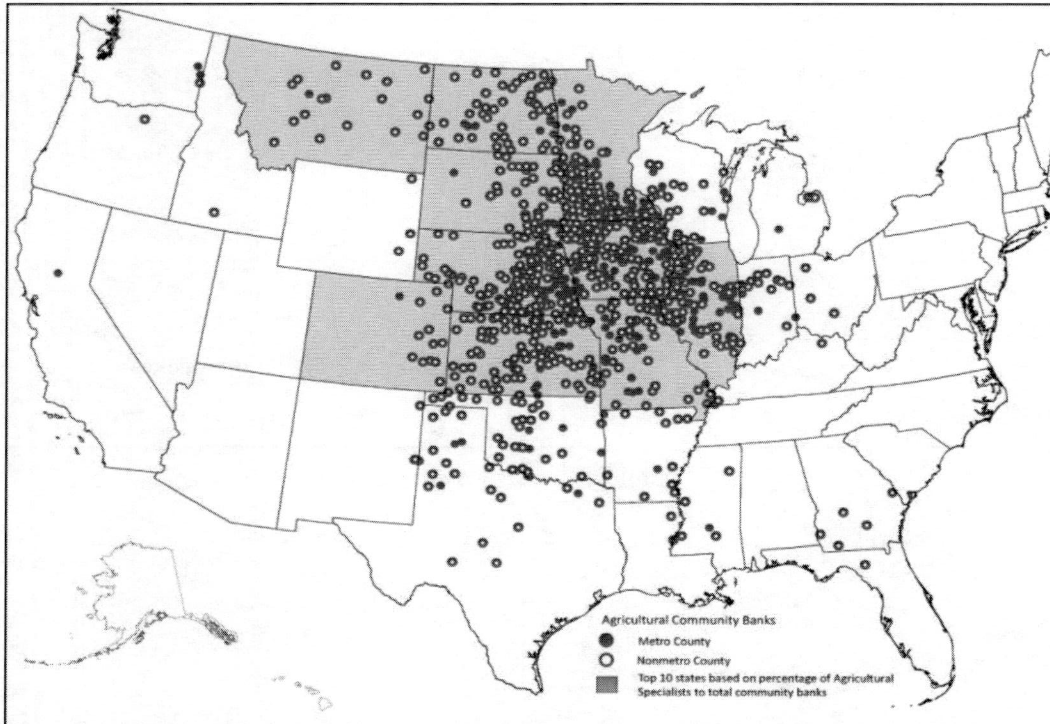

State	Agricultural Specialists %
NE	68%
SD	62%
ND	62%
IA	51%
KS	34%
MN	32%
MT	31%
MO	20%
CO	16%
IL	16%

Source: FDIC.

Map 5.3. Headquarters Locations of Agricultural Specialists, Year-End 2011.

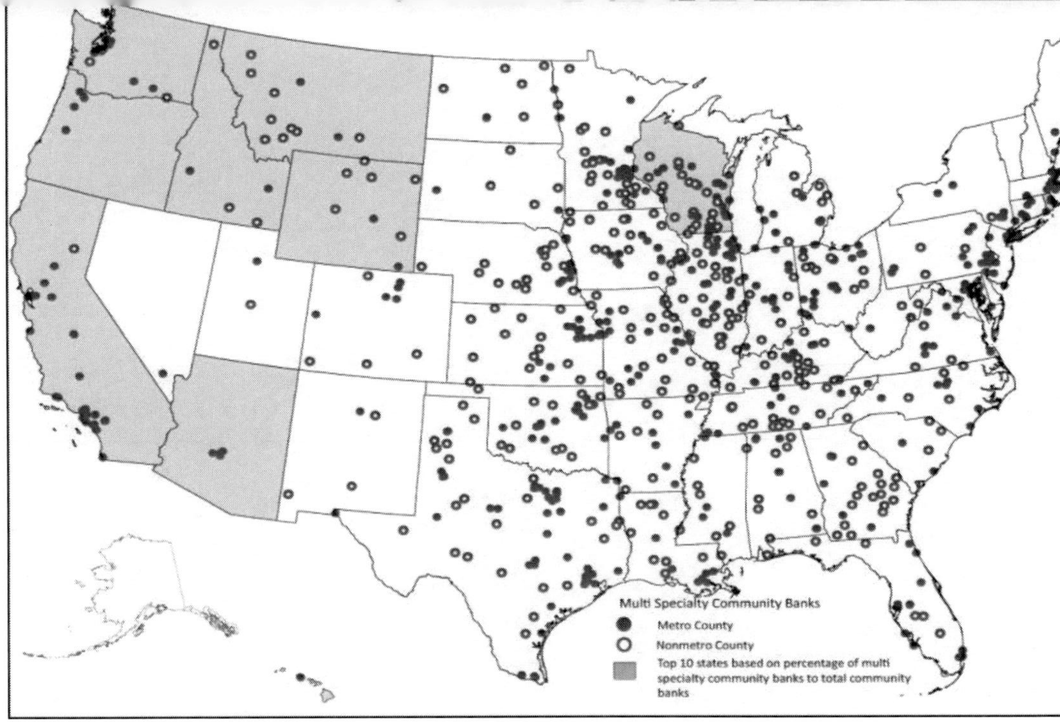

State	Multi-Specialists %
DE	36%
CA	31%
AK	24%
OR	22%
FL	20%
DC	17%
AZ	17%
UT	17%
NV	16%
NC	16%

Source: FDIC.

Map 5.4. Headquarters Locations of Community Banks That Are Multi-Specialists, Year-End 2011.

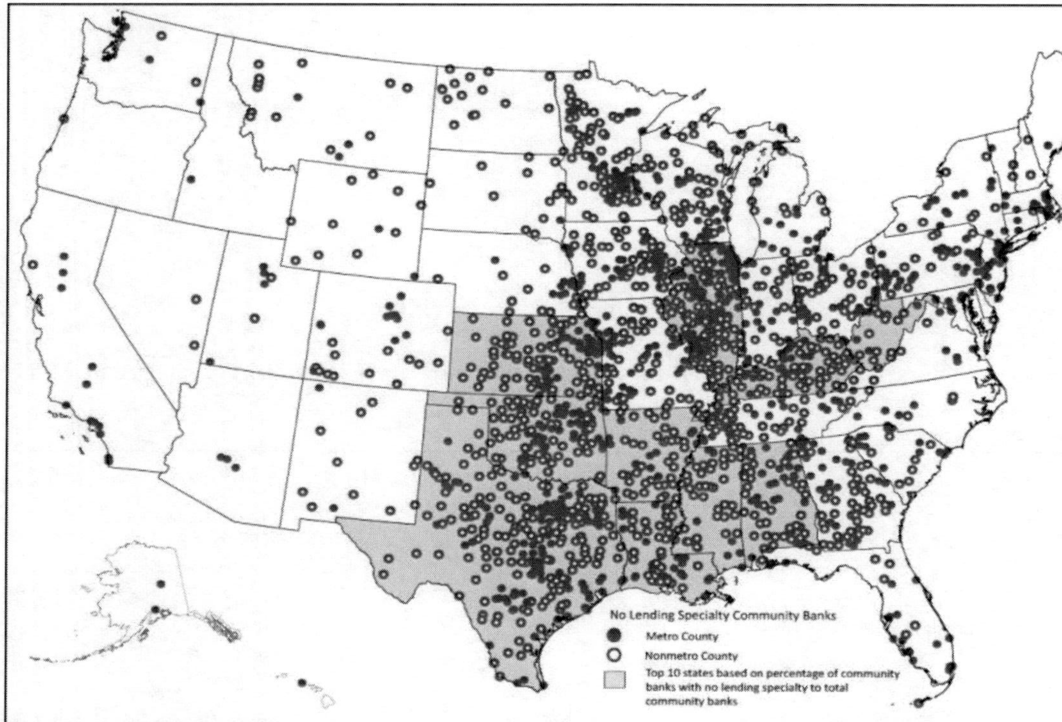

State	No Specialty %
AL	59
MS	58
TX	51
OK	48
AR	47
LA	47
KY	43
WV	41
IL	39
KS	39

Source: FDIC.

Map 5.5. Headquarters Locations of Community Banks With No Lending Speciality, Year-End 2011.

State	C&D Concentrated %
UT	31
NC	29
DE	22
SC	21
GA	19
VA	19
TN	16
WA	13
AZ	13
CO	12

Source: FDIC.

Map 5.6. Headquarters Locations of Community Banks With at Least 10 Percent of Total Assets in C&D Loans, Year-End 2011.

WHAT FACTORS EXPLAIN DIFFERENCES IN PRETAX ROA AMONG COMMUNITY BANKS?

Local economic conditions have important influences on pretax ROA, but individual bank management decisions do as well.

To evaluate which bank management decisions are most important in determining the pretax ROA of community banks, a model constructed for this study estimates the effects of factors such as bank underwriting standards, loan growth, capital base, funding mix, lending specializations, security investments, and staffing. Based on a sample period that extends from 1994 through 2011, the model also controls for changes in macroeconomic conditions over time, as well as differences between individual banks that do not change over time.[1] The model focuses on community banks that raise 50 percent or more of their deposits from a single county, which would typically imply that most of the banks' lending activity is also confined to this geographic area. By targeting these "very local" community banks, the model can control for local economic conditions by introducing county-level data on unemployment, home prices, credit card delinquencies, and wage growth.

The model finds that community banks that "stick to the basics" with regard to lending and deposit gathering typically perform better than other community banks. Higher ROAs are associated with higher loan volumes, as opposed to higher volumes of other assets such as securities, and a more diversified loan portfolio. Holdings of commercial and industrial (C&I), construction and development (C&D) and other commercial real estate (CRE) loans are associated with lower ROA compared with holdings of other asset types. Moreover, specializing in these commercial loan types especially hurts the earnings of "local" banks that do more business outside of their local area. Minimizing nonperforming loans also increases ROA, implying that solid underwriting and loan administration practices are important to community bank profitability.

Banks that limit their use of noncore funding and maintain lower overall funding costs also generate relatively higher returns. Last, community banks appear to benefit when retail banking in the county is concentrated in fewer institutions, indicating less competition in the local market area.

The model also provides a useful framework for testing the extent to which economies of scale exist for this set of local community banks. The model finds modest, but statistically significant, gains in ROA as banks exceed the average size. For the sample of banks that raised more than 75 percent of their deposits from one county, the gain is maximized when asset size approaches $1 billion.[2] The estimated increase in ROA that accrues from above-average size is relatively small—about 6 basis points in all—and most of this benefit is realized when asset size reaches about $600 million. Taken together, these results indicate that asset size offers very limited benefits in determining the financial performance of local community banks.

See: http://www.fdic.gov/regulations/resources/cbi/report/cbi-roa.pdf.

[1] Typically, this would be referred to as a 9 panel dataset.
[2] The ROA analysis adjusts asset size to constant dollars as of the fourth quarter of 2000.

As Map 5.1 shows, CRE specialists were primarily headquartered in metro counties (80 percent) and tended to be located in the West and the Southeast, where more than one-half of community banks had a CRE lending specialty. Nonetheless, only about one-quarter of CRE specialists were headquartered in the ten most concentrated states and the remaining CRE specialists are distributed across the country.

The Geography of the Lending Specialist Groups

Mortgage specialists also tended to be headquartered in metro counties (61 percent) and are largely located in the eastern half of the country as shown in Map 5.2. In particular, the Northeast and nearby states had the highest concentration of mortgage specialists. In Maine, Vermont, New Hampshire, and Massachusetts, mortgage specialists made up at least two-thirds of community banks.

Not surprisingly, agricultural specialists were largely headquartered in nonmetro areas (84 percent) and tightly clustered in the center of the country as shown in Map 5.3. In Nebraska, South Dakota, North Dakota, and Iowa, more than one-half of community banks were agricultural specialists. In total, the ten most concentrated states for agricultural specialists had 84 percent of all community banks with that specialty.

Map 5.4 shows that multi-specialists were distributed throughout the country, but were more likely to be found in metro counties (57 percent) than in nonmetro counties. States with the highest concentration of such institutions were clustered in the Pacific Northwest. However, multi-specialists were not as common as other lending specialties. Rhode Island and Idaho were the only states where multi-specialists made up more than one-quarter of community banks.

Community banks with no lending specialty were also widely distributed, but were more likely to be headquartered in nonmetro counties (59 percent) than in metro counties as shown in Map 5.5. States with the highest proportion of banks with no lending specialty were located in the South and Midwest. Over half of community banks in Alabama, Mississippi and Texas had no lending specialty.

Finally, community banks with at least 10 percent of assets in C&D loans were primarily located in metro areas (74 percent), and clustered in the Southeast and the West, as shown in Map 5.6. Utah, North Carolina, Delaware, and South Carolina were the only states where such institutions make up more than 20 percent of community banks.

Performance Comparisons across Community Bank Lending Specialty Groups

The long time series of data for community banks permits a comparative analysis of the performance of these lending specialties over the study period. This section examines pretax ROA, the income and expense components of pretax ROA, and the incidence of failures across the lending specialty groups.

Table 5.6 compares the weighted average pretax ROA for community banks in each lending specialty group over five-year intervals and for the entire study period. Agricultural specialists (with a weighted average pretax ROA of 1.4 percent) were the strongest performers over the entire study period, followed by the no specialty group (1.28 percent) and consumer specialists (1.27 percent). CRE specialists, with an average pretax ROA of 0.64 percent, were the weakest performers over the entire study period. In the middle were three groups with very similar overall performance in terms of pretax ROA: multi-specialists (0.98 percent), mortgage specialists (1 percent) and C&I specialists (1.03 percent).

Table 5.6. Pretax Return on Assets (ROA) by Lending Specialty Group, 1985-2011

Lending Specialty Group	Time Period						
	Five-Year Intervals					2011	All Years: 1985-2011
	1986-1990	1991-1995	1996-2000	2001-2005	2006-2010		
Agricultural Specialists	0.98%	1.68%	1.65%	1.50%	1.25%	1.38%	1.40%
Consumer Specialists	0.85%	1.55%	1.55%	1.44%	0.89%	2.22%	1.27%
C&I Specialists	0.60%	1.09%	1.50%	1.45%	1.04%	0.89%	1.03%
Mortgage Specialists	0.55%	1.24%	1.39%	1.33%	0.63%	0.69%	1.00%
CRE Specialists	-1.57%	0.75%	1.78%	1.68%	0.25%	0.37%	0.64%
No Specialty	0.88%	1.48%	1.62%	1.42%	1.05%	1.08%	1.28%
Multi-Specialists	0.28%	1.15%	1.65%	1.52%	0.69%	0.72%	0.98%
Total	0.47%	1.31%	1.56%	1.49%	0.60%	0.75%	1.02%

Source: FDIC.

Note: Figures represent weighted average pretax return on assets for federally insured community banks reporting in each group during the period.

Table 5.7. Net Interest Income to Average Assets by Lending Specialty Group, 1985-2011

Lending Specialty Group	Time Period						
	Five-Year Intervals					2011	All Years: 1985-2011
	1986-1990	1991-1995	1996-2000	2001-2005	2006-2010		
Consumer Specialists	4.14%	4.47%	4.41%	3.97%	3.84%	4.12%	4.25%
C&I Specialists	4.10%	4.36%	4.34%	4.01%	3.89%	3.35%	4.13%
Agricultural Specialists	3.90%	4.13%	3.97%	3.84%	3.67%	3.66%	3.86%
CRE Specialists	2.19%	4.07%	4.40%	3.96%	3.54%	3.53%	3.62%
Mortgage Specialists	2.38%	3.37%	3.34%	3.25%	3.01%	3.18%	2.99%
Multi-Specialists	3.08%	4.07%	4.16%	3.86%	3.57%	3.65%	3.66%
No Specialty	3.51%	3.96%	3.89%	3.51%	3.28%	3.27%	3.64%
Total	3.04%	3.82%	3.85%	3.67%	3.43%	3.43%	3.51%

Source: FDIC.

Note: Figures represent weighted average net interest income as a percent of average total assets for federally insured community banks reporting in each group during the period.

The worst average performance for all community banks and for every lending specialty group occurred during the 1986-1990 and 2006-2010 periods. These periods were marked by high credit losses and large numbers of bank failures. The three five-year intervals from 1991 through 2005 represent a time of comparatively strong performance across the lending specialty groups. Every lending specialty group reported an average pretax ROA of at least 1 percent in each five-year interval between 1991 and 2005 with one exception, when CRE specialists earned just 0.75 percent in the period 1991-1995. CRE specialists clearly experienced the most volatile earnings performance as shown in Table 5.6, reporting the lowest pretax ROA of any group in three intervals (1986-1990, 1991-1995, and 2006-2010), and the highest pretax ROA of any group in the other two intervals (1996-2000 and 2001-2005). However, this elevated volatility of earnings for CRE specialists was not accompanied with higher average earnings. Over the entire study period, the pretax ROA of CRE specialists trailed the community bank average by more than one-third.

Income and Expense Components of Pretax ROA

Comparing the components of pretax ROA (net interest income, noninterest income, noninterest expense, and provision expense, as described in Chapter 4) reveals sources of disparity among the ROAs of different lending specialties. Table 5.7 shows the net interest income component of ROA for the community bank lending specialty groups. Overall, net interest income showed considerable variation over time, peaking during the 1990s and steadily declining during the 2000s. Consumer specialists and C&I specialists recorded the highest levels of net interest income for the entire study period and for most of the five-year intervals. Agricultural specialists also earned higher-than-average levels of net interest income in every five-year interval. Conversely, mortgage specialists consistently earned the lowest levels of net interest income. CRE specialists contributed somewhat to the volatility of the community bank average, earning net interest income equal to just 2.19 percent of assets between 1986 and 1990, but well-above-average levels in each of the other five-year intervals.

Table 5.8 shows the noninterest income component of ROA across the community bank lending specialty groups. Consumer specialists earned more noninterest income than any other specialist group for the period as a whole and in every five-year interval. C&I specialists and community banks with no lending specialty also earned levels of noninterest income above the community bank average. The no specialty group earned a progressively higher level of noninterest income as a percent of assets in each of the five-year intervals. The average ratio for all community banks also increased in each of the five-year periods between 1986 and 2005, before declining during the 2006-2010 interval.

Table 5.9 shows that the mortgage specialists had the lowest noninterest expense ratio for the entire study period and for each of the five-year intervals, followed closely by agricultural specialists. Only these two lending specialty groups recorded average noninterest expense ratios lower than 3 percent for the entire study period. At the high end of the distribution for the entire study period and for each of the five-year intervals were consumer specialists and C&I specialists. CRE specialists, multi-specialists and community banks with no specialty occupied the middle of the distribution. Community banks as a group experienced little variation in their noninterest expense ratio over the entire study period. The highest community bank ratio (3.08 percent) was recorded in the 1991-1995 interval, while the ratios measured for the final three other five-year intervals were all very close to the study period average of 2.96 percent.

Table 5.8. Noninterest Income to Average Assets by Lending Specialty Group, 1985-2011

Lending Specialty Group	Time Period						
	Five-Year Intervals					2011	All Years: 1985-2011
	1986-1990	1991-1995	1996-2000	2001-2005	2006-2010		
Consumer Specialists	1.07%	1.31%	1.29%	1.20%	1.10%	2.69%	1.20%
C&I Specialists	0.95%	1.19%	1.09%	1.14%	0.94%	0.72%	1.04%
CRE Specialists	0.79%	0.92%	0.90%	0.92%	0.72%	0.65%	0.80%
Agricultural Specialists	0.61%	0.65%	0.71%	0.66%	0.65%	0.59%	0.65%
Mortgage Specialists	0.63%	0.57%	0.62%	0.67%	0.66%	0.80%	0.64%
No Specialty	0.81%	0.91%	0.92%	1.05%	1.16%	1.02%	0.95%
Multi-Specialists	0.89%	0.88%	0.97%	1.02%	0.88%	0.88%	0.93%
Total	0.77%	0.81%	0.84%	0.91%	0.82%	0.82%	0.83%

Source: FDIC.

Note: Figures represent weighted average noninterest income as a percent of average total assets for federally insured community banks reporting in each group during the period.

Table 5.9. Noninterest Expense to Average Assets by Lending Specialty Group, 1985-2011

Lending Specialty Group	Time Period						
	Five-Year Intervals					2011	All Years: 1985-2011
	1986-1990	1991-1995	1996-2000	2001-2005	2006-2010		
Mortgage Specialists	2.30%	2.55%	2.53%	2.60%	2.70%	2.93%	2.51%
Agricultural Specialists	2.88%	2.95%	2.83%	2.80%	2.72%	2.63%	2.80%
CRE Specialists	3.28%	3.65%	3.25%	2.98%	3.03%	3.06%	3.09%
C&I Specialists	3.68%	3.92%	3.53%	3.37%	3.26%	2.72%	3.57%
Consumer Specialists	3.73%	3.86%	3.67%	3.32%	3.46%	4.07%	3.68%
No Specialty	3.04%	3.23%	3.03%	3.00%	3.04%	2.93%	3.07%
Multi-Specialists	3.06%	3.43%	3.26%	3.12%	3.06%	3.18%	3.15%
Total	2.88%	3.08%	2.96%	2.94%	2.97%	3.00%	2.96%

Source: FDIC.

Note: Figures represent weighted average noninterest expense as a percent of average total assets for federally insured community banks reporting in each group during the period.

The previous three earnings ratios discussed also represent the components of the efficiency ratio, or the ratio of noninterest expense to net operating revenue. Table 5.10 compares weighted average efficiency ratios for the community bank lending specialty groups for the entire study period. Agricultural specialists stand out in this comparison for their strong, lower-than-average efficiency ratios. For the entire study period, agricultural specialists reported an average efficiency ratio of just 62 percent, compared with the overall community bank average of 68 percent. As discussed above, agricultural specialists have consistently demonstrated lower-than-average noninterest expenses and higher-than-average net interest income, setting them apart from the other specialists in terms of both ROA and the efficiency ratio. The highest average efficiency ratio over the entire study period was reported by CRE specialists at 70 percent. Moreover, the efficiency ratios of the CRE specialists were somewhat volatile over time, far exceeding the community bank average in the 1986-1990 and 1991-1995 intervals, and coming in under the average during the 1996-2000 and 2001-2005 intervals. As described above, much of the efficiency ratio volatility on the part of CRE specialists came from variation in net interest income.

Table 5.10. Efficiency Ratio by Lending Specialty Group, 1985-2011

Lending Specialty Group	Time Period						
	Five-Year Intervals					2011	All Years: 1985-2011
	1986-1990	1991-1995	1996-2000	2001-2005	2006-2010		
Agricultural Specialists	63.90%	61.66%	60.48%	62.19%	63.10%	61.99%	62.12%
Consumer Specialists	71.51%	66.80%	64.49%	64.33%	70.00%	59.81%	67.60%
C&I Specialists	72.70%	70.60%	64.95%	65.50%	67.46%	66.98%	69.03%
Mortgage Specialists	76.31%	64.59%	63.85%	66.40%	73.41%	73.42%	69.15%
CRE Specialists	110.17%	73.17%	61.37%	61.11%	71.21%	73.23%	69.75%
No Specialty	70.34%	66.34%	62.91%	65.93%	68.42%	68.48%	66.81%
Multi-Specialists	76.99%	69.17%	63.55%	64.02%	68.86%	70.37%	68.59%
Total	75.56%	66.62%	63.12%	64.03%	70.07%	70.54%	68.14%

Source: FDIC.

Note: Figures represent weighted noninterest expense as a ratio to net operating income for federally insured community banks reporting in each group during the period.

Table 5.11. Provision Expense to Average Assets by Lending Specialty Group, 1985-2011

Lending Specialty Group	Time Period						
	Five-Year Intervals					2011	All Years: 1985-2011
	1986-1990	1991-1995	1996-2000	2001-2005	2006-2010		
Mortgage Specialists	0.33%	0.27%	0.13%	0.12%	0.31%	0.42%	0.23%
Agricultural Specialists	0.71%	0.19%	0.21%	0.22%	0.34%	0.26%	0.33%
CRE Specialists	1.40%	0.71%	0.27%	0.26%	0.97%	0.80%	0.73%
Consumer Specialists	0.91%	1.04%	1.00%	0.99%	1.07%	1.30%	0.97%
C&I Specialists	1.06%	1.30%	1.10%	1.09%	1.08%	1.19%	1.11%
No Specialty	0.49%	0.24%	0.18%	0.20%	0.34%	0.34%	0.30%
Multi-Specialists	0.76%	0.51%	0.30%	0.30%	0.71%	0.68%	0.54%
Total	0.59%	0.33%	0.21%	0.22%	0.67%	0.56%	0.43%

Source: FDIC.

Note: Figures represent weighted average provision expense to average total assets for federally insured community banks reporting in each group during the period.

The lending specialty groups also showed substantial differences in provision expense for loan and lease losses (see Table 5.11). For the entire study period, the average provision expenses reported by agricultural specialists, multi-specialists and the no specialty group all remained relatively close to the overall community bank average. Mortgage specialists reported the lowest provision expense of any group of community banks over the entire period, averaging just 0.23 percent of total assets. Conversely, the highest average provision expenses were reported by C&I specialists (1.11 percent), consumer specialists (0.97 percent) and CRE specialists (0.73 percent). While provision expenses were relatively high for C&I specialists and consumer specialists in every five-year interval, provision expenses dipped sharply for CRE specialists in the 1996-2000 and 2001-2005 intervals, when generally strong real estate market conditions helped to keep CRE credit losses low. Mortgage specialists, agricultural specialists, multi-specialists and the no specialty group also experienced relatively low loan loss provision expenses during these intervals.

This discussion of expense ratios and efficiency naturally leads to the question of whether smaller institutions are at a competitive disadvantage as a result of *economies of scale* that enable larger institutions to operate at a lower average cost. Because this is such an important topic, additional FDIC analysis evaluated the importance of economies of scale among community bank lending specialty groups. The results of this analysis are summarized in the inset box "Do Economies of Scale Work Against Small Community Banks?" and show that while benefits of economies of scale do exist for community banks, they are exhausted when community banks reach a modest asset size.

Incidence of Failure

Another comparison of the performance of the lending specialty groups uses the *failure index* introduced in Chapter 2. The failure index for each group is calculated as the ratio of failures within that group to failures of all community banks, divided by the ratio of the number of banks in that group to the total number of community banks. A lending specialty group with a failure index of "1" indicates that those banks failed in numbers proportional to their share of all community banks during the period, while a lending specialty group with a failure index of "2" indicates that those banks failed twice as often as their share of community banks.

Table 5.12 shows that the lending specialty groups with the lowest failure indexes for the entire period were banks with no specialty (0.41) and agricultural specialists (0.53). Conversely, the groups with the highest failure indexes were CRE specialists (2.25), C&I specialists (2.19), and multi-specialists (1.71). Institutions in these three groups failed far more frequently than the average community bank. Table 5.12 also shows that the most important timeframes for determining the relative frequency of failure were 1986-1990 (1,328 community bank failures), 1991-1995 (441 failures) and 2006-2010 (270 failures). CRE specialists had a high frequency of failure, while C&I specialists were well above the overall community bank average during the period 1986-1990, when more than one-half of all community bank failures took place. C&I specialists were also well above the overall community bank average during the 1996-2000 and 2001-2005 five-year intervals. However, these high failure indexes represent a total of eight failures of C&I specialists during these two five-year intervals when relatively few community bank failures occurred. Multi-specialists were more than twice as likely to fail as the average community bank in all of the five-year intervals from 1986 through 2005.

Table 5.12. Community Bank Failure Index by Lending Specialty Group, 1985-2011

Lending Specialty Group	Time Period						
	Five-Year Intervals						
	1986-1990	1991-1995	1996-2000	2001-2005	2006-2010	2011	All Years: 1985-2011
CRE Specialists	3.34	4.62	0.00	0.72	2.30	3.42	2.25
C&I Specialists	1.87	1.58	3.02	6.27	0.53	0.51	2.19
Consumer Specialists	0.96	1.03	0.00	0.00	0.00	0.00	1.20
Mortgage Specialists	1.11	1.57	0.45	1.24	0.45	0.00	1.03
Agricultural Specialists	0.76	0.07	1.31	0.00	0.16	0.08	0.53
Multi-Specialists	2.02	2.34	2.54	2.24	1.27	0.42	1.71
No Specialty	0.42	0.39	0.80	0.19	0.19	0.09	0.41
Total	1.00	1.00	1.00	1.00	1.00	1.00	1.00
Number of Failures	1,328	441	20	17	270	88	2,284

Source: FDIC.

Note: The failure index for each group is calculated as failures within that group as a ratio to all failures, divided by institutions in that group as a ratio to all institutions in that period. Index values above 1 indicate that institutions in the group failed more often than their prevalence in the population, while index values less than 1 indicate that they failed less often. The failure index is calculated for federally insured community banks.

A Closer Look at Commercial Real Estate Lending by Community Banks

Chart 5.3 shows the types of loans that comprise total commercial real estate loans held by community banks at year-end 2011. The three main components are loans secured by nonfarm, nonresidential properties (73 percent of CRE loans), loans for the acquisition, construction and development of real estate (C&D loans, 16 percent of CRE loans), and loans secured by multifamily properties (11 percent of CRE loans). C&D loans can be further subdivided into those secured by 1-to-4 family residential projects and all other C&D projects, with all other C&D loans making up about three-quarters of the total in 2011.

CRE Specialists Increase in Importance

The most noteworthy change in community bank lending strategies over the study period was the large increase in CRE lending specialists. Between 1991 and 2007, the number of CRE specialists increased fivefold, from 474 to 2,274. The increase was even larger as a percent of all community banks. Chart 5.4 shows that CRE specialists were less than 4 percent of all community banks in 1991, in the wake of the regional real estate downturns of the late 1980s and early 1990s, but grew to almost 30 percent of community banks at their peak in 2007. The figures are even higher if the analysis also considers multi-specialists that have CRE as one of their lending specialties.

Chart 5.5 tracks the rise of community banks that met the CRE specialty designation criteria in each year based on whether the designation was derived from C&D lending, CRE lending, or both.[33] It shows that most of the large percentage increase between 1998 and 2008 occurred among community banks that held both C&D loans greater than 10 percent of assets and total CRE loans greater than 30 percent of assets. These institutions declined sharply after the onset of recession in 2008, because of large declines in C&D balances. After more than doubling between 2003 and 2007 to a peak level of $206 billion, total C&D loans held by community banks fell by almost 60 percent over the next four years.

Chart 5.6 shows that holdings of loans secured by nonfarm, nonresidential real estate grew steadily throughout most of the study period for community banks in every lending specialty group. While CRE specialists and multi-specialists held more nonfarm, nonresidential loans as a percent of assets than the other specialty groups in every year, all of the other lending specialty groups followed the same general pattern of rising nonfarm, nonresidential real estate loans over virtually the entire study period.

Previously, Chart 5.3 also showed that as of 2011, community banks held $183 billion of loans secured by owner-occupied commercial properties and another $199 billion of CRE loans secured by nonowner-occupied properties. This distinction is important because CRE loans secured by owner-occupied commercial real estate in many cases do not represent loans for which a rental income stream from the property is the primary source of repayment. In fact, community banks held more CRE loans secured by owner-occupied properties than C&I loans ($164 billion) in 2011.

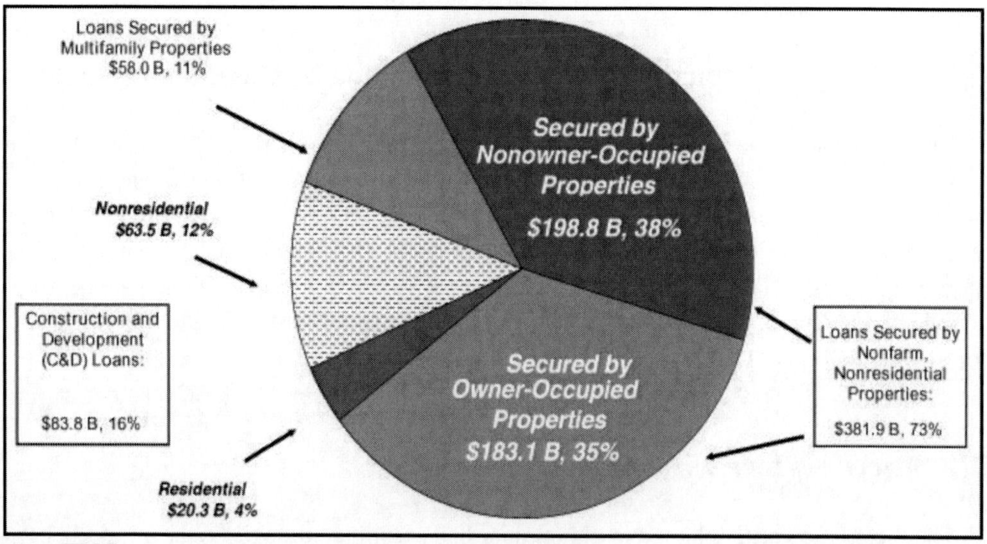

Source: FDIC.

Chart 5.3. Commercial Real Estate Loans Held by FDIC-Insured Community Banks, Year-End 2011.

While it would be very useful to know how much this owner-occupied CRE category contributed to the large increases in total CRE lending by community banks over the entire study period, this breakdown is available in the Call Report data only since 2007. As of 2011, these data show that owner-occupied loans made up 48 percent of all community bank CRE loans secured by nonfarm, nonresidential properties, a percentage that has remained virtually unchanged since 2008.[34]

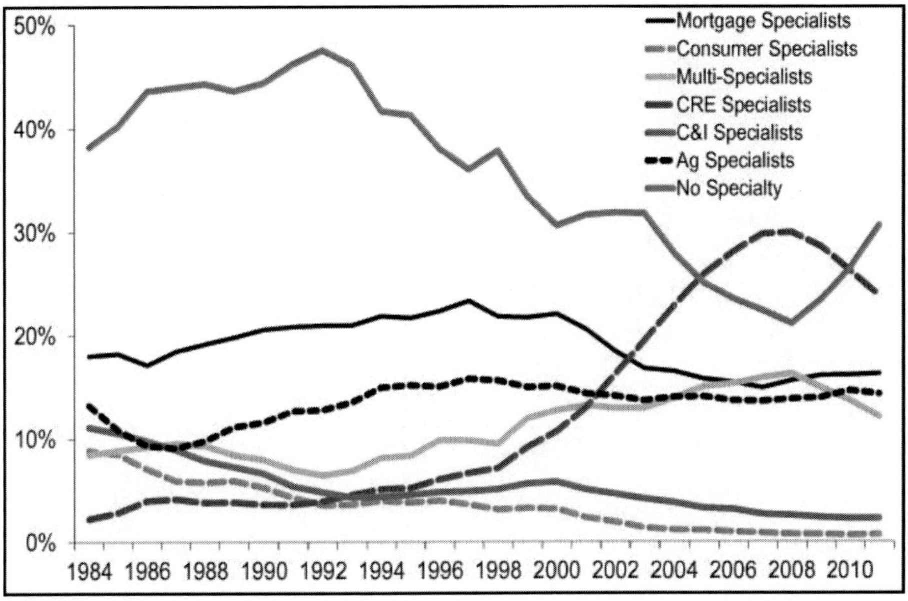

Source: FDIC.

Chart 5.4. Percent of Community Banks by Lending Specialty Group, 1984-2011.

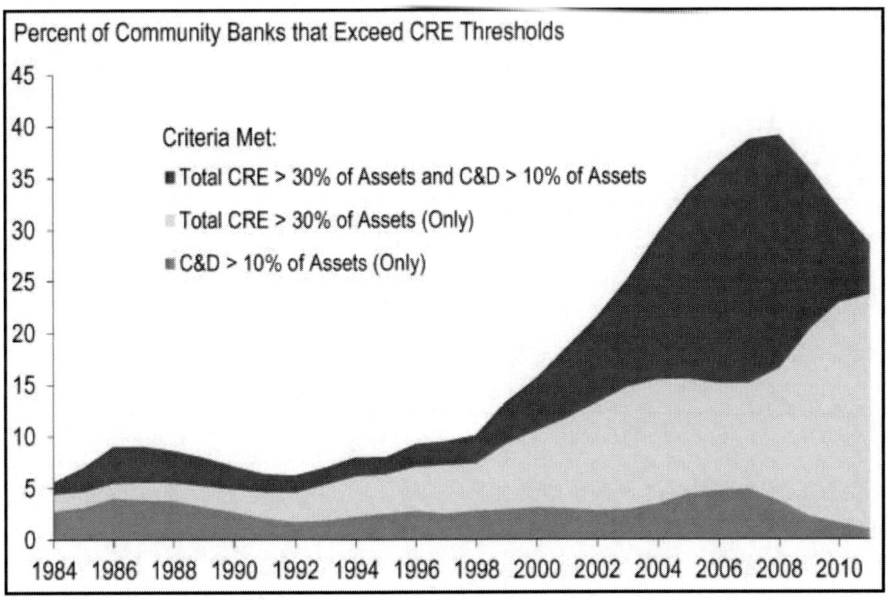

Source: FDIC.

Chart 5.5. The Most Notable Long-Term Development in Community Bank Lending Strategies Has Been the Shift Toward Commercial Real Estate Lending.

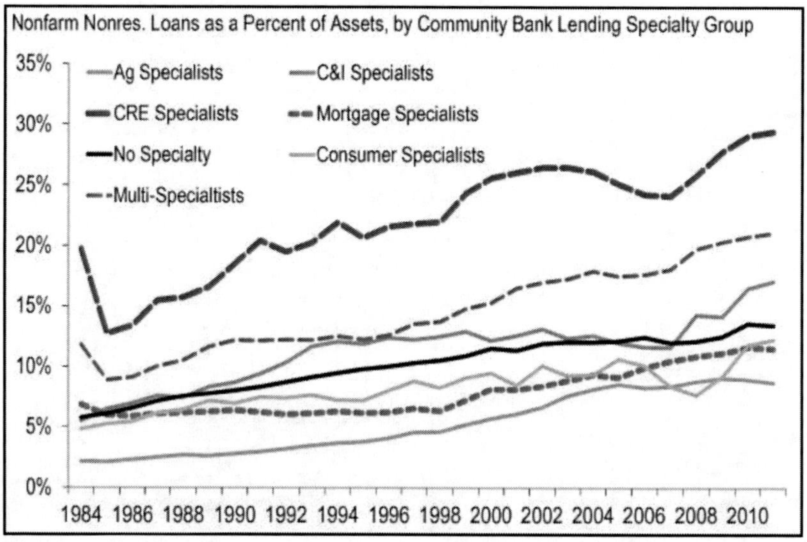

Source: FDIC.

Chart 5.6. CRE Loans Secured by Nonfarm, Nonresidential Properties Have Risen Steadily Over Time at Community Banks in Every Specialty Group.

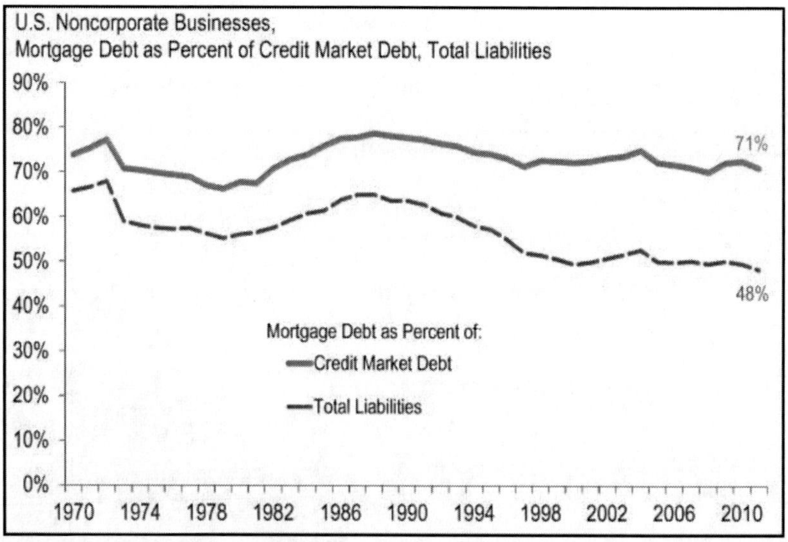

Source: Federal Reserve, *Flow of Funds*.

Chart 5.7. Mortgage Debt Has Consistently Made Up Well More Than Half of the Credit Market Debt of Noncorporate Businesses for More Than 40 Years.

CRE loans secured by owner-occupied properties more closely resemble C&I loans for which the commercial real estate collateral has been attached in an abundance of caution. This trend in owner-occupied CRE appears to represent an increasingly preferred method for community banks to make secured commercial loans to business customers that are not necessarily engaged in real estate activities. Therefore, the role of owner-occupied CRE lending must be taken into account when interpreting the overall increase in CRE lending by community banks, the rise in the number of CRE specialists, and the decrease in the number of C&I specialists, If one assumes that the loans secured by owner-occupied properties could be regarded as C&I loans rather than CRE loans, the share of the C&I lending specialty group among community banks would likely not have experienced the decrease shown in Chart 5.4.

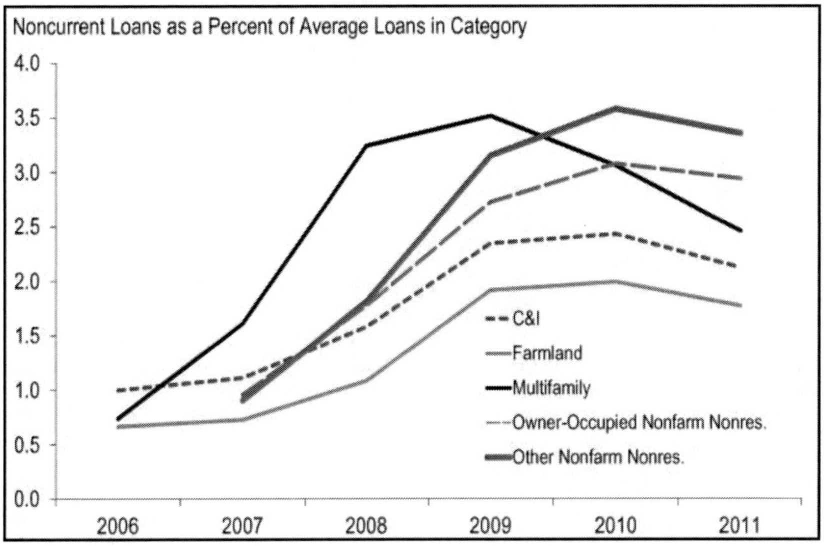

Source: FDIC.

Note: Noncurrent loans are loans 90 days or more past due or on nonaccrual status.

Chart 5.8. Performance Characteristics of Commercial Loans in Community Banks: Noncurrent Loan Rates, FDIC-Insured Institutions, 2006-2011.

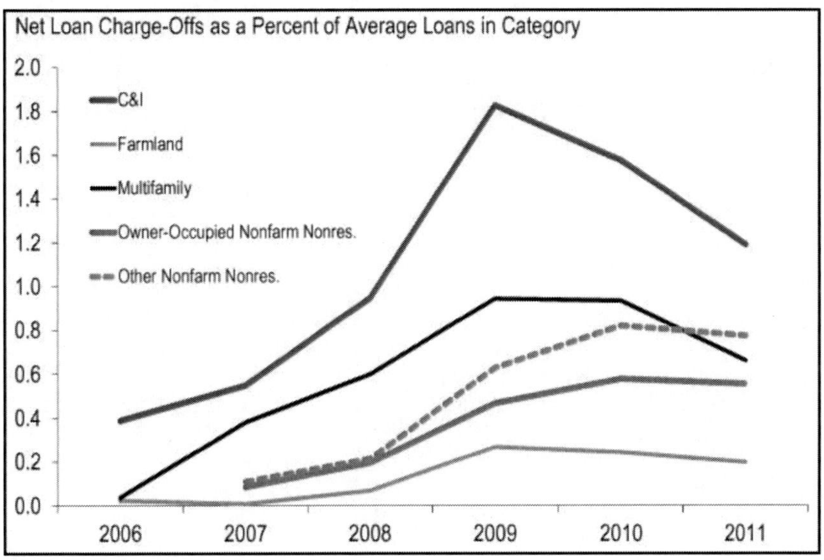

Source: FDIC.

Chart 5.9. Performance Characteristics of Commercial Loans in Community Banks: Net Charge-Off Rates, FDIC-Insured Institutions, 2006-2011.

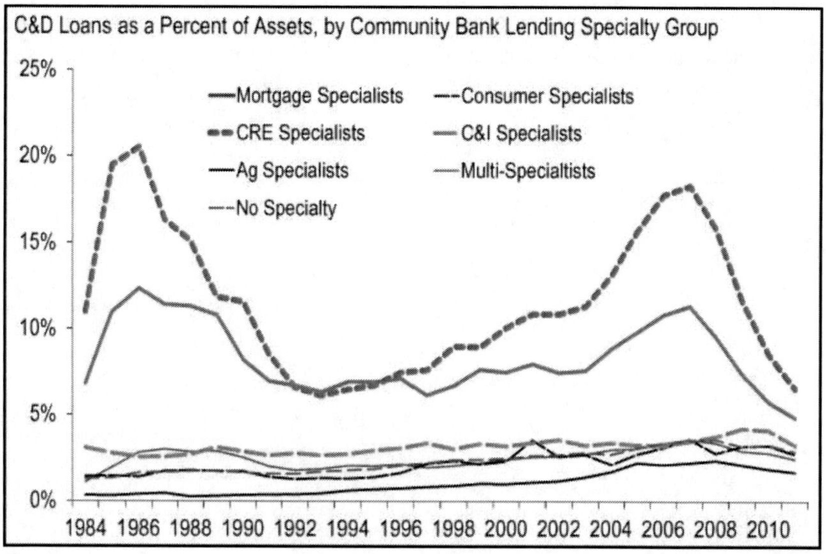

Source: FDIC.

Chart 5.10. Construction Lending by Community Banks Has Risen in Real Estate Boom Years, Led by CRE Specialists and Multi-Specialists.

There is other evidence to support the notion that owner-occupied CRE lending may be a substitute for C&I lending. The *Flow of Funds* data from the Federal Reserve show that real estate secured loans have long been an important source of credit to small businesses. In fact, mortgage credit has averaged 57 percent of the total liabilities of nonfarm, noncorporate businesses since 1970, and 73 percent of their credit market debt—percentages that have declined modestly from peak levels in the mid-1980s (see Chart 5.7).

Table 5.13. Failure Index for Federally Insured Community Banks by Select Lending Specialty Groups and by C&D Loans to Assets, 1985-2011

Lending Specialty Group		Time Period						
		Five-Year Intervals						
		1986-1990	1991-1995	1996-2000	2001-2005	2006-2010	2011	All Years: 1985-2011
CRE Specialists	C&D < 10%	2.59	4.38	0.00	1.51	1.01	1.70	1.37
	C&D > 10%	3.60	4.88	0.00	0.00	2.95	8.49	2.90
Multi-Specialists	C&D < 10%	1.92	1.79	3.23	3.03	0.62	0.20	1.33
	C&D > 10%	2.17	3.83	0.00	0.00	2.54	2.37	2.60
All Community Banks	C&D < 10%	0.87	0.86	1.06	1.14	0.41	0.42	0.83
	C&D > 10%	2.78	4.35	0.00	0.00	2.85	5.82	2.80
Number of Failures		1,328	441	20	17	270	88	2,284

Source: FDIC.

Note: The failure index for each group is calculated as failures within that group as a ratio to all failures, divided by institutions in that group as a ratio to all institutions in that period. Index values above 1 indicate that institutions in the group failed more often than their prevalence in the population, while index values less than 1 indicate that they failed less often. The failure index is calculated for federally insured community banks.

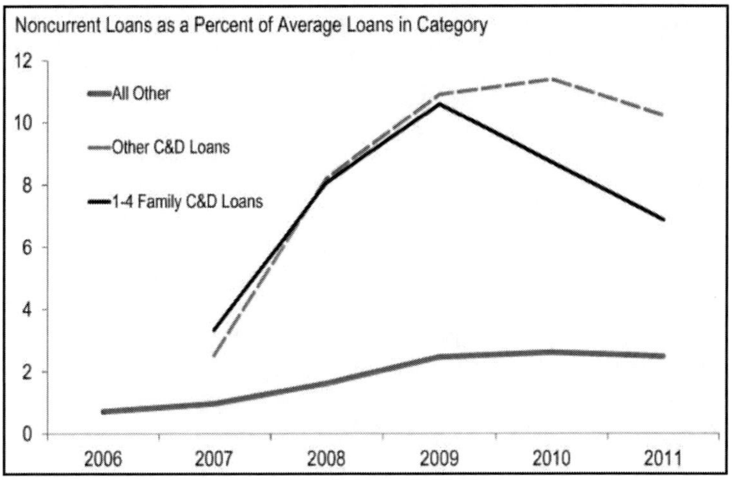

Source: FDIC.

Note: Noncurrent loans are loans 90 days or more past due or on nonaccrual status.

Chart 5.11. Performance Characteristics of C&D Loans in Community Banks: Noncurrent Loan Rates, FDIC-Insured Institutions, 2006-2011.

Performance of CRE and Other Commercial Loan Categories

Charts 5.8 and 5.9 trace noncurrent loans and net loan charge-offs at community banks, respectively, for five main classes of commercial loans since the beginning of 2006—CRE loans secured by owner-occupied nonfarm, nonresidential properties, CRE loans secured by other nonfarm, nonresidential properties, CRE loans secured by multifamily properties, farmland loans, and C&I loans. Each of the five loan categories, including CRE loans secured by nonfarm, nonresidential properties (both owner-occupied and otherwise), experienced increases in problem loans and loan charge-offs during the recent crisis, with improvement noted in 2011. Farmland loans experienced the best overall performance of any group, both in terms of the noncurrent loan ratio and the net loan charge-off ratio. The three CRE loan categories performed better than C&I loans in terms of net loan charge-off rates, but experienced higher noncurrent loan ratios, with CRE loans secured by owner-occupied nonfarm, nonresidential properties generally performing better than the other CRE loan categories. Although the net loan charge-off ratio was better at the peak of the recent crisis for the CRE loan categories compared with the ratio for C&I loans, data from the end of the last crisis (1991-1993) suggest that banks record charge-offs on C&I loans more quickly than charge-offs on nonfarm, nonresidential property loans, in part due to the length of the foreclosure process and ultimate sale of the foreclosed collateral. Taken together, these trends suggest that care must be taken to differentiate between CRE loans secured by income-producing properties and CRE loans secured by owner-occupied properties when evaluating the risk characteristics of CRE loan portfolios. The performance characteristics of C&D loans were markedly different from CRE loans secured by owner-occupied and other CRE properties during the last several years and are therefore reviewed separately.

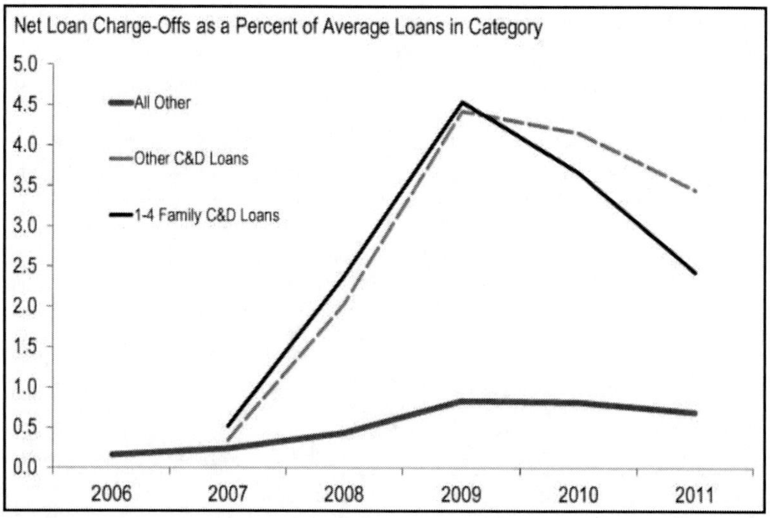

Source: FDIC.

Chart 5.12. Performance Characteristics of Commercial Loans in Community Banks: Net Charge-Off Rates, FDIC-Insured Institutions, 2006-2011.

The Role of C&D Lending at Community Banks

The patterns of C&D lending shown in Chart 5.10 suggests that C&D lending has been a highly cyclical activity pursued mostly by CRE specialists and multi-specialists. While C&D loans never exceeded 5 percent of total assets for any of the other specialty groups in any year, they totaled more than 5 percent of assets for CRE specialists and multi-specialists in every year until 2011, when the percentage for multi-specialists fell to 4.8 percent. Moreover, during the real estate booms of the mid-1980s and the early- to mid-2000s, holdings of C&D loans increased sharply as a percent of assets at CRE specialists and, to a lesser degree, multi-specialists, while holding steady among every other lending specialty.

C&D Loan Performance Deteriorated Significantly during the Financial Crisis

Charts 5.11 and 5.12 show that during the recent crisis, C&D loans held by community banks experienced much higher noncurrent loan and net loan charge-off ratios than the other classes of CRE and commercial loans presented in Charts 5.8 and 5.9. The noncurrent loan ratio for both 1-to-4 family C&D loans and other C&D loans peaked above 10 percent during the recent crisis, compared to a peak ratio of below 3 percent for the other CRE and commercial loan categories, when combined. The net loan charge-off ratio displays a similar pattern, peaking slightly above 4.5 percent for both 1-to-4 family C&D and other C&D loan categories. This compares with a peak net loan charge-off ratio under 1 percent for the combined other CRE and commercial loan categories. Both 1-to-4 family C&D and other C&D loan categories showed similar deterioration as the recent crisis intensified and both categories performed markedly worse than the other CRE and C&I loans.

Higher Levels of C&D Lending Are Associated with Higher Rates of Failure

During the crisis years of the late 1980s and early 1990s, as well as the interval starting in 2006, the subset of community banks with C&D loans greater than 10 percent of assets stands out even among the main lending specialist groups in terms of adverse financial performance. Table 5.13 compares the failure index for CRE specialists, multi-specialists and all community banks according to whether the members of each group held C&D loans greater than 10 percent of total assets.[35] For the entire study period, community banks with C&D loans greater than 10 percent of assets were 2.8 times more likely to fail than the average community bank, while those with C&D loans less than 10 percent of assets were less likely to fail than the average community bank. Even among the CRE and multi-specialist groups, those with C&D loans greater than 10 percent were far more likely to fail than other members of these groups. This was particularly the case in the 2006-2010 interval and in 2011, when banks with a 10 percent concentration in C&D loans were several times more likely to fail than other institutions.

Changes in Lending Strategy and the Financial Performance of Community Banks in the 2000s

Among the community bank lending specialty groups studied in this chapter, three groups stand out as representing the largest percentages of community banks as of 2000, and for exhibiting relatively strong and stable performance over most of the study period. Table 5.4 shows that the three largest groups of community banks in 2000 were the no specialty group (31 percent), mortgage specialists (22 percent), and agricultural specialists (15 percent). One of the reasons these three groups came to represent more than two-thirds of all community banks in 2000 was their consistently strong credit performance and low failure rates. Community banks in these groups reported a lower weighted average provision expenses to average assets ratio and a lower failure index than each of the other four lending specialty groups across the study period. In addition, agricultural specialists and the no specialty group reported higher weighted average ratios of pretax ROA than any of the other five groups across the study period.

Given the relatively strong long-term operating results of these three groups, additional analysis was performed using them as a baseline group. Hundreds of community banks shifted out of the three baseline groups and into other lending specialties after 2000. Those community banks that shifted out of the baseline groups were regarded as pursuing an alternative lending strategy. Between 2000 and 2005, the share of community banks in the baseline groups declined from 68 percent to 55 percent. Over the same period, the percent of community banks identified as CRE specialists increased from 11 percent to 26 percent. As depicted in Charts 5.4 and 5.5, the main vehicles for these shifts to alternative lending specialties were increases in holdings of C&D loans and other CRE loans.

Table 5.14. Changes in Community Bank Lending Strategies, 2000-2005

Community Banks in Baseline Lending Specialty Groups in 2000		Number of Community Banks in 2005								Community Banks Exiting Between 2000 and 2005	
		Remaining in Baseline Lending Specialty Groups				Pursuing Alternative Lending Strategies					
						Strategy 1:	Strategy 2:	Strategy 3:			
Lending Specialty Group	Number of Community Banks	Mortgage Specialists	Agricultural Specialists	No Specialty	Total	C&D Loans > 10% of Assets	Total CRE Loans > 30% of Assets	Other Changes in Specialty Group	Total	Failed	Other Exit
Mortgage Specialists	1,942	1,025	5	201	1,231	222	118	108	448	5	258
Agricultural Specialists	1,327	6	967	89	1,062	34	11	93	138	1	126
No Specialty	2,697	95	100	1,325	1,520	309	219	310	838	2	337
Total	5,966	1,126	1,072	1,615	3,813	565	348	511	1,424	8	721

Source: FDIC.

Note: Some institutions with C&D loans greater than 10 percent of assets are assigned to the No Specialty group if their total loans-to-assets ratio remains below 33 percent. Community banks meeting the criteria for Strategy 1 (C&D loans greater than 10 percent of assets) or Strategy 2 (total CRE loans greater than 30 percent of assets) by 2005 shifted into either the CRE lending specialist group or the multi-specialist group. Community banks listed under Strategy 3 include all community banks that shifted out of the three baseline specialty groups that did not meet the criteria for Strategy 1 or Strategy 2, including those that no longer qualified as community banks.

Table 5.15. Characteristics of Community Banks That Remained in Baseline Specialty Groups in 2000 and 2005 and Those That Shifted to Alternative Lending Strategy as of 2005

Characteristic of Community Bank	Number of Community Banks	Percent Remaining in Baseline Group as of 2005	Percent Shifting to Alternative Lending Strategy as of 2005
All Community Banks Belonging to Baseline Specialty Groups in 2000	5,237	73%	27%
Type of Corporate Organization			
C Corporation	3,144	69%	31%
S Corporation	1,527	74%	26%
Mutual	566	90%	10%

Age of Charter			
Established Before 1950	4,124	78%	22%
Established Between 1950 and 1979	522	64%	36%
Established in 1980 or Later	591	43%	57%
Geography of Headquarters Location			
Metro County	2,263	63%	37%
Micro County	1,172	75%	25%
Rural County	1,802	84%	16%
Within One of Ten High-Growth States[1]	457	55%	45%
Outside the Ten High-Growth States	4,780	75%	25%
Trust Preferred Securities (TruPS) Outstanding at Holding Company Level[2]			
Yes	352	50%	50%
No	4,885	74%	26%

Source: FDIC.

[1] High growth states defined according to the total increase in the Economy.com / Case-Shiller Home Price Index, 2000-2005. States include: AZ, CA, FL, HI, MD, NJ, NV, NY, RI, VA.

[2] Indicates TruPS outstanding at the holding company at any time between 2000 and 2005.

Table 5.16. Weighted Average Pretax ROA of Community Banks That Belonged to the Baseline Lending Specialty Groups in 2000 According to the Lending Strategy Pursued as of 2005

		Weighted Average Pretax ROA, by Year											
		2000	**2001**	**2002**	**2003**	**2004**	**2005**	**2006**	**2007**	**2008**	**2009**	**2010**	**2011**
Remained in Baseline Lending Specialty Groups	Mortgage Specialists	1.3%	1.3%	1.4%	1.4%	1.3%	1.2%	1.0%	0.8%	0.3%	0.4%	0.8%	0.8%
	Agricultural Specialists	1.6%	1.4%	1.5%	1.5%	1.5%	1.6%	1.4%	1.4%	1.2%	0.9%	1.2%	1.4%
	No Specialty	1.6%	1.5%	1.6%	1.4%	1.4%	1.4%	1.3%	1.2%	0.9%	0.7%	0.9%	1.0%
Pursued Alternative Lending Strategies	1: C&D Loans > 10% of Assets	1.4%	1.4%	1.6%	1.6%	1.5%	1.6%	1.5%	1.2%	-0.1%	-0.9%	-0.1%	0.3%
	2: Total CRE Loans > 30% of Assets	1.4%	1.5%	1.6%	1.6%	1.6%	1.6%	1.5%	1.3%	0.2%	-0.2%	0.4%	0.6%
	3: Other Changes in Strategy	1.5%	1.5%	1.7%	1.7%	1.6%	1.6%	1.7%	0.8%	0.3%	0.1%	0.9%	1.2%

Source: FDIC.

Table 5.17. Troubled Institutions as Percent of Community Banks That Belonged to Baseline Lending Specialty Groups in 2000 According to the Lending Strategy Pursued as of 2005

			Troubled Institutions as Percent of Community Banks in Group											
			2000	2001	2002	2003	2004	2005	2006	2007	2008	2009	2010	2011
Remained in Baseline Lending Specialty Groups	Mortgage Specialists		4%	5%	7%	5%	4%	5%	6%	7%	9%	14%	17%	17%
	Agricultural Specialists		5%	5%	5%	7%	5%	3%	3%	5%	7%	12%	15%	12%
	No Specialty		4%	4%	5%	5%	5%	5%	4%	3%	6%	12%	16%	14%
Pursued Alternative Lending Strategies	1:	C&D Loans > 10% of Assets	7%	5%	6%	7%	5%	4%	4%	9%	27%	51%	56%	52%
	2:	Total CRE Loans > 30% of Assets	7%	9%	8%	7%	6%	7%	5%	8%	19%	36%	44%	46%
	3:	Other Changes in Strategy	5%	5%	5%	5%	6%	5%	5%	8%	14%	23%	29%	25%

Source: FDIC.

Note: Troubled institutions are defined as those rated 3, 4 or 5 at their most recent examination.

Table 5.18. Troubled Institutions as Percent of Community Banks That Pursued C&D and CRE Lending Strategies

Strategy Group			Troubled Institutions as Percent of All Community Banks in Group											
			2000	2001	2002	2003	2004	2005	2006	2007	2008	2009	2010	2011
Shifted from Baseline Specialty Group in 2000 to Alternative Strategy as of 2005	1:	C&D Loans > 10% of Assets	7%	5%	6%	7%	5%	4%	4%	9%	27%	51%	56%	52%
	2:	Total CRE Loans > 30% of Assets	7%	9%	8%	7%	6%	7%	5%	8%	19%	36%	44%	46%
Already Engaged in Lending Strategy as of 2000	1:	C&D Loans > 10% of Assets	7%	8%	8%	8%	6%	4%	5%	9%	39%	58%	64%	58%
	2:	Total CRE Loans > 30% of Assets	10%	9%	9%	8%	7%	7%	6%	8%	26%	51%	57%	52%

Source: FDIC.

Table 5.14 shows the number of community banks in each of the three baseline groups in 2000, as well as those that shifted to alternative lending specialties or exited the industry by 2006. In defining the shift in lending strategy, Table 5.14 first identifies community banks that left one of the three baseline groups because they accumulated C&D loans greater than 10 percent of total assets, followed by those that accumulated total CRE loans greater than 30 percent, and finally those that left one of the three baseline groups for any other reason, including if they were no longer designated as a community bank.[36] These shifts in lending strategy are labeled Strategy 1 (C&D loans greater than 10 percent of assets), Strategy 2 (total CRE loans greater than 30 percent of assets), and Strategy 3 (all other specialty group changes). Table 5.14 shows that more than 1,400 community banks shifted out of one of the baseline groups between 2000 and 2005, with the largest number of them doing so by accumulating C&D loans greater than 10 percent of assets (Strategy 1).

Characteristics of Community Banks That Shifted Strategies

Table 5.15 provides further detail comparing the characteristics of community banks that remained in one of the three baseline groups as of 2005 and those that shifted to one of the alternative lending strategies. Overall, 27 percent of them made such a shift, but the percentages were higher for those community banks in the baseline groups that were: organized as C corporations (31 percent); established between 1950 and 1979 (36 percent) or established in 1980 or later (57 percent); headquartered in a metro county (37 percent) or headquartered in one of ten fast-growing states (45 percent); or reported Trust Preferred Securities (TruPS) outstanding at the holding company level (50 percent).[37] While not every community bank followed this profile, these characteristics tended to distinguish banks that shifted lending strategies from those that remained in one of the baseline groups.

Outcomes for Alternative Lending Strategies

A comparison of pretax ROA across the decade confirms that the first half of the 2000s was an inopportune time to shift from one of the three baseline groups to pursue an alternate lending strategy (see Table 5.16). Community banks that pursued another lending specialty generally outperformed those that remained in one of the three baseline groups by a modest margin between 2000 and 2006. During this period, U.S. real estate prices rose rapidly, with S&P Case-Shiller 20-City Home Price Index rising by a total of 82 percent. However, as real estate prices began to decline after 2006, the earnings performance of community banks pursuing Strategy 1 (C&D lending) and Strategy 2 (CRE lending) deteriorated. These groups underperformed the three baseline groups by a substantial margin from 2008 through the end of the study period. Community banks pursuing Strategy 3 (all other shifts in lending specialty) also generally underperformed the three baseline groups in 2008 and 2009, but recovered to post a weighted average pretax ROA above 1 percent in 2011.

Table 5.17 shows that an even larger disparity in performance exists between the three baseline groups and the alternative lending strategies when comparing rates of troubled institutions (those rated 3, 4 or 5 at their last examination). Community banks that remained in the three baseline groups through 2005 did experience increases in the level of troubled institutions after the onset of recession and lower real estate prices in 2007. However, community banks that shifted to one of the three alternative lending strategies were far more likely to become troubled. In 2010 and 2011, more than half of community banks that shifted to Strategy 1, and that had not already failed were troubled, as were more than 40 percent of banks that had shifted to Strategy 2.

Chart 5.13 compares the incidence of failure for community banks in the three baseline groups and those that shifted to one of the three alternative lending strategies. The failure index indicates the prevalence of failed banks in each group relative to the prevalence of that group in the larger population of community banks. Between 2006 and 2011, failures among community banks that shifted to Strategy 1 (C&D lending) were almost five times higher than their share of the overall population, while failures among those that shifted to Strategy 2 (CRE lending) were almost double their share of the population. Meanwhile, community banks that remained in one of the three baseline groups failed at rates significantly below their share of all community banks in the population.

Did Newcomers Fare Worse in the Real Estate Downturn?

Given the underperformance of community banks that shifted from one of the three baseline groups to one of the alternative lending strategies, it is natural to ask whether community banks that were already engaged in these lending strategies in 2000 fared better because of their longer track record with that strategy. The data suggest that this is not the case. Table 5.18 calculates troubled institutions as a percent of community banks that shifted to Strategy 1 (C&D lending), Strategy 2 (CRE lending) and those that were already pursuing these strategies as of 2000. The results indicate that community banks that became engaged earlier in the C&D or CRE lending strategies actually fared worse than those that later shifted to those strategies.

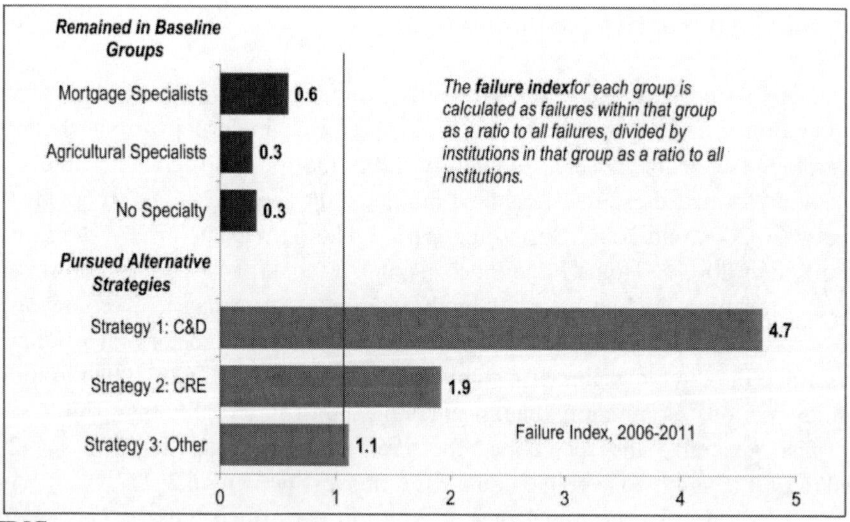

Source: FDIC.

Chart 5.13. Failure Index 2006-2011 Community Banks That Belonged to Baseline Specialty Groups in 2000 According to 2005 Lending Strategy.

One possible reason the longtime C&D and CRE lenders fared as bad as or worse than the newcomers is that they had more time to build up higher concentrations of C&D and total CRE loans. Table 5.19 compares the failure index for the years 2006 through 2011 for community banks engaged in Strategy 1 or Strategy 2 according to whether they shifted to one of those strategies from one of the three baseline groups or if they were already engaged in one of those strategies in 2000. The table also breaks down community banks in each of these groups according to their degree of concentration in that loan type as of 2005. The results not only confirm that the incidence of failure was frequently higher for banks that were already engaged in Strategy 1 or 2 in 2000, but also that the degree of concentration is an important determinant of the incidence of failure in each group. The higher the concentration in C&D or total CRE lending in 2005, before the real estate downturn began, the higher the incidence of failure after 2005.

What Were the Lending Strategies of New Banks, and How Did They Fare?

To complete the evaluation of lending strategies in the 2000s, Table 5.20 places community banks that were established between year-end 2000 and year-end 2005 into one of the three baseline groups or one of the three alternative lending strategies. Almost half of the community banks established between 2000 and 2005 were pursuing the C&D strategy as of 2005, while another 13 percent held total CRE loans equal to at least 30 percent of assets. Just under 20 percent of new community banks were members of one of the three baseline groups. Similar to existing community bank charters, the performance of new banks in the baseline specialty groups was somewhat better than that of new community banks pursuing Strategy 1 (C&D) or Strategy 2 (CRE), although new community banks pursuing Strategy 3 also performed well.

Table 5.19. Failure Index: 2006-2011 Community Banks That Pursued C&D and CRE Lending Strategies by Degree of Lending Concentration

Alternative Lending Strategy		Shifted to Strategy Between 2000 and 2005	Already Engaged in Strategy by 2000
Strategy 1: C&D Loans > 10% of Assets		**Failure Index: 2006-2011**	
Concentration of C&D Loans to Assets as of 2005	10 to 20 Percent	1.6	2.4
	20 to 30 Percent	4.8	4.4
	Greater Than 30 percent	12.8	9.9
Strategy 2: Total CRE Loans > 30% of Assets		**Failure Index: 2006-2011**	
Concentration of Total CRE Loans to Assets as of 2005	30 to 40 Percent	0.9	0.7
	40 to 50 Percent	1.1	1.6
	Greater Than 50 percent	1.1	1.6

Source: FDIC.

Notes: Excludes community banks chartered after 2000.

Table 5.20. Lending Strategies of New Community Banks, 2001-2005 and Performance Indicators, 2006-2011

Lending Strategy as of 2005		New Charters, 2001-2005		Performance Measures, 2006-2011		
		Number	Percent of Total	Pretax ROA (WA)	Percent Troubled (WA)	Failure Index
Baseline Lending Specialty Groups	Mortgage Specialists	29	4.5%	-0.30%	28%	0.76
	Agricultural Specialists	3	0.5%	1.01%	N/A	0.00
	No Specialty	92	14.2%	0.02%	26%	1.14
Alternative Lending Strategies	1: C&D Loans > 10% of Assets	299	46.2%	-0.67%	38%	4.53
	2: Total CRE Loans > 30% of Assets	87	13.4%	-0.52%	32%	1.73
	3: Other Strategies	137	21.2%	0.69%	23%	0.97

Source: FDIC.

Note: WA indicates weighted average. N/A indicates data withheld to avoid disclosing confidential information.

Summary

Community banks shifted the composition of their loan portfolios from retail loans to commercial loans during the study period, and this shift was mainly due to an increase in the share of loans secured by CRE. Agricultural specialists, consumer specialists, and banks with no lending specialty generally performed best among lending specialty groups, while CRE specialists were the worst performers over the entire study period. CRE specialists performed slightly better than the average for all community banks in good economic times, but performed significantly worse during the periods that coincided with banking crises. The largest segment of CRE lending was secured by nonfarm, nonresidential properties. About half of these loans at community banks were secured by properties that depend upon rental income for repayment and the other half were secured by owner-occupied properties. The loans secured by owner-occupied properties have many similarities to C&I loans. During the recent crisis, both types of nonfarm, nonresidential CRE loans had lower loss rates than C&I loans. Another important segment of CRE lending was C&D lending, which has been one of the poorest performing loan types in periods of economic distress. While C&D lending rose mainly at banks that focused on that product, the prevalence of nonfarm, nonresidential loans rose across all types of community banks. The performance of CRE specialists was marked by volatile net interest income and high credit costs. Most notably, banks that had high levels of C&D loans performed significantly worse than other banks.

Lending strategy is an important factor in community bank success, and it proved to be especially so in the tumultuous second half of the 2000s decade. More than two-thirds of community banks entered the decade as members of one of three baseline lending specialty groups that demonstrated consistently strong performance across the study period.

Nonetheless, hundreds of community banks left these baseline groups in the first half of the decade as the U.S. real estate boom was nearing a peak and pursued alternative lending strategies built on C&D or CRE lending. These institutions slightly outperformed those that remained in the baseline lending groups while real estate prices were rising. After 2007, community banks that shifted to these alternative lending strategies underperformed those that remained in one of the three baseline groups by a substantial margin, as did community banks that began the decade already engaged in the C&D and CRE lending strategies. Finally, almost 60 percent of community banks chartered between 2000 and 2005 also were engaged in the C&D or CRE lending strategies by 2005, and these institutions also generally underperformed new community banks that pursued one of the three baseline lending strategies.

The implication of these results is that community banks that stuck to one of the three baseline lending strategies performed well, on average, across the study period as a whole and even during the crisis years of the late 2000s. Community banks that abandoned those lending specialties for the small bit of extra yield that could be obtained from C&D and other CRE lending during the boom proved to be much more vulnerable to the effects of the crisis once it occurred.

6. Capital Formation at Community Banks

Overview

This chapter discusses the role of capital at community banks, with a focus on how community banks build their capital over time. First, the role of retained earnings as a source of capital is discussed and the rate of earnings retention is compared across various types of banks. Next is a discussion of capital raising from external sources. While this strategy for adding to capital is used less frequently than earnings retention, the discussion shows that community banks have been able to raise external capital when needed.

Do Economies of Scale Work Against Small Community Banks?

Economies of scale exist when the average cost of producing a unit of output declines as the volume of output increases. In sectors such as manufacturing, where physical inputs and outputs can be easily identified and measured, it is relatively straightforward to estimate economies of scale. In service industries like banking, it becomes more difficult to define economies of scale, in part because it is less clear what constitutes a unit of input or output. For example, a demand deposit could be considered either an input or an output. Due to such ambiguities, there are many possible ways to measure banking output and average costs. Nonetheless, there are reasons to suspect that economies of scale could indeed arise in some segments of the banking industry. Larger banks may be better able to diversify risks, especially when they can operate across many geographic regions that differ in their degree of correlation with the national economic business cycle. Larger banks may also be able to lower their funding costs by issuing debt directly to the capital markets. Moreover, there may be opportunities for larger banks to spread fixed costs, such as those associated with technology and information processing, across a large portfolio made up of multiple lines of business.

If economies of scale were to be found in banking, larger institutions would reap ongoing cost advantages, and the potential of achieving these advantages could serve as an impetus for consolidation among smaller institutions. Besides economies of scale, there is evidence that many banks operate with less than optimal efficiency compared with similarly sized institutions.

The existence of inefficient banks also serves as an impetus for consolidation as efficient banks may gain by acquiring less efficient institutions and altering management practices. Following a merger, it can be difficult to identify whether gains are achieved from improved operating efficiency or from enhanced scale benefits. The empirical evidence suggests that consolidation can lead to improved efficiency. Stiroh (1999) finds that banking industry consolidation in the early 1990s reallocated assets toward more profitable institutions while the least profitable institutions exited the industry. Boyd and Graham (1998) also find that small-bank mergers from this period were associated with significant improvements in cost and profit efficiency.

For the most part, the literature that uses bank data from the 1980s finds that banks achieve a minimum level of average costs somewhere between $75 million and $300 million in total assets.[1] Numerous studies from this period also find evidence of diseconomies of scale (increasing average costs) for the largest institutions. Stiroh (1999) finds that consolidation over the second half of the 1990s, a period characterized by mergers among larger institutions, was associated with reduced profitability as the largest bank mergers underperformed. Boyd and Graham (1998) also find that consolidation among the largest banks produced little evidence of cost or profit efficiency gains over this period. However, subsequent research has identified methodological limitations that may call into question the evidence for diseconomies of scale.

Newer approaches to this topic have shifted the modeling approach away from an assumption that banks simply minimize costs and toward a framework in which bank managers maximize profits. Additionally, the literature has increasingly focused on estimating the importance of scale economies at the largest bank holding companies, especially since the financial crisis. Many of these newer studies find evidence that the very largest institutions do benefit from economies of scale (e.g., Hughes and Mester [2011], Hughes [2011], Wheelock and Wilson [2012]).

In light of the lack of recent studies relating to economies of scale in community banks, the FDIC conducted research specifically designed to determine if economies of scale exist among community banks.[2] This analysis places particular emphasis on whether scale economies are important enough to prompt community banks to try to lower their average costs through consolidation.

In the FDIC analysis, a bank's average cost of producing output is measured as total bank costs divided by bank balance sheet assets. Total costs are defined as the sum of interest expenses, provisions for loan and lease losses, and noninterest expenses.

The FDIC analysis uses a non-parametric regression model to estimate the form and shape of the average cost curve for community banks. The cost curve is measured for two years, 2006 and 2009 (both measured in 2011 dollars) to capture years of both economic expansion and recession. Separate analysis was conducted for different lending specialist groups because they may have unique costs and technologies that lead to distinctive patterns of scale economies.

Cost curves for two of the community bank lending specialist groups, CRE and agriculture, are shown in the following charts. In each of the charts, the center line represents an estimated average cost curve that varies with asset size, while the outer lines represent a 95 percent confidence interval constructed by the regression model. Among the lending specialist groups, CRE specialists have the largest potential benefit from economies of scale, as their 2006 average costs decline by about 400 basis points between asset sizes of $10 million and $10 billion (see Chart 5.14). However, the estimated curve shows little difference in average costs between community banks with assets between $100 million and $1 billion, and very small benefits beyond $1 billion. In other words, the majority of efficiency gains are achieved by $100 million in total assets. The average cost curve estimated for CRE specialists for 2009 looks somewhat different from the 2006 cost curve because of changes in the composition of the group, not the least of which was the failure of 88 community bank CRE specialists during that interval (see Chart 5.15). Nevertheless, the 2009 cost curve still shows that the average costs level off above $500 million, indicating that most cost advantages are realized at that size.

For the agricultural lending specialty group, there is less evidence of economies of scale (see Charts 5.16 and 5.17). There is very little difference in estimated costs between the smallest and largest banks, and there are no statistically significant cost advantages beyond $100 million in total assets. Analysis of other community bank specialty lending groups shows that, while the cost-minimizing scale varies between $75 million and $300 million depending on the lender specialty, there is no evidence of economies of scale for any specialty group beyond $500 million.

These results using 2006 and 2009 data are consistent with the findings of many banking studies that use data from the 1980s.

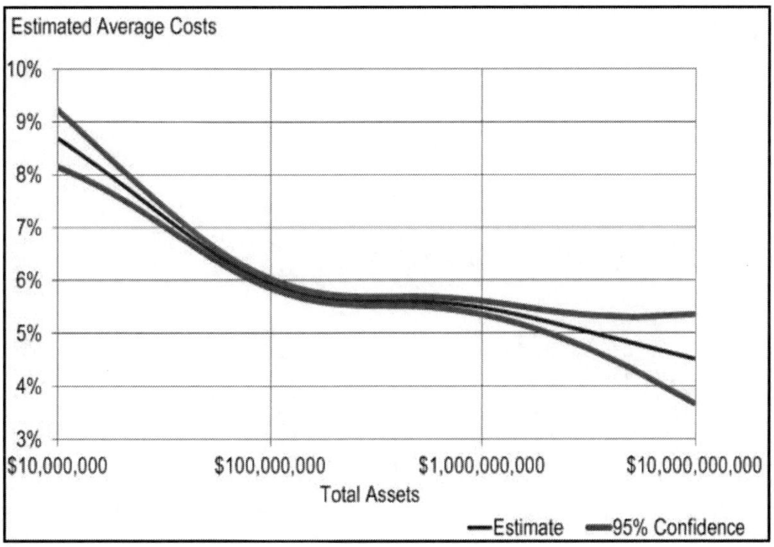

Source: FDIC.

Chart 5.14. Estimated Average Total Costs as a Function of Asset Size FDIC-Insured Community Banks (CRE Lending Specialists), 2006.

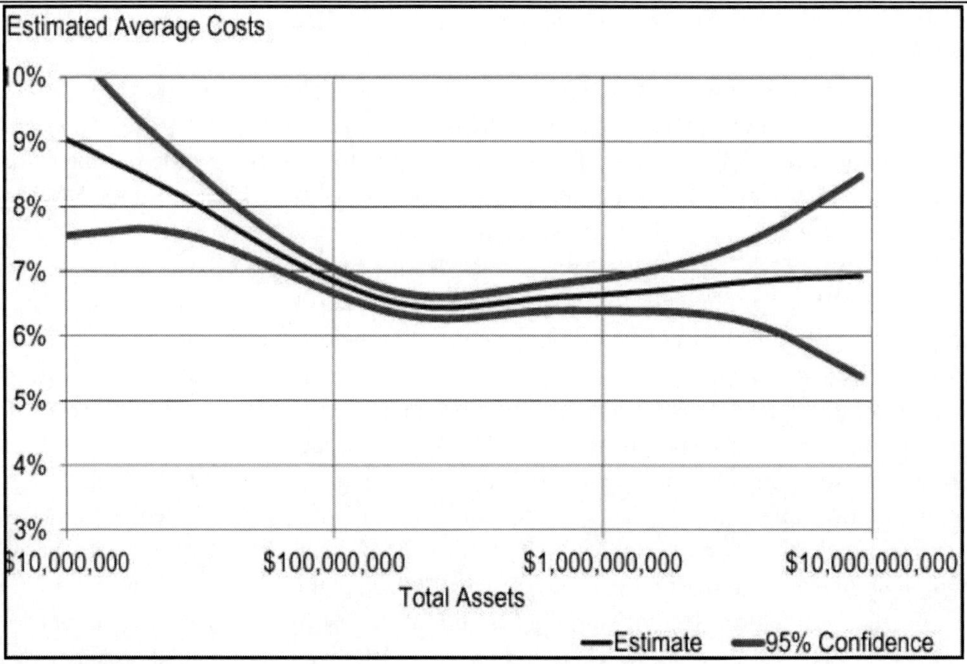

Source: FDIC.

Chart 5.15. Estimated Average Total Costs as a Function of Asset Size FDIC-Insured Community Banks (CRE Lending Specialists), 2009.

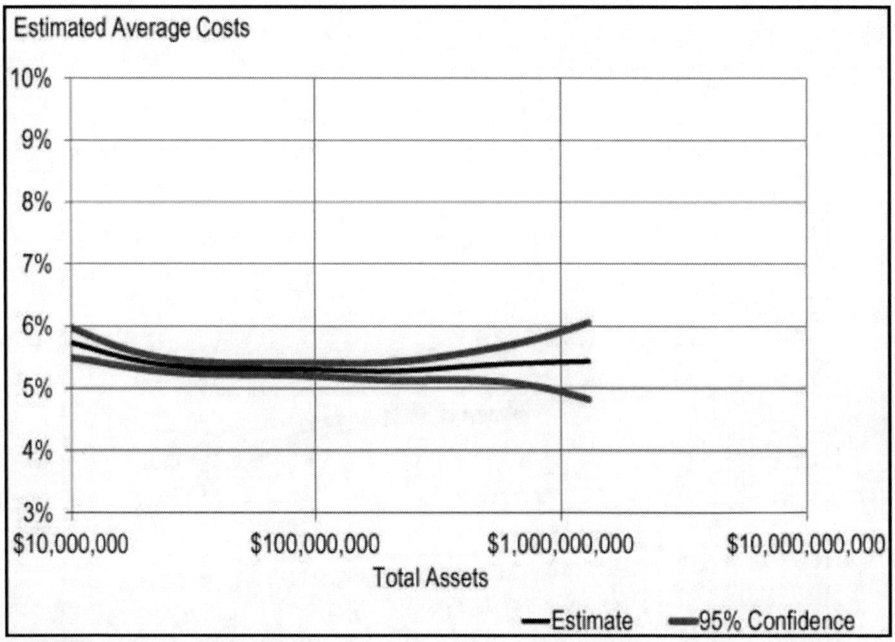

Source: FDIC.

Chart 5.16. Estimated Average Total Costs as a Function of Asset Size FDIC-Insured Community Banks (Agricultural Lending Specialists), 2006.

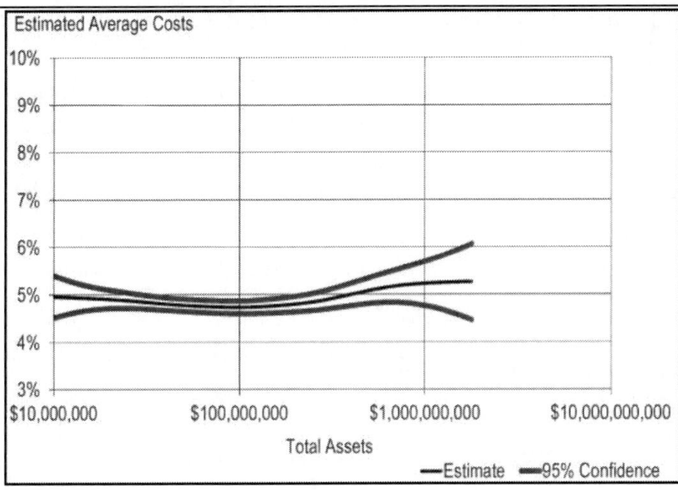

Source: FDIC.

Chart 5.17. Estimated Average Total Costs as a Function of Asset Size FDIC-Insured Community Banks (Agricultural Lending Specialists), 2009.

These results show that while some small community banks may be able to reduce their average costs through growth, there is no indication of any significant benefit beyond $500 million in asset size. Much of the benefit from economies of scale appears to dissipate once community banks reach $100 million in total assets. Therefore, while economies of scale may create incentives for banks to grow toward $100 million to $300 million in assets, depending on lending specialty, scale considerations are probably not the most important factor driving consolidation above that size threshold.

[1] See Berger, Hunter Timme, 1993.

[2] Paul Kupiec and Stefan Jacewitz, 2012.

Long-Term Trends in Bank Capital Ratios

Capital is generally measured relative to a bank's assets and risk exposures. The most basic measure is the l*everage ratio*, which measures common equity, certain types of preferred equity and retained earnings as a percentage of total assets. Beyond this basic measure, perhaps the most frequently cited is the *total risk-based capital ratio*, which uses a broader regulatory definition of capital in the numerator and adjusts total assets in the denominator to reflect a range of on- and off-balance-sheet risk exposures.

Based on either the leverage ratio or total risk-based capital, community banks consistently maintained higher capital levels than noncommunity banks over the study period (Charts 6.1 and 6.2). Capital levels at both community and noncommunity banks increased sharply in the early 1990s as the industry recovered from the banking and thrift crisis that began in the 1980s and as banks conformed to new capital standards under the first Basel capital agreement and Prompt Corrective Action (PCA).[38] Leverage capital ratios for both groups rose more gradually during the years between the banking crises that bookend the study period, as the industry posted record earnings. Average leverage capital ratios fell—for noncommunity banks in 2007 and 2008, and for community banks in 2008 and 2009—around the onset of the recent crisis before rising again as capital flowed in both from government programs and private sources.

By contrast, the average total risk-based capital ratio actually declined steadily for community banks during the years between banking crises, as risk-weighted assets rose faster than equity capital. Still, the total risk-based capital ratio remained higher at community banks than at noncommunity banks throughout this period. The total risk-based capital ratio rose sharply for both groups in the wake of the recent financial crisis as the industry raised capital and shed higher-risk assets. By the end of 2011, the total risk-based capital ratios for both groups exceeded 15 percent and were approaching historic highs.

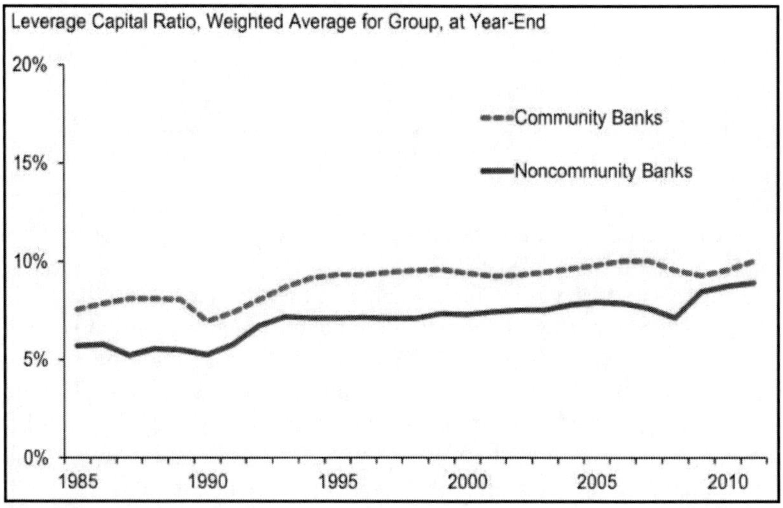

Source: FDIC.

Chart 6.1. Leverage Capital Ratio, Federally Insured Community and Noncommunity Banks, 1985-2011.

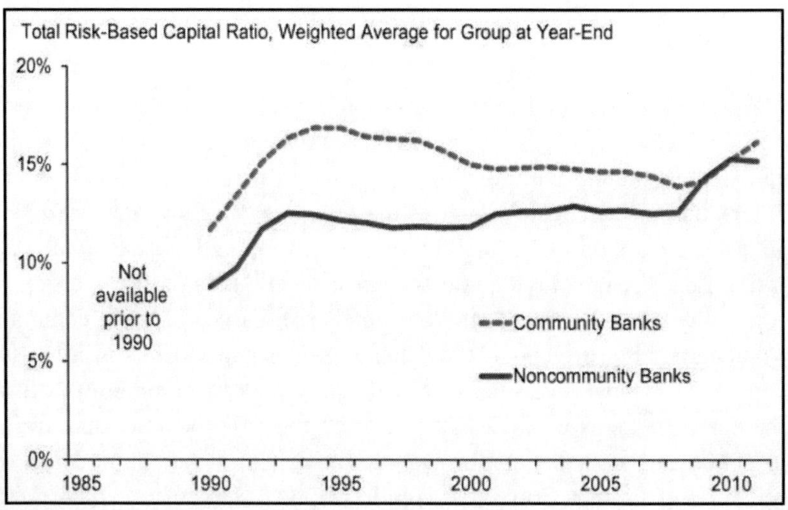

Source: FDIC.

Chart 6.2. Total Risk-Based Capital Ratio, Federally Insured Community and Noncommunity Banks, 1990-2011.

Sources of Capital for Community and Noncommunity Banks

Capital formation at banks takes place through two main channels.[39] The first is the internal generation of new capital through *retained earnings*. Retained earnings are the amount of net income remaining after common and preferred dividends are paid. To the extent that most banks report positive earnings each year, they are usually in a position not only to pay dividends to their shareholders, but also to add to their capital stock through retained earnings. The second channel through which capital formation takes place at banks is *raising of capital from external sources.*[40]

Table 6.1 and Charts 6.3 and 6.4 break down the total changes in equity capital from retained earnings and external capital at community and noncommunity banks during the study period. Community banks were much more dependent on retained earnings for capital formation than noncommunity banks during the study period. Community banks obtained almost 48 percent of their total capital formation through retained earnings, compared with 29 percent for noncommunity banks. As a share of prior period equity, community banks and noncommunity banks increased capital through retained earnings by about 3.6 percent and 3.5 percent per year, respectively. However, increases from external capital raises represented an average of 5 percent of prior year equity at noncommunity banks, compared with only 3.5 percent at community banks.

While both community and noncommunity banks have become more dependent on external capital over the past decade, community banks continued to be almost twice as reliant as noncommunity banks on retained earnings as a source of increase in equity capital. In the last ten years, retained earnings made up 41 percent of additions to equity capital at community banks, compared with 23 percent at noncommunity banks.

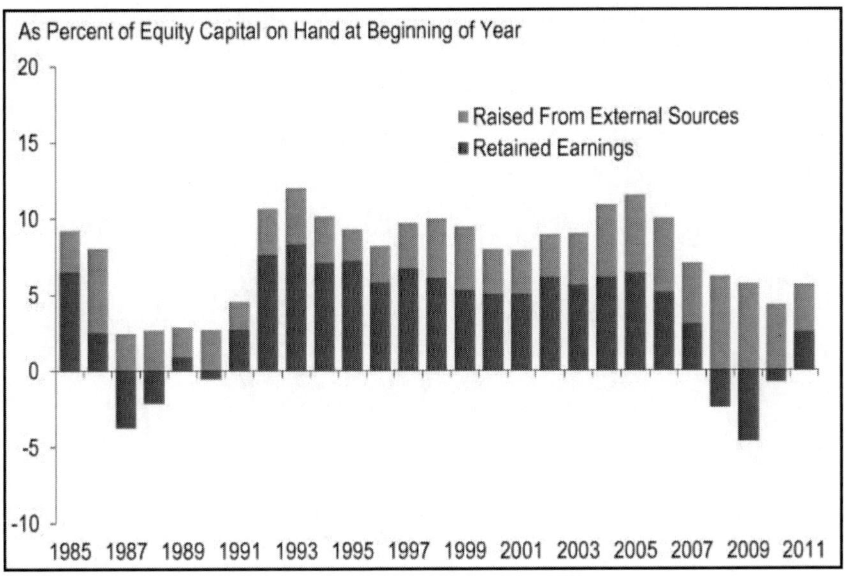

Source: FDIC.

Chart 6.3. Contributions to Annual Changes in Equity Capital All Community Banks.

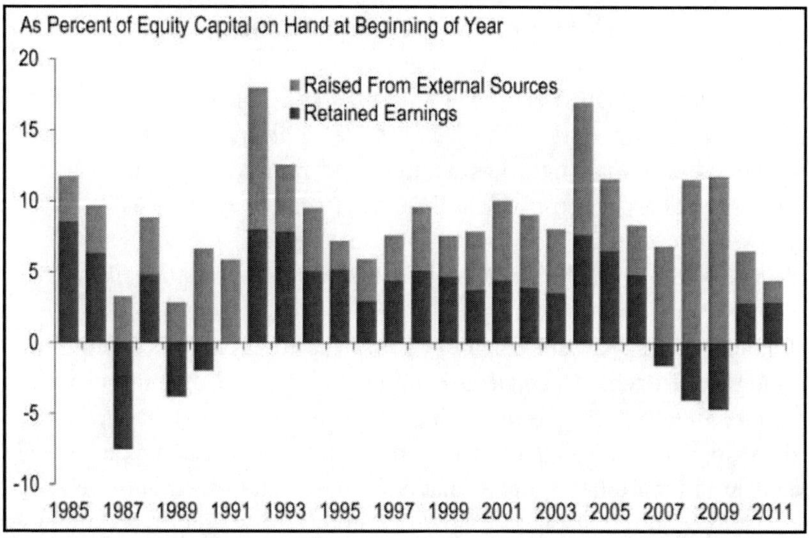

Source: FDIC.

Chart 6.4. Contributions to Annual Changes in Equity Capital All Noncommunity Banks.

Because of the large financial losses incurred during the recent crisis, both community and noncommunity banks had to offset three years of negative retained earnings (2007-2009 for noncommunity banks, 2008-2010 for community banks) with large volumes of capital raised from external sources. By 2011, as industry earnings began to normalize, both groups had managed to re-establish a more normal mix of additions to capital through internal and external sources.

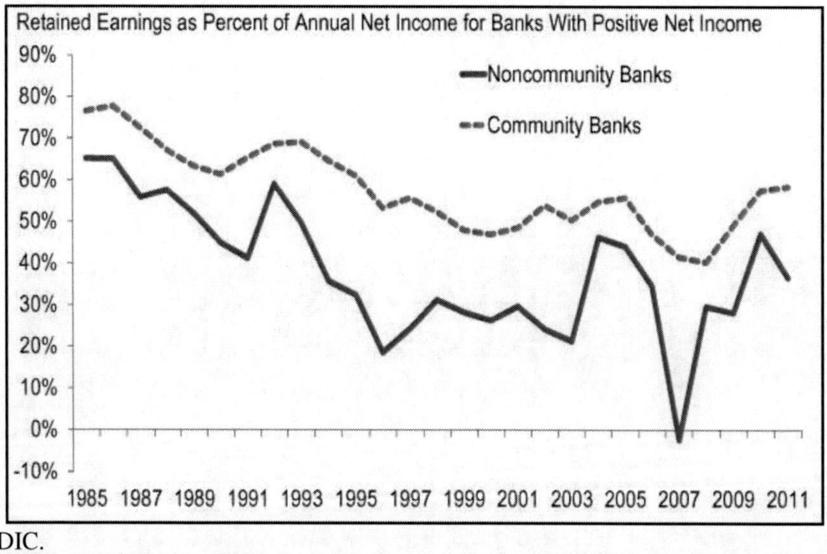

Source: FDIC.

Chart 6.5. Community Banks With Positive Net Income Consistently Retain a Higher Percent of Earnings Than Noncommunity Banks.

Capital Formation through Retained Earnings

Most federally insured banks and thrift institutions report positive annual net income in most years. Of the more than 332,000 year-end financial reports submitted by federally insured banks and thrifts since 1985, more than 291,000, or 88 percent, showed positive earnings for the year, with the remainder reporting zero or negative net income (see Table 6.2). In all, the total annual net income reported by all federally insured banks and thrifts since 1985 has amounted to $1.67 trillion.

Table 6.1. Total Additions to Equity Capital Through Retained Earnings and New Capital Raised From External Sources, 1985-2011

Group	Additions to Capital Through:				Total
	Retained Earnings		New Capital Raised From External Sources		
	$ Billions	% of Total	$ Billions	% of Total	$ Billions
Community Banks	$116	48%	$127	52%	$243
Noncommunity Banks	$303	29%	$734	71%	$1,037
Total	$419	33%	$861	67%	$1,280

Source: FDIC.

For the industry as a whole, most of this net income was paid out to common and preferred shareholders in the form of dividends. Of all federally insured banks and thrifts with stock charters that reported during the study period, 71 percent reported dividend payments. Banks organized as mutual institutions have no stockholders and typically do not pay dividends. (For a fuller discussion of bank ownership structures, see the inset box "Bank Ownership Structure and Access to External Capital.") In total, banks and thrifts paid out almost $1.26 trillion in dividends over the study period, for an aggregate industry dividend payout rate of 75 percent. The average payout rate over the study period was 58 percent of net income for community banks, substantially lower than the 78 percent rate for noncommunity banks. More than 60 percent of the year-end financial reports filed by all federally insured stock institutions during the study period showed both positive retained earnings and dividends.

Banks face a balancing act between adding to their capital base through retained earnings and paying regular dividends. In the 80 percent of total year-end financial reports where net income was larger than dividends paid during the study period, total additions to equity capital through retained earnings amounted to $942 billion. By contrast, in the 20 percent of all year-end reports where dividends exceeded net income, the amount of negative retained earnings amounted to $525 billion. Thus, the net addition to total industry equity capital through retained earnings during the study period was $417 billion.

BANK OWNERSHIP STRUCTURE AND ACCESS TO EXTERNAL CAPITAL

Banks can be organized either as stock corporations or as mutual institutions. In a stock corporation, an owner's interest in the company is represented by shares of stock.

There are two main forms of stock ownership, S corporations and C corporations. Banks and thrifts were made eligible to choose the Subchapter S form of ownership in 1996. Subchapter S status allows qualifying organizations to enjoy the limited liability of corporations while passing their tax liability directly to shareholders.[1] Because Subchapter S status includes restrictions on the number and type of shareholders, banks organized as S corporations may be limited in their ability to raise capital from new investors. Those stock corporations that have not chosen S corporation status are commonly referred to as C corporations. C corporations are subject to taxation of earnings at the corporate level in addition to taxation of any dividends distributed to shareholders. However, because C corporations are not subject to the same legal limits on shareholders, they have more flexibility than S corporations in seeking capital from new investors.

Under the mutual form of ownership, there are no shareholders; the bank is owned by its depositors and typically managed by trustees. Most mutual institutions are located in the northeastern United States, where mutual savings banks have a long history. Because mutual institutions do not issue stock, their options for increasing capital are generally limited to retained earnings.

The vast majority of community banks hold stock charters (Chart 6.6). C corporations represent the largest number of community banks, as they made up about 41 percent of community banks at year-end 2011. However, a significant number have chosen the Subchapter S form of ownership. The number of community banks organized as S corporations increased from 598 (6 percent of all community banks) in 1997 to 2,278 (34 percent) at the end of 2011. The share of community banks holding mutual charters has gradually declined over time, from 15 percent in 1984 to just under 7 percent in 2011.

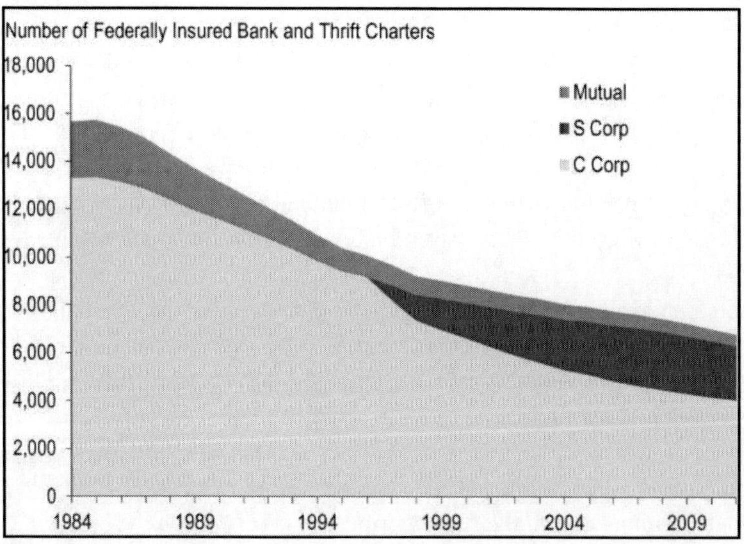

Source: FDIC.

Chart 6.6. Community Banks by Ownership Type, 1984-2011.

Most banks operate within bank holding companies, which typically own all or most of the common stock of one or more subsidiary banks.[2] To the extent that outside capital is sought by a subsidiary bank, the holding company is almost always the vehicle for raising that capital from existing or new shareholders. Funds can then be "downstreamed" to subsidiary banks. In cases where a single bank holding company operates a number of individual banking subsidiaries, issuance by the holding company not only allows for the centralization of capital raising, but it may also confer the advantage of stock issuance by a larger entity with a greater presence in the capital markets. Before the relaxation of state branching restrictions and limits on interstate banking in the 1980s and 1990s, bank holding companies were often used to operate geographically dispersed banking franchises through multiple charters. However, as described in Chapter 2, the relaxation of these restrictions led to a wave or mergers and consolidations that greatly reduced the total number of federally insured bank and thrift charters.

Most noncommunity banks belong to organizations that are publicly traded. At year-end 2011, about 65 percent of noncommunity bank charters, representing 92 percent of noncommunity bank assets, were publicly traded or were subsidiaries of publicly traded companies.[3] As a result, the shares of these companies tend to be relatively liquid, and their banks have ready access to additional capital through issuance of new shares.

Compared with noncommunity banks, the shares of community banks are more likely to be privately owned and closely held. At year-end 2011, an estimated 84 percent of community banks were privately held. The remaining 16 percent, representing about 34 percent of community bank assets, were in organizations that were publicly traded—though typically not on major exchanges.[4] As a result, even the publicly traded shares of community banks tend to be less liquid than the shares of noncommunity banks.

[1] The Small Business Job Protection Act of 1996 amended the Internal Revenue Code to allow qualifying financial institutions to elect Subchapter S status for federal income tax purposes. To qualify as an "S corporation," a bank or thrift must qualify as a "small business corporation" under section 1362(a) of Title 26. See 26 U.S.C. § 1361(a) (1). There are five requirements that must be met to qualify as a "small business operation." They are: (i) the institution must not use the reserve method of accounting for bad debts described in 26 U.S.C. § 585; (ii) the institution must not have more than 100 shareholders; (iii) the institution must not have as a shareholder a person who is not an individual, except as permitted by 26 U.S.C. § 1361(c); (iv) the institution must not have as a shareholder a nonresident alien; and (v) the institution must not have more than one class of stock. See 26 U.S.C. § 1361(b)(1)-(2). For purposes of determining how many shareholders a bank or thrift has, a husband and wife, and all members of a family, shall be treated as one shareholder. See 26 U.S.C. § 1361(c)(1). For purposes of determining how many classes of stock a bank or thrift has, "a corporation shall not be treated as having more than 1 class of stock solely because there are differences in voting rights among the shares of common stock." 26 U.S.C. § 1361(c)(4).

[2] At year-end 2011, at least 333 community banks and 59 noncommunity banks were in thrift holding companies. Because complete data for thrift holding companies were not available, thrift holding companies were not used to group organizations for purposes of this study. Thrift holding companies are diverse, ranging from noncomplex companies with limited activities to complex, multinational corporations. Unlike bank holding companies, thrift holding companies are not yet subject to consolidated capital requirements.

Also, a small segment of the industry consists of mutual holding companies. There were over 150 mutual holding companies operating at the end of 2011. Mutual holding companies are formed to permit some stock ownership in a bank that was previously entirely mutually owned. Shareholders, who own a percentage of the holding company, elect part of the board, and depositors elect the remainder. In these structures, the subsidiary banks are stock banks that are wholly owned by the mutual holding company.

[3] FDIC calculations based on data from SNL Financial. For purposes of this analysis, publicly traded institutions are considered to be companies that are either traded on a major exchange or in over-the-counter trading. The vast majority of publicly traded noncommunity banking organizations are listed for trading on major exchanges. Privately held banks are considered to be part of institutions that are not traded on a major exchange or in over-the-counter trading.

[4] Of those remaining 16 percent, only about one-third (5 percent of all community banks, representing 21 percent of community bank assets) belonged to organizations listed for trading on a major exchange.

Source: FDIC calculations based on data from SNL Financial.

Table 6.2. Federally Insured Banks and Thrifts Reporting Positive Net Income, Dividends and Retained Earnings by Ownership Type, 1985-2011

Community Banks					
	Percent of Year-End Financial Reports With:				
Ownership Type	Net Income > 0	Retained Earnings > 0	Dividend > 0	Dividend and Retained Earnings > 0	Dividend > 0 and Dividend > Net Income
Stock	88%	80%	72%	62%	10%
Mutual	88%	88%	0%	0%	0%
Total	88%	81%	65%	56%	9%
Noncommunity Banks					
Stock	87%	73%	67%	50%	17%
Mutual	81%	80%	3%	2%	1%
Total	87%	73%	66%	50%	17%

Source: FDIC.

Note: Mutuals may issue preferred stock and pay cash dividends in exceptional cases.

The Importance of Retained Earnings for Community Banks. There are important differences between community and noncommunity banks in the allocation of net income between dividends and retained earnings. These differences can be seen most clearly in the case of institutions reporting positive net income for the year. Chart 6.5 depicts how profitable community and noncommunity banks allocated net income to retained earnings in each year of the study period. It shows that profitable community banks consistently retained a higher percentage of current earnings than noncommunity institutions. On a weighted average basis for the entire study period, profitable community banks retained 57 percent of net income, compared with just 34 percent for noncommunity institutions.

Chart 6.5 also illustrates that retained earnings as a percent of net income have generally trended downward over most of the study period. Retained earnings as a percent of net income clearly fell during crisis episodes. However, looking at how different groups of community banks allocate net income between dividends and retained earnings also helps to explain this trend.

There are important differences in earnings retention between community banks organized as mutual organizations, C corporations and S corporations. As noted earlier, mutual organizations by definition retain virtually 100 percent of net income as retained earnings. Both C corporations and S corporations may pay dividends, but retained earnings are generally substantially higher at C corporations (Chart 6.7). One factor that contributes to this difference is that the tax obligations of banks organized as S corporations are passed through to shareholders. A higher dividend payout rate, and a correspondingly smaller percentage of income retained, is a means by which a bank organized as an S corporation can provide shareholders with the cash needed to cover these tax obligations.

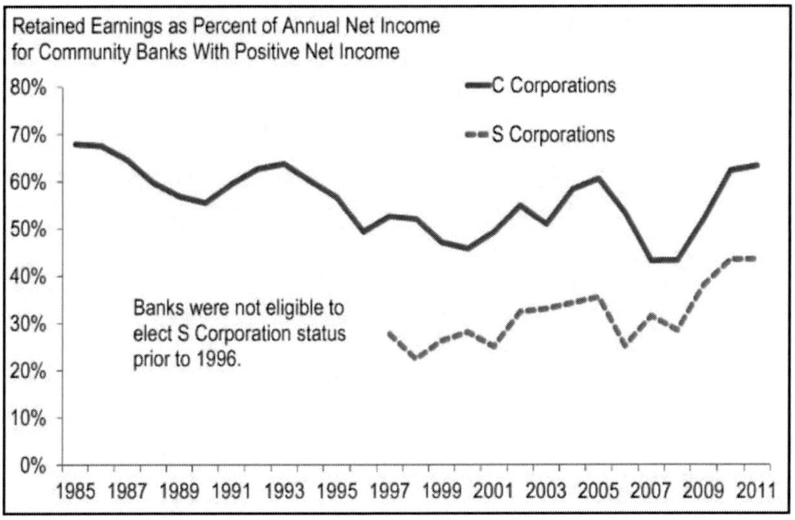

Source: FDIC.

Chart 6.7. Community Banks That Have Adopted S Corporation Status Retain a Smaller Portion of Earnings Than C Corporations.

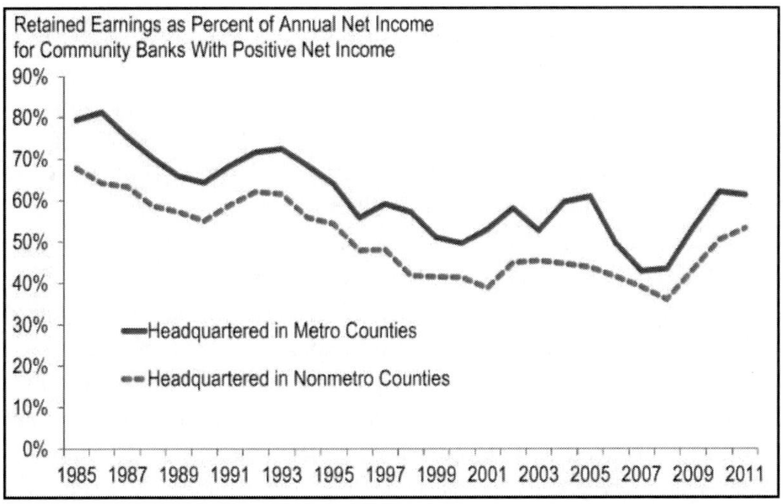

Source: FDIC.

Chart 6.8. Community Banks Headquartered in Metro Counties Have Consistently Retained a Higher Percentage of Earnings Than Nonmetro Banks.

A smaller, yet still consistent, difference can be observed in the percentage of net income retained by community banks headquartered in metro and nonmetro counties (Chart 6.8). In every year, profitable community banks headquartered in metro counties retained a higher percentage of net income than community banks headquartered in nonmetro counties. For the entire study period, the metro community banks with positive earnings retained 60 percent of their net income on a weighted average basis, compared with 48 percent for nonmetro community banks. Community banks operating in metro areas have a higher overall rate of asset growth and therefore have a greater incentive to add to capital through retained earnings. Over the study period, community banks headquartered in metro counties grew at a weighted average annual rate of 8.4 percent, versus 6.8 percent for community banks headquartered in nonmetro counties.

Table 6.3 shows five-year annual averages for retained earnings as a percent of net income for profitable community banks by the lending specialty groups introduced in Chapter 5. The highest overall rates of retained earnings are found among mortgage specialists (69 percent for the entire study period), followed by CRE specialists and multi-specialists. Higher retained earnings for mortgage specialists are largely explained by the fact that mutual institutions, which typically retain 100 percent of net income, are more prevalent among mortgage specialists than among community banks in general. In fact, mortgage specialists with stock charters typically have lower retained earnings than community banks with other lending specialties that have stock charters.

Meanwhile, the lowest percentages for retained earnings are found among agricultural specialists (42 percent of net income for the entire study period). An important factor driving this low rate of earnings retention is the prevalence of S corporations, which made up 58 percent of agricultural lending specialists in 2011, compared with 34 percent of all community banks. For the remaining lending specialties, the split between dividends and retained earnings among profitable community banks was generally even.

Capital Formation by Accessing External Sources

The second main source of capital for both community and noncommunity banks is from external sources. External capital raises include both the issuance of new equity instruments to investors by a bank and, more commonly, the downstreaming of funds from a holding company to a bank subsidiary, which may or may not be associated with the issuance of equity or debt by the holding company. Just over 10 percent of the year-end financial reports filed by all banks during the study period showed material increases in equity capital from external sources.[41] When community banks raise capital from external sources, many do so through private placements that are subscribed by the current owners and directors of the bank or other local investors who have unique knowledge of and interest in the institution.

A 2012 report by the Government Accountability Office (GAO) analyzed sources of capital for small banks.[42] The GAO found that a majority of banks they surveyed expressed confidence that they could raise new capital from their board members or members of their community.[43] Far smaller percentages expressed confidence that they could successfully raise capital by issuing common stock through either a public offering or a private placement. According to estimates by the GAO for its report, 27 percent of banks surveyed thought they could raise capital through a public common stock offering while 46 percent thought they could raise capital through a private placement.[44] However, the survey found that most community banks have been able to raise external capital when it has been necessary to do so.[45]

Table 6.3. Weighted Average Retained Earnings as a Percent of Annual Net Income for Community Banks with Positive Net Income by Lending Specialty Group, 1985-2011

Lending Specialty Group	All Community Banks						
	Time Period						
	Five-Year Intervals					2011	All Years: 1985-2011
	1986-1990	1991-1995	1996-2000	2001-2005	2006-2010		
Mortgage Specialists	88.9%	78.7%	53.9%	57.6%	55.8%	65.4%	68.9%
CRE Specialists	80.9%	72.2%	58.2%	58.8%	51.2%	66.7%	58.2%
C&I Specialists	56.3%	63.5%	57.1%	47.9%	42.7%	72.3%	55.3%
Consumer Specialists	51.0%	61.8%	39.6%	48.3%	47.2%	33.0%	51.0%
Agricultural Specialists	52.3%	48.8%	37.0%	37.0%	39.9%	49.1%	41.9%
Multi-Specialists	76.0%	65.3%	56.6%	56.5%	51.3%	55.8%	59.0%
No Specialty	56.5%	58.0%	46.7%	44.2%	33.9%	52.8%	49.6%
Total	69.0%	65.8%	51.2%	52.8%	46.8%	58.7%	56.8%
Community Banks Organized as C Corporations							
CRE Specialists	78.3%	70.0%	60.6%	64.3%	57.4%	73.3%	63.2%
C&I Specialists	56.3%	63.5%	61.7%	53.3%	49.3%	83.2%	58.7%
Mortgage Specialists	73.0%	66.3%	38.8%	43.8%	43.5%	56.0%	52.9%
Consumer Specialists	50.9%	61.7%	41.1%	50.8%	59.0%	35.5%	52.6%
Agricultural Specialists	52.3%	48.8%	42.8%	47.6%	50.0%	64.0%	48.4%
Multi-Specialists	70.4%	62.8%	59.0%	60.7%	56.8%	60.1%	61.5%
No Specialty	55.3%	57.1%	48.4%	47.5%	37.1%	58.0%	51.6%
Total	60.9%	60.5%	49.4%	54.9%	50.6%	63.6%	55.7%

Source: FDIC.

Raising of External Capital by New Charters. Newly chartered institutions require an adequate level of starting capital to commence operations. During the study period, a total of 3,649 new community banks were chartered.[46] In total, these new community banks reported $25.5 billion in total equity capital at the end of their first year of operation, along with negative retained earnings of $3.2 billion. Netting out these two figures results in an estimated $28.7 billion in equity capital that was presumably raised from external sources. The weighted average year-end leverage ratio for these new community banks was 22.2 percent, much higher than the industry averages depicted in Chart 6.1.[47]

Raising of External Capital by Existing Institutions. After banks have advanced past their first year of operations, they may choose to raise additional capital from external sources. These "existing" community banks may be categorized into three groups according to the frequency with which they raised capital from external sources during the study period. The first such category includes community banks that never raised material amounts of capital from external sources. Community banks that have raised capital from external sources can be further divided into two additional groups: those that raised capital *occasionally* and those that did so *frequently*. The "frequent raisers" are defined as those that raised external capital more than one time and did so in more than 20 percent of the years they operated during the study period. "Occasional raisers" are defined as those banks that raised external capital at least once but in no more than 20 percent of the years they operated.

Chart 6.9 shows the percent of community banks and their total assets that fall into each of these three capital raising categories in 2011. It shows that 42 percent of community banks, with 28 percent of community bank assets, have never raised material amounts of capital from external sources after their first year of operation. Another 40 percent of community banks, with 46 percent of community bank assets, can be considered occasional raisers, while another 19 percent of community bank charters with 25 percent of total assets can be considered frequent raisers. This breakdown shows that a relatively small proportion of community banks count on the ability to add to their capital by accessing external sources on a regular basis.

Charts 6.10 and 6.11 track the percent of existing community and noncommunity banks, respectively, that raised capital from external sources each year, and indicates whether they were frequent or occasional raisers. Chart 6.10 shows that in the early years of the study period, the percentage of all community banks that raised external capital each year remained relatively small, never exceeding 10 percent until 2002. However, this percentage increased somewhat after 2000, and then rose further after the onset of the financial crisis in 2008. In all, 61 percent of the instances of community banks raising external capital during the study period involved frequent raisers, the group that also made up more than half of raisers in every year after 1986.

A similar time path of capital raising can be observed for noncommunity banks in Chart 6.11. Noncommunity banks raised external capital more frequently than community banks in every year, and nearly twice as frequently on a weighted average basis over the entire study period. Capital raises by noncommunity banks were also dominated by frequent raisers, which made up 65 percent of the instances of capital raising by noncommunity banks during the study period.

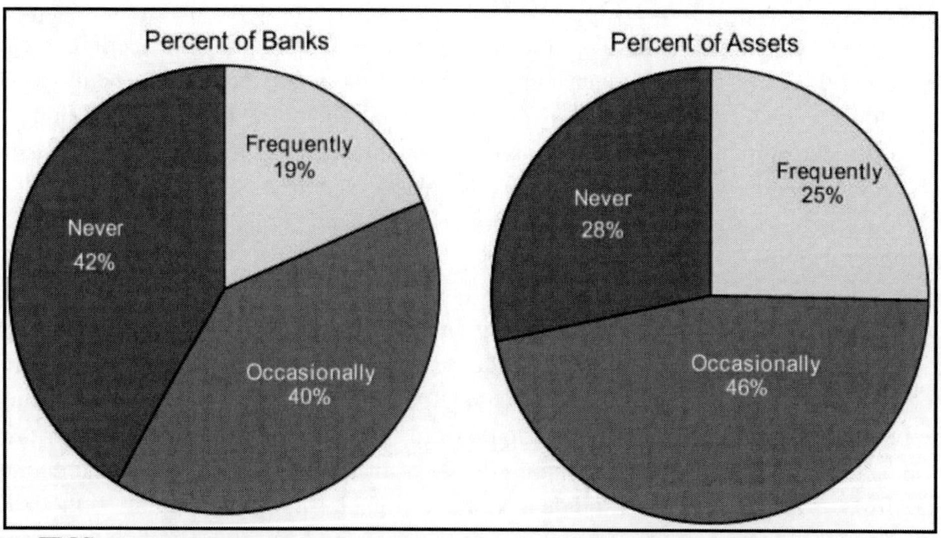

Source: FDIC.

Note: For banks reporting at year-end 2011. Excludes raises by new institutions in first year. Shares do not add to 100 due to rounding.

Chart 6.9. Community Banks by Lifetime Frequency of Raising External Capital, 2011.

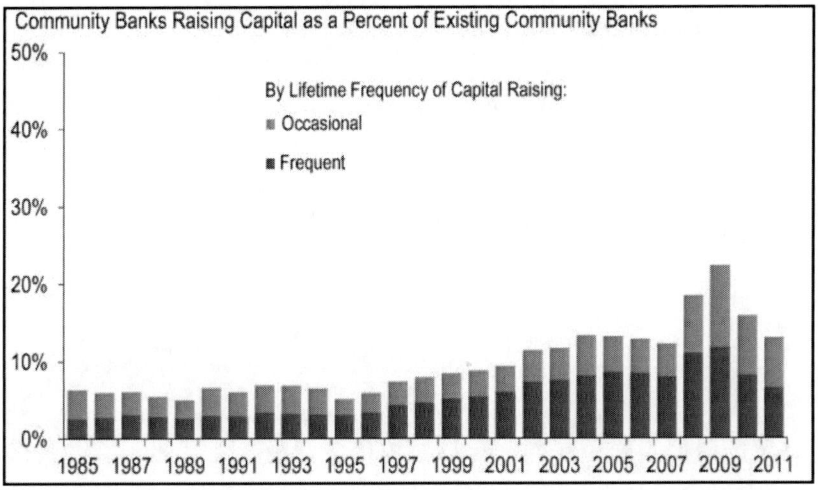

Source: FDIC.

Note: Excludes institutions in their first year of existence.

Chart 6.10. A Relatively Small Percentage of Community Banks Raises Capital From External Sources in Any Given Year.

Charts 6.12 and 6.13 track the volumes of external capital raised by community and noncommunity banks by year relative to their equity capital at the end of the prior year. Over the entire study period, community banks raised an average of 3.5 percent of their prior-year equity, while noncommunity banks raised an average of 5 percent. The volumes raised by community banks relative to equity rose at community banks in the middle 2000s, while both community and noncommunity banks raised substantial volumes after the onset of the financial crisis in 2008.

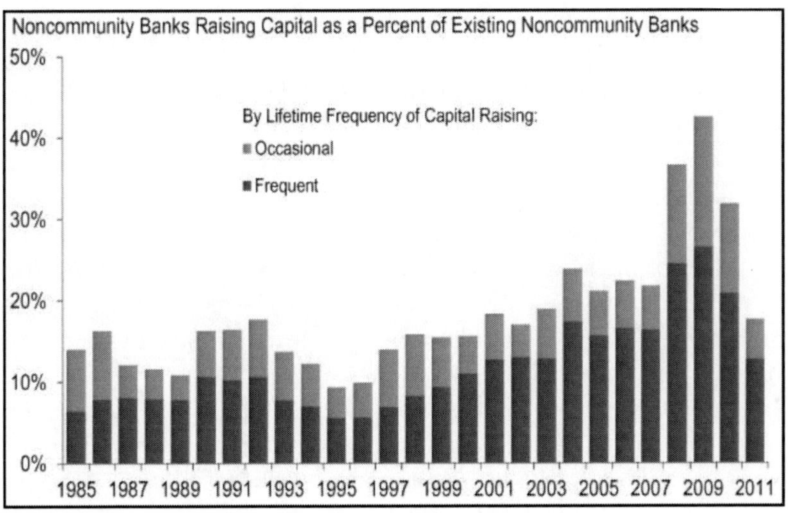

Source: FDIC.

Note: Excludes institutions in their first year of existence.

Chart 6.11. Noncommunity Banks Have Raised External Capital With Greater Frequency Than Community Banks.

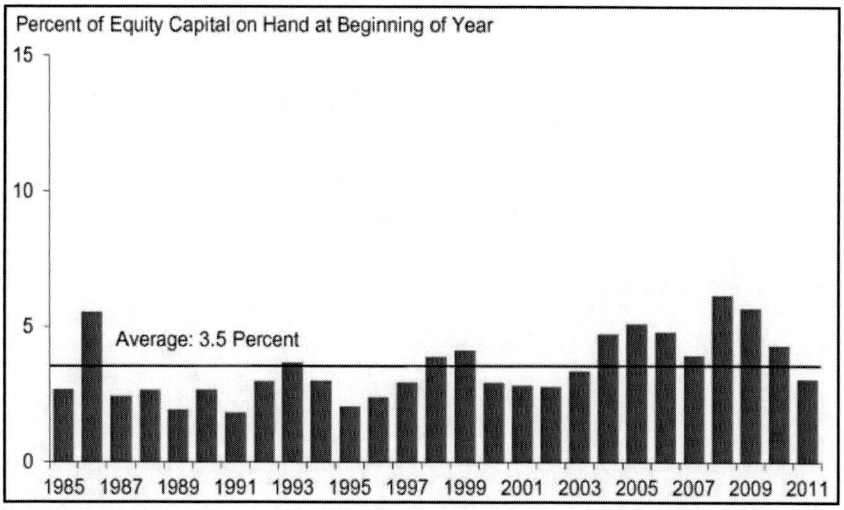

Source: FDIC.

Chart 6.12. Annual Volume of External Capital Raised All Community Banks.

While the holding companies of noncommunity banks issued them in much higher volumes, TruPS also became an important vehicle for raising capital at community banks. Between 2000 and 2007, TruPS made up almost half of the total volume of public equity issuance for community banks, and about three-quarters of issuance for noncommunity banks.[49] Although many community bank holding companies were too small to issue their own TruPS in public markets, by the early 2000s investment banks were increasingly securitizing small TruPS into collateralized debt obligations (CDOs). Noncommunity banks continued to issue large volumes of TruPS through 2009. Public issuance of TruPS by community bank holding companies peaked in 2003 at $2.1 billion, but remained over $1 billion annually through 2007 before declining sharply.[50]

Raising Capital Through Trust Preferred Securities. Much of the increase in capital raised by community and noncommunity banks between 2000 and 2007 was driven by the increased issuance of Trust Preferred Securities (TruPS). First issued in the early 1990s, TruPS are debt-like instruments issued by bank holding companies to raise funds that may then be downstreamed to bank subsidiaries as equity capital. Payments to TruPS investors were tax deductible for the holding companies that issued them, and the issuances were not dilutive to existing common shareholders. TruPS began to be more widely issued after a 1996 ruling by the Federal Reserve Board allowing them to be counted as Tier 1 capital at the holding company level.[48]

By October 2010, about one-third of the dollar volume of TruPS used to collateralize CDOs had either defaulted or deferred dividend payments.[51] The deteriorating performance of many community bank TruPS and declining investor confidence in CDOs made community bank TruPS difficult to issue in highly risk-averse capital markets. Subsequent regulatory changes have further discouraged the issuance of TruPS. The Wall Street Reform and Consumer Protection Act of 2010 (Dodd-Frank Act) required that regulators take steps to exclude TruPS from the definition of Tier 1 capital for many bank holding companies.[52]

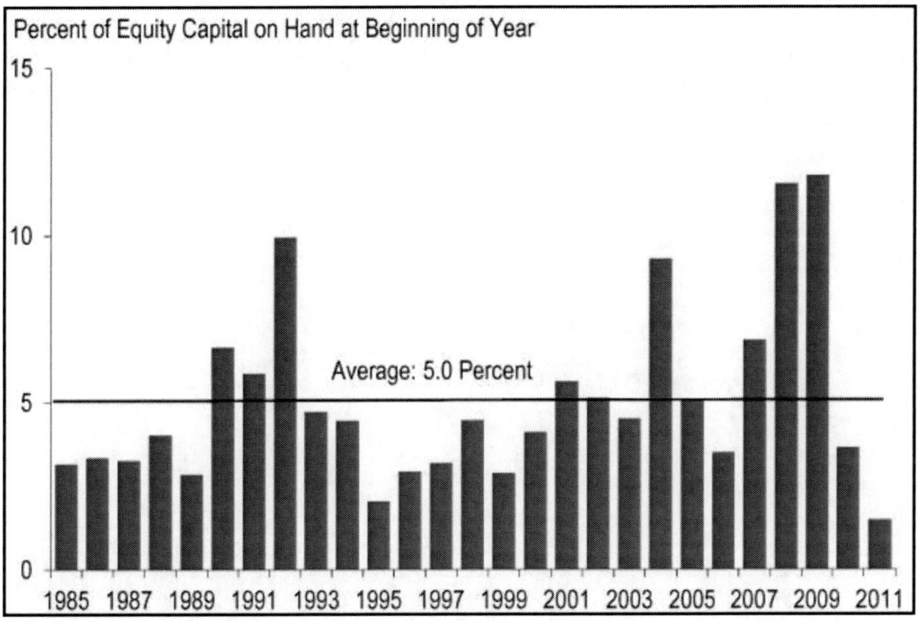

Source: FDIC.

Chart 6.13. Annual Volume of External Capital Raised All Noncommunity Banks.

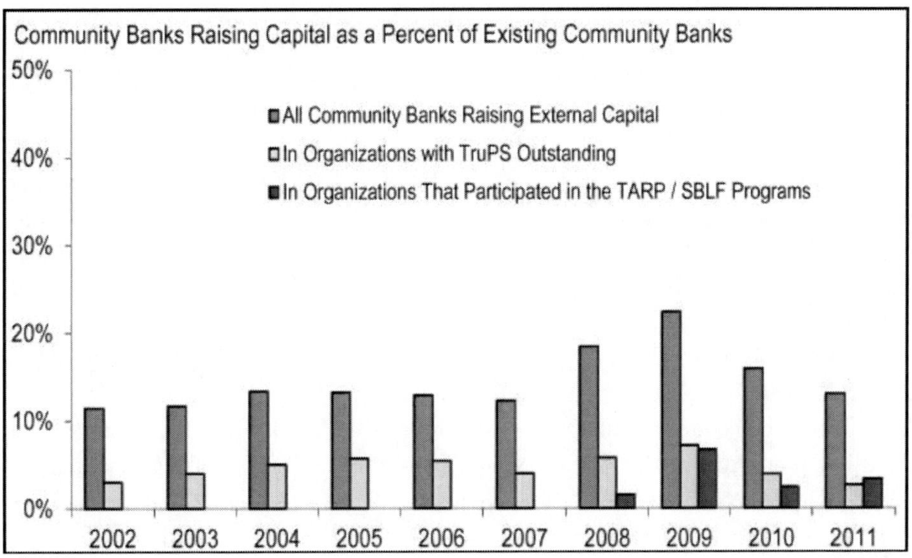

Source: FDIC.

Note: Excludes institutions in their first year of existence.

Chart 6.14. Community Banks in Organizations That Issued TruPS or That Participated in the TARP and SBLF Programs Made Up a Substantial Portion of Capital Raises Over the Past Decade.

Federal Programs to Facilitate Capital Raising. The financial losses associated with the crisis led both community and noncommunity banks to seek external capital more frequently and in greater amounts. As depicted in Charts 6.12 through 6.15, the annual frequency and volume of capital raising increased markedly during the crisis for both community and noncommunity banks. Overall, 2,712 existing community banks raised external capital at least once between 2008 and 2010, adding $27.4 billion to their equity capital. During that same interval, some 535 noncommunity banks raised a total of $277.5 billion. Overall, the volume of external capital raised by community and noncommunity banks between 2008 and 2010 exceeded the amount that they had collectively raised in the previous six years combined.

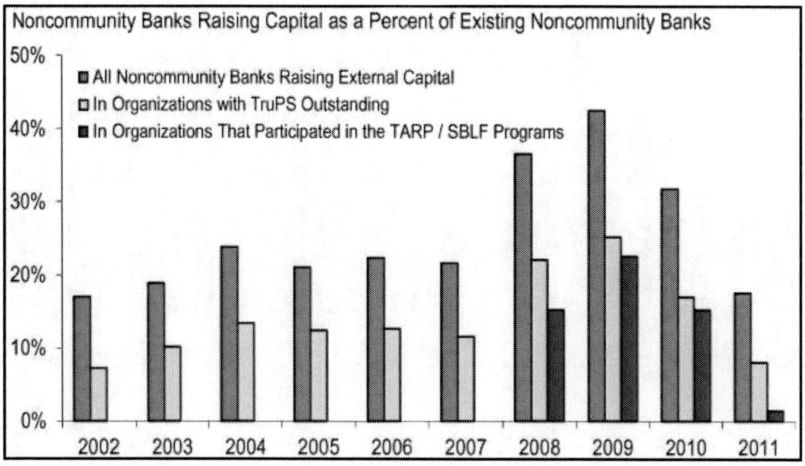

Source: FDIC.

Note: Excludes institutions in their first year of existence.

Chart 6.15. TruPS and the TARP / SBLF Programs Were More Frequent Sources of Capital to Noncommunity Banks Over the Past Decade Than to Community Banks.

The substantial increase in external capital raising after 2007 was largely made possible by two federal programs designed to facilitate bank access to capital during period of financial market instability. First, the Troubled Asset Relief Program (TARP) was authorized in October 2008.[53] The Treasury Department created the Capital Purchase Program (CPP) under TARP to stabilize the financial system by directly providing capital to financial institutions. In 2008 and 2009, Treasury invested approximately $205 billion under the CPP by purchasing preferred stock or subordinated debentures in 707 financial institutions.[54] Second, the Small Business Lending Fund (SBLF) was created in 2010. The SBLF was authorized as a $30 billion fund from which Treasury could make capital investments in qualified banks and community development loan funds with assets of less than $10 billion in order to increase the availability of credit for small business.[55] Treasury invested $4 billion of SBLF funds into 307 banks in 2011; 137 of these banks used SBLF funds to repay CPP capital.[56]

The combined influence of TruPS and the TARP and SBLF can be seen in Charts 6.14 and 6.15, which depict the total frequency of capital raising for community and noncommunity banks, respectively, since 2002, as well as the frequency of capital raising for banks in organizations that had issued TruPS and those that participated in the TARP or SBLF programs.[57] The charts show that between 2002 and 2011, community banks in holding companies that had TruPS outstanding represented one-third of all community banks that raised external capital and 40 percent of the total volume of capital raised. For noncommunity banks, the numbers were even higher, with banks in organizations with TruPS outstanding representing 55 percent of the number of noncommunity banks raising capital as well as the total volume of capital raised. It should be noted that while the ability to issue new TruPS declined rather precipitously during the crisis, the number of banks with TruPS outstanding at the holding company level has declined more slowly.

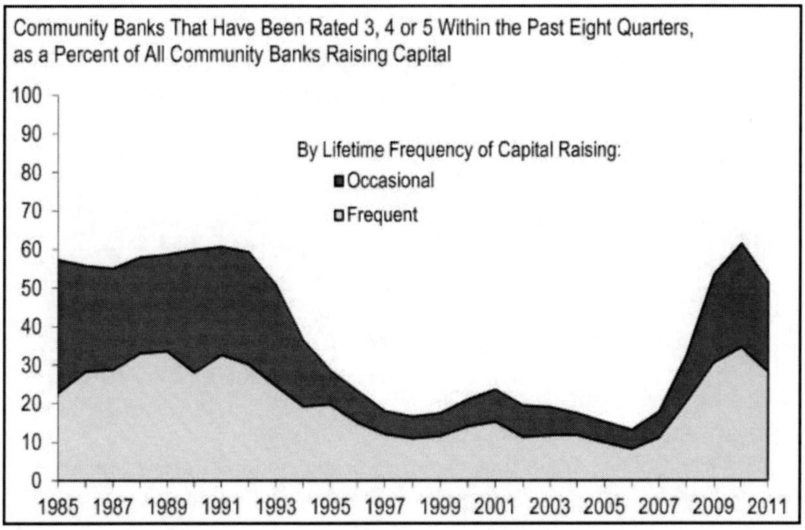

Source: FDIC.

Note: Excludes institutions in their first year of existence.

Chart 6.16. During Periods of Distress, Half or More of Community Bank Capital Raises Are Undertaken by Institutions That Have Been Rated 3, 4 or 5.

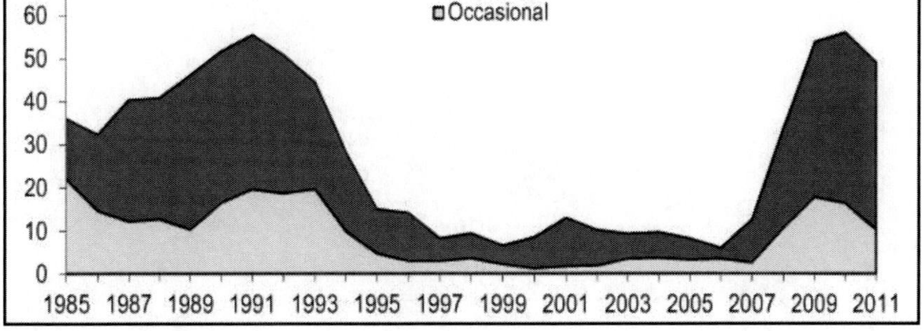

Source: FDIC.

Note: Excludes institutions in their first year of existence.

Chart 6.17. Capital Raises by Troubled Noncommunity Banks Also Increase in Crisis Periods, but to a Lesser Extent Than at Community Banks.

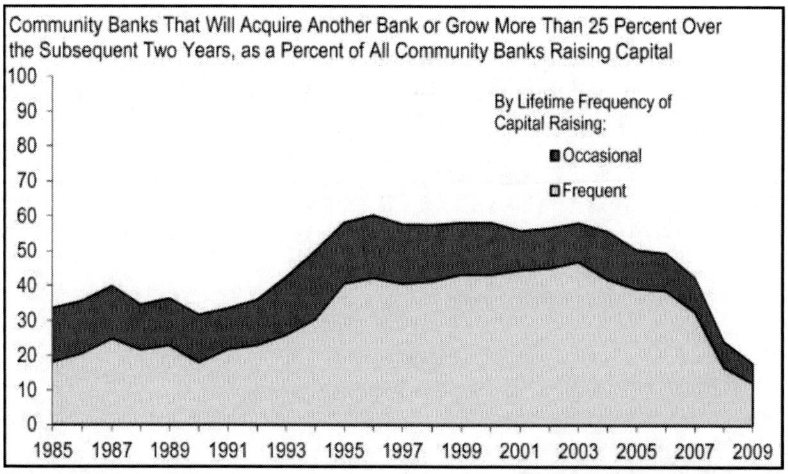

Source: FDIC.

Note: Excludes institutions in their first year of existence.

Chart 6.18. During Non-Crisis Periods, More Than Half of Community Bank Capital Raises Are Undertaken by Banks Set Up to Grow Rapidly or Make Acquisitions.

Between 2008 and 2011, years that encompass the financial crisis and its aftermath, the TARP and SBLF provided significant amounts of capital to both community banks and noncommunity banks. While the total proportion community banks raising capital during that period rose to a historic high of 17.5 percent, one-fifth of the community banks that did so were participants in the TARP or SBLF programs. Some 40 percent of the total capital raised by community banks between 2008 and 2011 was raised by TARP or SBLF participants. While one-third of noncommunity banks raised external capital during this period, 44 percent of those that did so were part of the TARP or SBLF programs. These institutions accounted for 75 percent of the total capital raised by noncommunity banks during this period.

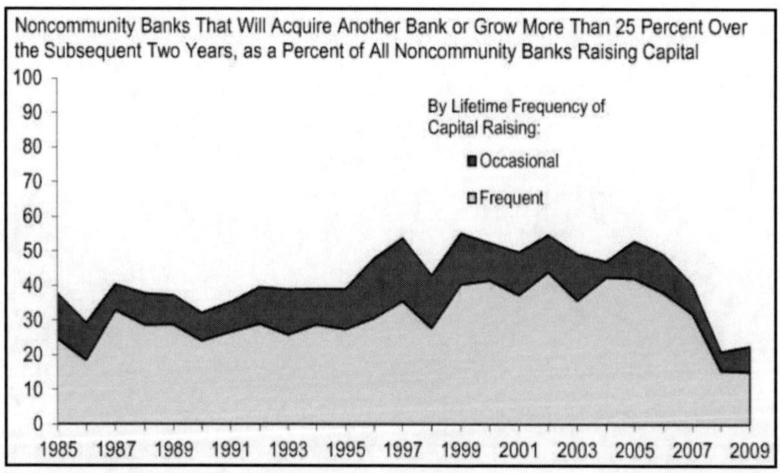

Source: FDIC.

Note: Excludes institutions in their first year of existence.

Chart 6.19. Prior to the Recent Crisis, a Steadily Rising Share of Noncommunity Bank Capital Raises Were Made by Institutions Set to Grow or Make Acquisitions.

Access to external capital during the crisis years was not exclusively limited to institutions that issued TruPS or participated in the TARP and SBLF programs. Between 2008 and 2011, 1,882 community banks that did not belong to organizations that issued TruPS and did not participate in the government programs raised $16 billion in external capital, while 206 noncommunity banks that did not use these two sources raised a total of $66 billion.

Reasons for Capital Raising. While most community banks never raised capital from external sources, or did so only infrequently, it is important to understand some of the circumstances surrounding the external capital raises that did take place. Two of the most common situations are when community banks become troubled and when they acquire other banks or grow rapidly. Together, these two situations account for a large percentage of institutions that raised external capital during the study period.

Charts 6.16 and 6.17 depict the share of capital raises by troubled banks with supervisory ratings of 3, 4 or 5 sometime in the two years preceding the year of the capital raising. The share of capital raises for troubled community banks and noncommunity banks was very low during the non-crisis years between the mid-1990s and the mid-2000s. However, during the crisis years of the late 1980s and early 1990s, as well as the period since 2008, troubled institutions represent a much higher proportion of capital raisers. Across the entire study period, troubled institutions accounted for 33 percent of all capital raises and 25 percent of the volume of capital raised at community banks, while they accounted for 28 percent of capital raises and 36 percent of the volume of capital raised at noncommunity banks. The higher proportion of troubled institutions among capital raisers during crisis periods reflects their greater prevalence as a proportion of all community banks in those periods, but it also indicates that many troubled institutions are able to access external sources of capital.

Another reason a bank may want to raise capital is to strengthen its balance sheet to prepare for a period of growth or to acquire another institution. Charts 6.18 and 6.19 depict the percent of capital raises carried out by community and noncommunity banks that either made acquisitions or experienced asset growth of more than 25 percent in the two years following the year of the capital raise. Chart 6.18 shows that the share of capital raises by community banks that are related to growth or acquisition rose somewhat in the non-crisis years from the mid-1990s through the mid-2000s compared with the crisis years.[58] This pattern is in some respects the mirror image of the share of capital raises by troubled community banks, which were the highest in the crisis years. Still, in most years, more than one-quarter of community bank capital raises preceded a period of significant growth or an acquisition.

Noncommunity banks directly acquired 2,401 institutions during the study period, and access to external capital was in many cases part of the balance sheet strategy associated with acquisition. In all, 34 percent of capital raises by noncommunity banks preceded a period of rapid growth or an acquisition, with the percentage stedily increasing between the mid-1980s and the mid-2000s. Most of these capital raises were made by frequent raisers of capital, which also accounted for 86 percent of the dollar volume of raises that preceded growth or acquisition by noncommunity banks.

For both community and noncommunity banks, growth and acquisition became a much less important factor in motivating capital raises after the mid-2000s, mainly because growth and acquisitions became much less prevalent toward the end of the decade. While the total assets of community banks grew by 19.5 percent between 2004 and 2007, their asset growth slowed to just 2.5 percent in the next four-year period, from 2008 through 2011. The slowdown was even more pronounced for noncommunity banks, from asset growth of 40.3 percent between 2004 and 2007 to growth of just 0.03 percent after 2008.

While troubled banks and those preparing for growth or acquisition represented large percentages of capital raises for both community and noncommunity banks during the study period, a substantial number of capital raises took place where neither situation appeared to be a factor. Across the entire study period through 2009, there were a total of 10,835 capital raises (40 percent of the total) by community banks where the bank was neither troubled before the raise nor an acquirer or fast grower after the raise. Just over 5,700 of these raises by community banks were carried out by frequent raisers. For noncommunity banks, there were a total of 2,953 capital raises (44 percent of the total) where the bank was neither troubled before the raise nor an acquirer or fast grower after the raise. Just over 1,700 of these raises by noncommunity banks were carried out by frequent raisers. These comparisons show that while a small portion of community banks have raised capital from outside sources in the normal course of their business, this practice is somewhat more prevalent among noncommunity banks.

Summary

Both community and noncommunity banks rely on a mix of retained earnings and outside capital to add to their capital stock over time. Community banks set aside 57 percent of their net income during the study period as retained earnings, and retained earnings accounted for 59 percent of all additions to equity capital from internal and external sources, percentages that were in both cases substantially higher than for noncommunity banks. During periods when assets and earnings are growing at roughly the same rates, community banks can generate most of the capital they need from internal sources. Accordingly, the most important factor in ensuring that capital is made available to facilitate the growth of community banks is a steady stream of earnings from which to generate new capital.

Community banks became somewhat less dependent on internally generated capital over the last decade of the study period, when retained earnings made up just 41 percent of additions to their equity capital. Community banks have retained a smaller portion of their net income as retained earnings over time, as fewer of them came to be organized as mutual institutions and more of them adopted Subchapter S status. TruPS became a fairly common vehicle for community and noncommunity banking organizations to raise external capital in the years leading up to the recent financial crisis. As TruPS issuance rapidly diminished after the onset of this crisis, and as financial losses made it necessary for more institutions to raise external capital, federal programs made capital available to community and, especially, noncommunity banks.

As the effects of the financial crisis recede, both community and noncommunity banks are beginning to re-establish a more normal pattern of adding to their equity capital through both internal and external sources. As retained earnings once again become the most important vehicle for capital formation at community banks, it is worth noting that community banks have long demonstrated the ability to raise external capital in a variety of situations where they have needed to in starting new banks, in troubled bank situations, in preparation for growth and acquisition, and for reasons other than these.

APPENDIX A. DETAILS OF THE RESEARCH DEFINITION OF THE COMMUNITY BANK

To capture the essential qualities of community banks in a workable definition, the study reviewed and compared several alternative methods of employing the available bank financial reporting data. The following series of five steps demonstrate how to assemble and filter the available data in order to arrive at the research definition of community bank. This definition was developed during 2011 using year-end 2010 financial and demographic data but can be replicated using future data by following the five steps.

Step 1: Aggregate Bank-Level Data Reported under Each Holding Company into a Single Banking Organization

Although community banks are designated at the level of the banking organization, most of the data used to make that designation are reported at the bank level.[59] Therefore, the first step in applying the definition is to aggregate the bank-level data to the level of the organization. For some very small banks and banks not in a holding company, the bank itself represents the organization. For banks in a bank holding company, all banks under the holding company are combined into one organization. This applies both to balance-sheet measures and the branch structure describing the number and location of banking offices.

Banks are grouped at the organization level in order to take into account the activity of the entire banking organization, not just an individual subsidiary. Considering the entire organization is particularly important when evaluating data from the time before states eased or eliminated restrictions on intrastate branching and before the passage of the Riegle-Neal Interstate Banking and Branching Efficiency Act in 1994, the federal law that eliminated restrictions on interstate banking. Before laws allowed for inter- or intrastate branching, individual banks in a holding company often functioned as substitutes for branches.

At year-end 2010, 7,658 FDIC-insured banking charters operated within 6,914 separate banking organizations. Under the designation process, if a banking organization is designated as a community bank, every bank reporting under that organization is also considered a community bank.

Step 2: Exclude Specialty Banks

Five categories of specialty banks are excluded from the definition of community banks: credit card specialists, consumer nonbank banks, industrial loan companies, trust companies, bankers' banks, and banking organizations holding 10 percent or more of total assets in foreign offices.[60]

For purposes of the study, holding companies in which more than 50 percent of total bank assets reside within a specialty bank qualify at the organizational level as a specialty bank. In that event, the banking organization as a whole is designated as a noncommunity bank, as are all of the individual banks that operate within that organization. In addition, banking organizations with either no loans or no core deposits are also excluded.

When applying these exclusions to banking organizations operating at year-end 2010, 126 organizations are excluded from the community bank definition. Chart A.1 depicts how the reasons for excluding specialty banks have evolved over time. Most of the exclusions were made due to a single reason. In the earliest years of the sample period, the most prevalent reason was holding foreign assets greater than 10 percent of total assets. Over the past 20 years, specialty banks have represented the most prevalent case of excluded banks. Since 2001, having no loans has been the second most prevalent single reason for exclusion, explaining 22 percent of all excluded banking organizations in 2010 (see Chart A.1).

Step 3: Include Organizations That Engage in Basic Banking Activities

Because the conceptual definition of the community bank begins with the essential functions of lending and deposit gathering, minimum levels for the ratio of loans-to-assets (33 percent) and core-deposits-to-assets (50 percent) are imposed on each banking organization.[61] The thresholds are applied uniformly for each year-end data period. The thresholds are waived for small institutions as described in Step 5 below. Charts A.2 and A.3 depict the share of all banking organizations that fall short of these thresholds in any given year.

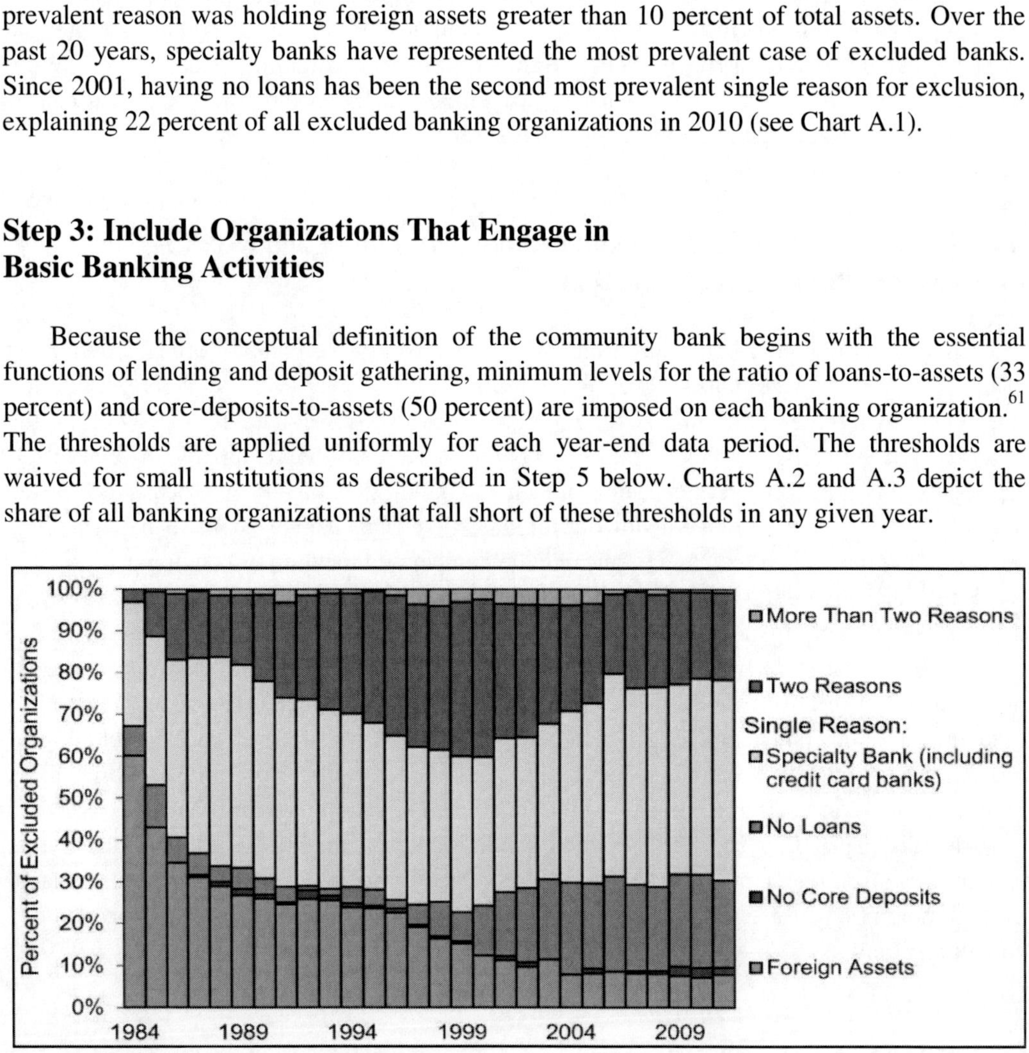

Source: FDIC.

*ILC, Nonbank Bank, Banker's Bank or Trust.

Chart A.1. Excluded Banking Organizations by Reason for Exclusion, 1984-2011.

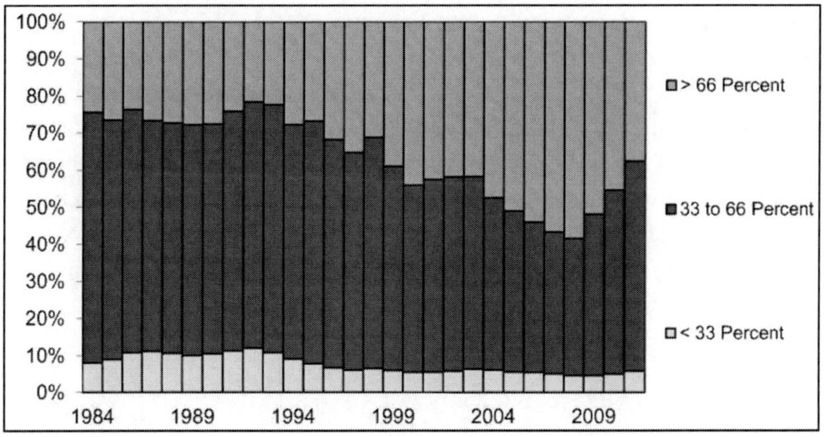

Source: FDIC.

Chart A.2. Percentages of FDIC-Insured Banking Organizations by Loans-to-Assets Ratio, 1984-2011.

The charts show that the vast majority of banking organizations meet both of these thresholds for basic banking activities. More banks, however, are excluded under the 33 percent loans-to-assets requirement than under the 50 percent core-deposits-to-assets requirement. FDIC analysis of the historical data shows that community banks typically raise core deposits in their local markets, but some institutions with an apparent community focus hold low levels of loans on their balance sheets, particularly during times of economic distress. Therefore, the 33 percent loans-to-assets threshold is chosen in lieu of a higher value in order to avoid making this requirement too restrictive.

Step 4: Include Organizations with a Limited Geographic Scope of Operations

A combination of thresholds was imposed to establish that the institution operates within a limited market area and is therefore in a better position to operate under a relationship lending approach than an institution with more widespread operations. A number of these thresholds are indexed over time to reflect how technological advances have enabled the average institution to gradually increase its geographic reach. As was the case with the thresholds imposed in Step 3, these geographic limits are waived for small institutions as described in Step 5 below.

Number of Banking Offices. The organization must have more than one office but not more than a maximum number of banking offices that varies over time, from 40 in 1985 to 75 in the baseline year of 2010. The maximum number of banking offices slowly increases based on a compound annual growth rate of 2.55 percent and is rounded to the nearest whole number. These thresholds are designed to allow for the fact that some institutions with fairly extensive branch networks can still operate under a community banking model. Beyond these thresholds, it would be difficult for an institution to operate with the degree of local autonomy typical of a community bank. The maximum office threshold encompasses approximately 98 percent of all banking organizations during the time period from 1985 to 2010 (see Chart A.4).[62]

While the minimum office requirement appears to exclude organizations with only one office from the community bank definition, Step 5 below describes how balance sheet and geographic requirements are waived for small institutions. As a result, small institutions with only one office are still defined as community banks. Institutions too large for the waiver described in Step 5 must meet the minimum office requirement, which helps to ensure that the institution primarily gathers deposits locally and does not rely excessively on the internet or other automated means to obtain funding.

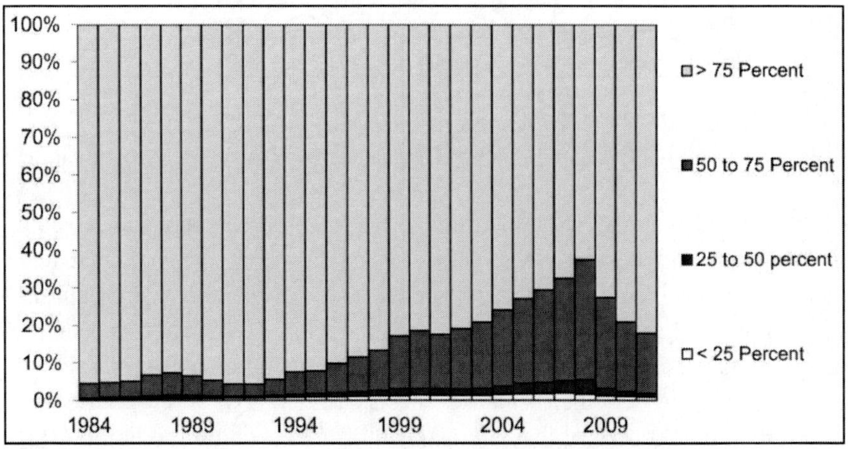

Source: FDIC.

Chart A.3. Percentages of FDIC-Insured Banking Organizations by Core Deposits-to-Assets Ratio, 1984-2011.

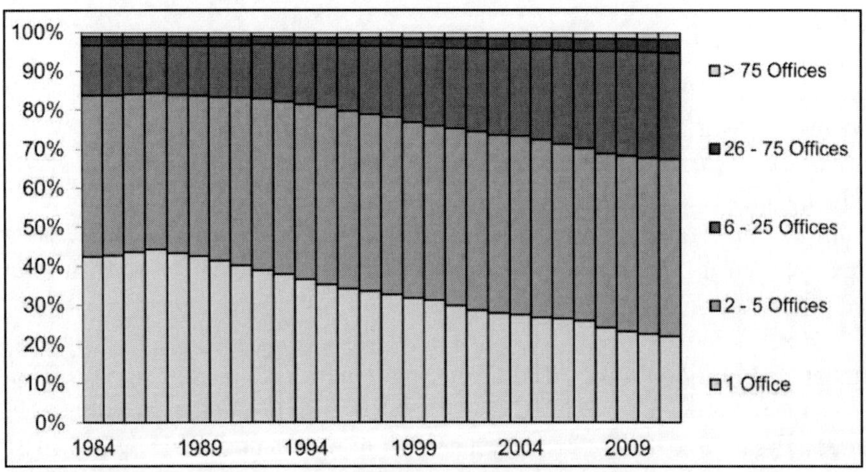

Source: FDIC.

Chart A.4. Percentages of FDIC-Insured Banking Organizations by Total Number of Banking Offices, 1984-2011.

Number of States and Large Metro Areas. The institution must maintain offices in no more than three states and no more than two large metropolitan areas.[63] These criteria further help to ensure that the bank headquarters and its branch offices are not located so far apart as to interfere with the bank's ability to make credit and other management decisions as a relationship lender. At the same time, allowing for offices in up to three states helps to ensure that community banks located near state lines are not unnecessarily excluded from the definition. Chart A.5 and Chart A.6 show that relatively few institutions exceed these maximums for offices in multiple states and large metro areas, respectively.

Deposits in a Single Office. To further ensure that the institution primarily gathers deposits locally and does not rely excessively on the internet or other automated means to obtain funding, a limit is placed on the dollar volume of deposits the organization can hold in any one banking office.[64] This threshold varies over time, from $1.25 billion in 1985 to $5 billion in 2010. The maximum slowly increases based on an annual compound growth rate of 5.7 percent.

Step 5: Establish an Asset Size Threshold below Which the Limits on Banking Activities and Geographic Scope are Waived

The preceding steps (Steps 3 and 4) go beyond asset size alone as a criteria for designating community banks and impose limits on banking activities and geographic scope. After imposing these conditions, 94 percent of banking organizations with total assets less than $1 billion in 2010 (and that had not been excluded as specialty banks) meet these criteria.[65] Accordingly, our definition is liberalized somewhat to exempt in 2010 all banking organizations with total assets less than $1 billion from the thresholds imposed on banking activities and geography in Steps 3 and 4 above. Moreover, since the median and average bank size changes over time with inflation, economic growth, and the size of the banking industry, the asset-size threshold for this exemption is indexed back over time to a level that equaled $250 million as of year-end 1985.[66] Similarly, as is the case in the 2010 data, more than 90 percent of banking organizations with total assets below the 1985 asset-size threshold (and that had not been excluded as specialty banks) meet the criteria in Steps 3 and 4.

Conclusion

The net effect of allowing this asset-size exemption is to make the research definition similar in some respects to previous studies that have imposed a size threshold of $1 billion. By comparison, however, the research definition is more restrictive in that it indexes that size threshold backward over time, and it is more permissive in that it includes any banking organization with assets greater than $1 billion that also meets the definitional requirements for banking activities and geographic scope of operations.

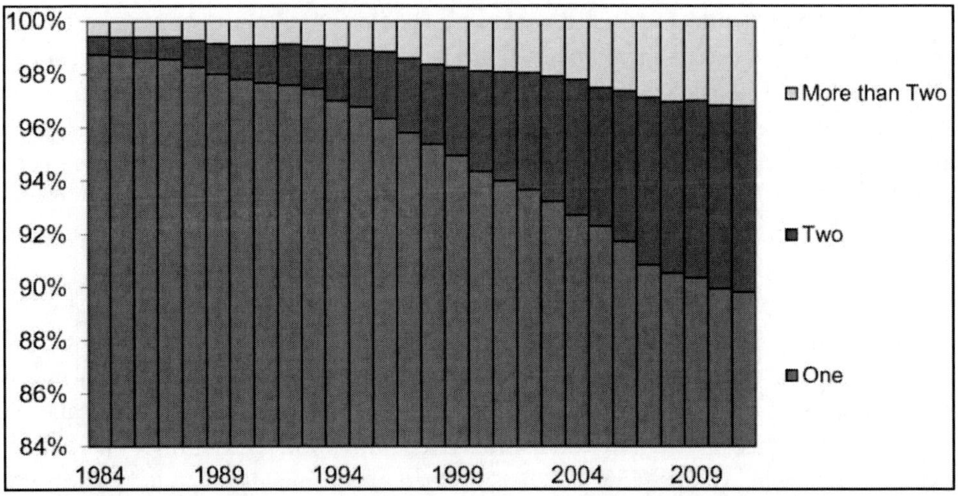

Source: FDIC.

Chart A.5. Percentages of FDIC-Insured Banking Organizations by Number of States in Which an Organization Has Offices, 1984-2011.

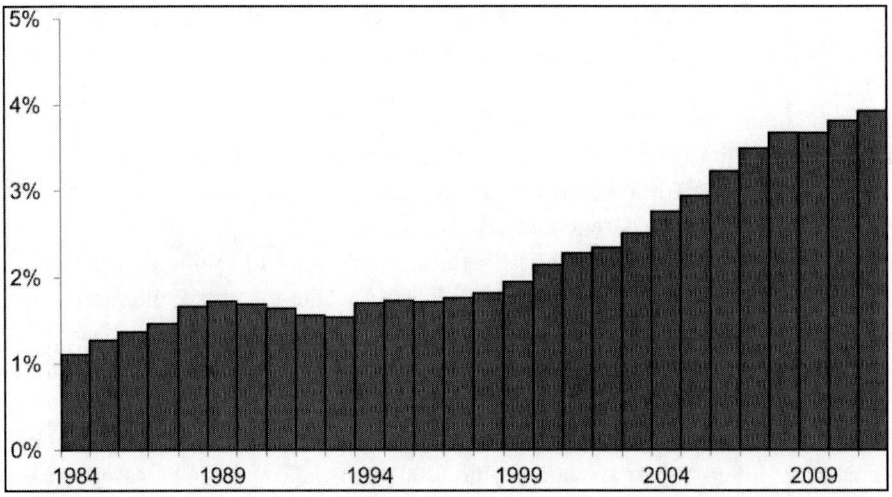

Source: FDIC.

Chart A.6. Percentages of FDIC-Insured Banking Organizations Located in More Than Two Large Metro Areas, 1984-2011.

APPENDIX B. REGULATORY COMPLIANCE COSTS – A SUMMARY OF INTERVIEWS WITH COMMUNITY BANKERS

The cost of regulatory compliance and its effect on profitability and competitiveness is a frequent topic of discussion among community bankers.[67, 68] It was also a common topic for discussion at the six Roundtable discussions hosted by the FDIC in 2012 as part of the Community Banking Initiative. While regulatory compliance could affect the cost structure of community banks, particularly compared with noncommunity banks, Call Reports and other regulatory filings do not provide specific data regarding these costs.

Because of the limited data available to evaluate the cost of regulatory compliance, the FDIC's Division of Insurance and Research conducted interviews with nine community bankers to understand what drives the cost of regulatory compliance and, where possible, obtain actual financial data to better understand how regulation and supervision affects bank performance. The interviews were conducted throughout October and November 2012.[69]

Study Concentration: Regulatory Compliance Questions

The interviews focused on three main areas: (1) noteworthy events or financial trends that had an effect on the operations of community banks; (2) specific regulations or supervisory practices that have affected regulatory costs; and (3) cost of regulatory compliance. Questions were developed to address these main areas and each bank was interviewed with the same set of questions.

(1) The majority of the interview participants identified September 11, 2001, and the recent financial crisis and recession as the most significant events or financial trends affecting the operations of community banks within the past 20 years. Interview participants noted that after the events of September 11, 2001, the banking industry faced new regulations related to the Bank Secrecy Act and the USA Patriot Act. While the interview participants generally understood why these regulations were needed, many stated that a significant amount of resources are needed to adequately comply with them. Most interview participants also noted that the recent financial crisis and recession had affected their operation, but that the full impact of the Dodd-Frank Act and other significant regulatory changes in the consumer protection area was still uncertain.

(2) Interview participants were asked several questions to determine what drives regulatory compliance costs at their institution and, specifically, which rules, regulations, and supervisory practices had the greatest effect on their operations. Most interview participants stated that no one regulation or practice had a significant effect on their institution. Instead, most stated that the strain on their organization came from the cumulative effects of all the regulatory requirements that have built up over time. To support this statement, many of the interview participants indicated that they have increased staff over the past ten years to support the enhanced responsibility associated with regulatory compliance. In addition, at least one-half of the interview participants noted that because of the cumulative effects of regulations on their institution, the amount of time each employee, not just those focused solely on compliance, spent completing duties associated with regulatory compliance had increased over the past five years.

    While the interview participants generally felt that the cumulative effects of regulations were driving their overall regulatory compliance costs, several bankers did identify specific regulations that require significant attention because of their business focus. These regulations included the Home Mortgage Disclosure Act,

Unfair and Deceptive Acts and Practices, Fair Lending, Bank Secrecy Act, USA Patriot Act, Privacy Notices, and Electronic Funds Transfers Act.

Interview participants were asked what steps the FDIC, as their primary federal regulator, could take to alleviate their concerns regarding regulatory compliance without affecting the FDIC's statutory role to ensure compliance with laws, rules, and regulations. The majority of interview participants indicated a desire for additional outreach by the FDIC to help them gain a better understanding of the proper ways to implement new or changing regulations and maintain compliance. The interview participants indicated that previous FDIC outreach events that were beneficial to their organizations included regional or nationwide conference calls, regional director's colleges, and contact with field office management, case managers, or review examiners.

(3) In an attempt to quantify the cost of regulatory compliance at their institution, interview participants were asked whether they tracked regulatory compliance costs within their internal cost structure. All the interview participants indicated that they did not actively track the various costs associated with regulatory compliance, because it is too time-consuming, costly, and is so interwoven into their operations that it would be difficult to break out these specific costs. Most of the interview participants indicated that they consider regulatory compliance as part of the normal cost of conducting business.

Consistent with the notion that these costs were a normal part of business, the interview participants noted that their overall business model and strategic direction had not changed or been affected by the regulatory compliance cost issues. In addition, the majority of interview participants stated that they had not discontinued offering products or services because of regulatory compliance, with the exception of overdraft protection and certain high-risk mortgage products.

Most interview participants indicated that while they do not specifically track and report on these costs to their board of directors, they can identify the direct costs associated with regulatory compliance from their general ledger. Direct costs are straightforward and easily identifiable to the extent that they can be separated from similar items not associated with compliance. Examples of direct costs include: compliance personnel salaries, employee training, consulting fees, external and internal audit fees, and specific software and hardware costs that are directly associated with compliance regulations.

Conversely, the interview participants noted that it is extremely difficult for them to identify indirect costs from their general ledger because they are not easily segregated between compliance and other areas. Examples of these costs include: noncompliance personnel time associated with regulatory compliance duties; software and hardware costs associated with responsibilities that might include compliance; and employee time associated with attending training that includes both compliance and noncompliance issues.

Common Themes Identified across the Interviews

While the primary goal of the interviews was to identify what drives regulatory compliance costs at community banks, two related themes emerged. A majority of the interview participants discussed their increasing reliance on consultants and their dependence on service providers.[70]

The interview participants indicated that as the regulatory environment continues to change, they have become more reliant upon consultants to assist with interpreting and implementing new or changing rules and regulations. Many of the interview participants stated that their increasing reliance on consultants is driven by their inability to understand and implement regulatory changes within required timeframes and their concern that their method of compliance may not pass regulatory scrutiny. Several of the interview participants indicated that greater outreach or technical assistance from the regulatory agencies could alleviate some of their increased reliance on consultants.

With regard to dependence on service providers, each of the interview participants noted that they had contracted with at least one firm to provide products and automated processes that provide a cost-effective means of complying with certain regulations. While these service providers are considered beneficial to their bank's operations, interview participants noted that these firms have few incentives to make timely changes to their software to meet new regulatory requirements. These time delays could affect their bank's ability to comply with new or changed rules. The interview participants expressed a strong desire to comply with outstanding rules and regulations; however, they feel dependent on service providers to provide the means for compliance. To potentially alleviate some of the effects of this dependency, the interview participants recommended that regulators communicate with service providers prior to the issuance of new regulation to ensure that these firms can provide the necessary products and services to institutions in a timely manner.

Conclusion

The goal of these interviews was to obtain specific information about what drives the cost of regulatory compliance and, where possible, actual financial data to begin to understand how regulation may affect bank performance. These interviews revealed that it is the cumulative effect of regulations and not one specific regulation that has had the greatest impact on the operations of the interview participants. Interview participants do not specifically track or report on the cost of regulatory compliance for their boards of directors. The majority of interview participants indicated that while direct costs can be more easily identified, it would be very costly to separate indirect costs from normal operational costs.

Every interview participant indicated that they understand the importance of being in full compliance with outstanding regulations and that they each spend considerable resources to achieve this. However, the interview participants felt that they would benefit from additional outreach and technical assistance from the regulatory agencies to assist them in their efforts to reduce their growing reliance on consultants and dependence on third-party service providers.

REFERENCES

Aguirregabiria, Victor, Robert Clark & Hui Wang. (2012). Diversification of Geographic Risk in Retail Bank Networks: Evidence from Bank Expansion after the Riegle-Neal Act.

Working Paper 465, University of Toronto, Department of Economics. http://www.economics.utoronto.ca/ public/workingPapers/tecipa-465.pdf.

Anderlik, John & Jeffrey Walser. (2004). Rural Depopulation: What Does It Mean for the Future Economic Health of Rural Areas and the Community Banks That Support Them? *FDIC Banking Review*, *16*, No. 3:57-95.

Berger, A. N., Hunter, W. C. & Timme, S. G. (1993). The efficiency of financial institutions: a review and preview of research past, present and future. *Journal of Banking & Finance*, *17*(2), 221-249.

Berger, Allen N. & Udell, Gregory F. (2001). Small Business Credit Availability and Relationship Lending: The Importance of Bank Organisational Structure. Board of Governors of the Federal Reserve System, FEDS Working Paper No. 2001-36. http://papers.ssrn.com/sol3/ papers.cfm?abstract_id=285937.

Boyd, J. H. & Graham, S. (1998). Consolidation in US banking: Implications for efficiency and risk. *Bank Mergers and Acquisitions*, 113-35.

Critchfield, Tim, Tyler Davis, Lee Davison, Heather Gratton, George Hanc, & Katherine Samolyk. (2004). Community Banks: Their Recent Past, Current Performance, and Future Prospects. *FDIC Banking Review*, *16*, no. 3:1-56. http://www.fdic.gov/ bank/analytical/banking/2005jan/ article1.html.

DeYoung, Robert, Hunter, William C. & Udell, Gregory F. (2004). The Past, Present and Probable Future of Community Banks. *Journal of Financial Services Research*, *25*, no. 2/3:85-133.

Hein, Scott E., Koch, Timothy W. & Scott MacDonald, S. (2005). On the Uniqueness of Community Banks. Federal Reserve Bank of Atlanta, E*conomic Review*, First Quarter, 15-36. http://www.frbatlanta.org/ filelegacydocs/hein article-final.pdf.

Hughes, Joseph P. & Mester, Loretta J. (July 31, 2011). Who Said Large Banks Don't Experience Scale Economies? Evidence from a Risk-Return-Driven Cost Function. FRB of Philadelphia Working Paper No. 11-27. Available at SSRN: http://ssrn.com/ abstract=1904527 or http://dx.doi.org/ 10.2139/ssrn.1904527.

Hughes, Joseph P. (2011). "*The elusive scale economies of the largest banks and their implications for global competitiveness*." Paper presented at the 14th annual banking conference, Federal Reserve Bank of Chicago, October.

Kahn, George A. et. al. (2003). The Role of Community Banks in the U.S. Economy. Federal Reserve Bank of Kansas City, *Economic Review*, Second Quarter, 15-36. http://www.kc.frb.org/Publicat/ECONREV/Pdf/ 2q03keet.pdf.

Ostergaard, Charlotte, Ibolya Schindele & Bent Vale. (2009). Social Capital and the Viability of Stakeholder-Oriented Firms: Evidence from Norwegian Savings Banks. EFA 2009 Bergen Meetings Paper. http://ssrn.com/abstract=1344495.

Philip E. Strahan. (2002). The Real Effects of U.S. Banking Deregulation. Wharton Financial Institutions Center Working Paper 02-39. http://fic.wharton.upenn. edu/fic/papers/ 02/0239.pdf

Stiroh, Kevin J. (1999). *Compositional Dynamics and the Performance of the U.S. Banking Industry*. Federal Reserve Bank of New York Staff Reports, February 2000, Number *98*.

Wheelock, D. C. & Wilson, P. W. (2012). Do Large Banks have Lower Costs? New Estimates of Returns to Scale for U.S. Banks. *Journal of Money, Credit and Banking*, *44*(1), 171-199.

End Notes

[1] Source: Federal Reserve, *Flow of Funds*, Table L.1.

[2] Source: Federal Reserve, *Flow of Funds*, Tables L.218 and L.222.

[3] FDIC calculations based on data from the Bureau of Economic Analysis. Each percentage point equals approximately $150 billion in 2011 U.S. economic output.

[4] Source: *Inside Mortgage Finance*.

[5] Paul Kupiec and Stefan Jacewitz, Community Bank Efficiency and Economies of Scale, FDIC, December 2012, http://www.fdic.gov/regulations/resources/cbi/report/cbi-eff.pdf. This study of efficiency and economies of scale was limited to the universe of community banks, and does not provide comparisons of cost with noncommunity banks, which are frequently much larger in size.

[6] Based on the lifetime frequency of community banks not in their first year of operation raising capital from external sources between 1984 and 2011. The reported figures add up to 101 percent due to rounding.

[7] For purposes of this study, the term bank refers to FDIC-insured banks and thrifts.

[8] Numerous studies refer to and describe the concept of relationship banking. See, for example, Hein, Koch and MacDonald (2005); Critchfield, Davis, Davison, Gratton, Hanc, and Samolyk (2004); Berger and Udell (2001), and DeYoung, Hunter and Udell (2004).

[9] See, for example, Ostergaard, Schindele, and Vale (2009).

[10] An example of this approach is found in Hein, Koch and MacDonald (2005).

[11] DeYoung, Hunter and Udell (2004) apply a $1 billion limit at the charter level, while Critchfield, Davis, Davison, Gratton, Hanc, and Samolyk (2004) apply the $1 billion limit at the level of the banking organization. The 2003 study by the Federal Reserve Bank of Kansas City also takes the latter approach.

[12] See, for example, Statement by Maryann F. Hunter, Deputy Director, Division of Banking Supervision and Regulation Community, Federal Reserve Board, Before the Subcommittee on Financial Institutions and Consumer Protection, Committee on Banking, Housing, and Urban Affairs, U.S. Senate, Washington, DC, April 6, 2011, http://www.federalreserve.gov/ newsevents/testimony/hunter20110406a.htm.

[13] Credit card banks are defined as institutions with credit card loans plus securitized receivables in excess of 50 percent of total assets plus securitized receivables. A consumer nonbank bank is a financial institution with a limited-purpose charter that can make commercial loans or take deposits, but not both. Industrial loan companies can be owned by commercial firms that are not regulated by a federal banking agency. A trust company is a corporation whose function is to act as a trustee, fiduciary, or agent for individuals or firms. A bankers' bank is a financial institution that provides financial services to other banks.

[14] As defined by the Office of Management and Budget, a metropolitan statistical area (MSA) contains a core urban area of 50,000 or more in population. For purposes of the study, a large MSA is defined as one with a population of more than 500,000.

[15] In 2010, after excluding specialty banks and banks that did not meet the minimum office requirement, 94 percent of banking organizations with assets less than $1 billion met the requirements for banking activities and limited geographic scope. The minimum office requirement is effectively waived for institutions that fall under the asset size threshold applied during step 5.

[16] The study period extends from year-end 1984 through year-end 2011. Time series analysis of stock variables (variables measured at a point in time) reported at year-end will extend from 1984 through 2011. Time series analysis of flow variables (variables measured across a period of time) will extend from 1985 through 2011.

[17] An additional 365 institutions (about 2 percent of charters) self-liquidated or otherwise exited the industry without failure or merger during this period.

[18] Source: Strahan (2002). The District of Columbia is not included in these state counts.

[19] Source: Strahan (2002).

[20] The Riegle-Neal Act required that every state allow interstate branching by 1997, but included an opt-out provision that was invoked only by Texas and Montana. Both states subsequently adopted interstate branching. See Aguirregabiria, Clark and Wang (2012) p. 11.

[21] Direct acquisitions refer to acquisitions or consolidations where the bank or banking organization is the target (bank or banking organization being acquired) in the merger transaction. Indirect acquisitions refer to banks or banking organizations that were previously acquired by the target bank or banking organization in a merger transaction.

[22] Data on total banking offices are collected annually through the Summary of Deposits (SOD), which provides a detailed record of each individual banking office, its location and total deposits, starting in 1987. The SOD covers all FDIC-insured institutions, including insured U.S. branches of foreign banks. For purposes of this study, banking offices are defined to include all offices and facilities that actually hold deposits, and do not include loan production offices, computer centers, and other nondeposit installations, such as automated teller machines.

[23] These designations are based on definitions for county equivalents made by the U.S. Office of Management and Budget (OMB) using Census Decennial population data. While most of the United States is divided into

counties, not all of it is (for example, Louisiana has parishes). For administrative purposes, the government allocates all jurisdictions not in counties into county equivalents. In this study, the FDIC combines counties and county-

equivalents and refers to them as counties to encompass all U.S. states and major territories, including American Samoa, Federated States of Micronesia, Guam, Mariana Islands, Puerto Rico, and the U.S. Virgin Islands.

[24] Anderlik and Walser (2004) categorized declining counties as those that lost population over the 30-year study period and accelerated declining counties as those that not only lost population, but did so more rapidly toward the end of the period.

[25] A focus on pretax ROA, as opposed to return on assets after tax, facilitates comparisons between banks organized as C corporations, which are taxed at the bank level, and S corporations, in which tax obligations pass through to shareholders.

[26] Beginning in 2001, FDIC-insured institutions that filed Call Reports began reporting more detailed data on noninterest income components. Similar data are not available for Thrift Financial Report (TFR) filers. To show TFR filers' share of the industry, as of December 31, 2011, TFR filers represented 8.5 percent of community banks and 10.8 percent of community bank assets, 11.1 percent of noncommunity banks and 5.6 percent of noncommunity bank assets. As of December 31, 2001, TFR filers represented 10.4 percent of community banks and 16.1 percent of community bank assets, 12.1 percent of noncommunity banks and 11.7 percent of noncommunity bank assets.

[27] The minimum level is an amount greater than $25,000 and exceeding 3 percent of total noninterest income. Examples of items that might be reported as all other noninterest income include income and fees from the printing and sale of checks, earnings on or the increase in value of cash surrender value of life insurance, income and fees from automated teller machines, rent and other income from other real estate owned, safe deposit box rent, net change in the fair values of financial instruments accounted for under a fair value option, bank card and credit card interchange fees, and gains on bargain purchases.

[28] The Dodd-Frank Wall Street Reform and Consumer Protection Act (Dodd-Frank), enacted on July 21, 2010, provides temporary unlimited deposit insurance coverage for noninterest-bearing transaction accounts from December 31, 2010, through December 31, 2012, regardless of the balance in the account and the ownership capacity of the funds. The unlimited coverage is available to all depositors, including consumers, businesses and government entities. The coverage is separate from, and in addition to, the insurance coverage provided for a depositor's other accounts held at an FDIC-insured bank.

[29] Paul Kupiec and Stefan Jacewitz, "Community Bank Efficiency and Economies of Scale," FDIC, December 2012, http://www.fdic.gov/regulations/resources/cbi/report/cbi-eff.pdf. The analysis was conducted using median values rather than averages weighted by assets or simple averages in order to isolate the experience of typical community banks and noncommunity banks and to eliminate the skewing effects of very large institutions. The median value of a distribution is the value that is halfway between the smallest and the largest value when the data are ranked by magnitude.

[30] Small loans to business are nonfarm, nonresidential and C&I loans in amounts under $1 million and farmland and agricultural production loans in amounts under $500,000. Prior to the March 31, 2010, Call Report, they were reported annually on the June 30 Call Report.

[31] Banks are also considered to be multi-specialists if they hold total retail loans or total commercial loans greater than 40 percent of total assets. Banks with total loans less than 33 percent of assets are grouped into the no specialty category.

[32] In this geographic analysis, states include the District of Columbia, but do not include U.S. Territories.

[33] Chart 5.5 includes any community bank that met the CRE specialty definition, even community banks that were identified as multi-specialists.

[34] Call Report reporting requirements for the breakout of nonfarm, nonresidential real estate loans in 2007 were subject to a de minimis test. Banks with less than $300 million in assets whose total commercial real estate loans were less than 150 percent of equity capital did not have to report the breakout.

[35] According to the definitions of the lending specialty groups, any bank with C&D loans greater than 10 percent of assets cannot belong to the mortgage, consumer, C&I or agricultural specialties. In rare cases, it is possible for a bank with C&D loans greater than 10 percent of assets to belong to the no specialty group if that institution has total loans less than 33 percent of assets.

[36] Some institutions with C&D loans greater than 10 percent of assets may remain in the No Specialty group if their total loans-to-assets ratio remains below 33 percent. Community banks meeting the criteria for Strategy 1 (C&D loans greater than 10 percent of assets) or Strategy 2 (total CRE loans greater than 30 percent of assets) by 2005 have shifted into either the CRE lending specialist group or the multi-specialist group. Community banks listed under Strategy 3 include all community banks that shifted out of the three baseline specialty groups that did not meet the criteria for Strategy 1 or Strategy 2, including those that no longer qualified as community banks.

[37] For a more complete description of the various organizational forms of community banks, see "Bank Ownership Structure and Access to External Capital" in Chapter 6. For a more complete discussion of TruPS as a source of external capital, see "Raising Capital Through Trust Preferred Securities" in Chapter 6.

[38] *Prompt Corrective Action*, or PCA, refers to the provision of the Federal Deposit Insurance Corporation Improvement Act of 1991 that requires bank supervisors to take certain action in the event a bank falls below the definition of "well-capitalized" as defined by regulation. Under PCA, a bank is categorized as well-capitalized if it has a total risk-based capital ratio of 10 percent or greater; has a Tier 1 risk-based capital ratio of 6 percent or greater; and has a leverage ratio of 5 percent or greater. The bank also must not be subject to any written agreement, order, capital directive, or prompt corrective action directive to meet and maintain a specific capital level for any capital measure. See Part 325 of the FDIC Rules and Regulations http://www.fdic.gov/regulations/laws/rules/2000-4500.html - fdic2000part325103

[39] Although the term capital formation is frequently used in national income accounting to describe increases in the stock of physical capital, it is used here to represent additions to equity capital by individual financial institutions.

[40] It should be noted that banks report other changes to equity capital, some of which are relatively large, but they do not represent net capital formation and are not part of the analysis in this chapter.

One is "Changes Incident to Business Combinations," which occurs when a bank purchases or combines with another bank or business or, if certain conditions are met, is purchased but retains its separate corporate existence. The total reported effect of these changes over the 27-year study period is over $1 trillion at noncommunity banks and about $46 million at community banks. At banks that have acquired another bank or business, changes incident to business combinations represent the fair value of stock issued to execute the purchase (or the historical cost of the acquired entity's equity capital at the end of the prior year in transactions during the study period—generally before July 1, 2001—accounted for as poolings of interests). While these changes incident to business combinations represent an increase in the capital of the acquiring bank, the increase is largely offset by the elimination of equity capital at the target institution. For banks that have been acquired in transactions in which push-down accounting is applied, changes incident to business combinations generally represent the net difference (positive or negative) between the acquired bank's capital at the end of the prior year and its equity capital as restated to reflect the purchase price of the bank's stock acquired in the transaction and the fair value of any of the bank's stock not acquired.

Another is "Other Comprehensive Income," which represents changes in equity that are not due to capital contributions from or distributions to owners and that are not captured in net income. At most community banks, the most important component of other comprehensive income is the change in net unrealized gains or losses in available for-sale securities. Under current regulatory standards, accumulated other comprehensive income is included in a bank's total equity as required by generally accepted accounting principles, but it is not included in any definitions of regulatory capital. Over the study period, other comprehensive income has totaled negative $6.1 billion at noncommunity banks and $3.4 billion at community banks.

[41] This study sought to isolate increases in bank capital that originated outside insured banks by identifying possible stock sales or funds downstreamed from a holding company. To do this, the study examined Call Report and Thrift Financial Report line items that report the sale, conversion, acquisition, or retirement of capital stock and other bank transactions with their parent holding companies. The study isolated increases in bank capital stock and surplus from these sources as capital raises. However, many values reported in these items are very small and may not be appropriate to include in the definition of a capital raise. In fact, for one-third of community banks that reported positive values for these items in the years 1985 through 2011, the amount reported accounted for less than 0.25 percent of bank assets reported the year before the raise. To eliminate *de minimis* raises, this study considers a capital raise to be an increase in capital stock and surplus that exceeds 0.25 percent of the bank's prior-year assets.

These data are reported in the Call Report on Schedule RI-A, Changes in Bank Equity Capital. They are found in the following line items:

"5. Sale, conversion, acquisition, or retirement of capital stock, net
6. Treasury stock transactions, net
11. Other transactions with parent holding company"

In addition to capital from investors, other transactions with parent holding company (line item 11) may include funds received from selling affiliate banks, selling branches, selling real estate to the holding company and other non stock transactions.

These data are reported in the Thrift Financial Report in the following schedules and line items:

Schedule SI, Supplemental Information, reported 1996 through 2011: Stock issued (SI640) - Stock Retired (SI650).

Schedule CA, Capital, reported 1990 through 1995: Perpetual Preferred Stock Issued (CA120) - Perpetual Preferred Stock Retired (CA130) - Common Stock Issued (CA220) - Common Stock Retired (CA230) - Treasury Stock Acquired (CA240) + Other Adjustments (CA250).

Schedule SI, Supplemental Information, reported 2004 through 2011: Capital Contributions (SI655).

The definition also includes the beginning capital reported by new entrants, defined as total equity less any reported retained earnings.

42 *Hybrid Capital Instruments and Small Institution Access to Capital*, Government Accountability Office, January 2012, p. 57 and 67. The GAO sampled 794 stand-alone banks and thrifts (those with no holding company) and top-level bank holding companies and thrift holding companies with total assets of less than $10 billion out of a universe of 6,733 institutions. The survey was conducted from June 15, 2011, to August 15, 2011. The GAO reports that it received valid responses from 510 (64 percent) out of the 794 sampled institutions. For more information about the GAO's methodology for designing and distributing the survey, see Appendix I of the GAO Report.

43 *Ibid*, Table 10: p. 67. The combined total of "Very likely" and "Somewhat likely" (70 percent).

44 *Ibid*, Table 10: p. 67. The combined total of "Very likely" and "Somewhat likely" for public offering (27 percent) and private placement (46 percent).

45 *Ibid*, p. 48. *A Majority of Smaller Institutions Report No Unmet Capital Need*

"Most smaller institutions have not raised capital since January 1, 2008, and the majority of those reported no need for or interest in additional capital (see fig. 10). Specifically, we estimate that 65 percent of smaller institutions have not raised capital since January 1, 2008, and 88 percent of those did not need or want to raise more regulatory capital. Only 3 percent of smaller institutions that had not raised capital since January 1, 2008, attempted to raise capital but were unable to do so."

46 This figure includes only new charters that did not exist in any other form (such as uninsured status) prior to becoming a federally insured bank or thrift.

47 Newly chartered institutions are frequently required to carry higher levels of capital at inception than regulatory minimums because it often takes several years for them to become profitable.

48 Federal Reserve press release, October 21, 1996, http://www.federalreserve.gov/boarddocs/press/bcreg/1996/19961021/default.htm

49 Source: SNL Financial.

50 Source: SNL Financial.

51 "Fitch Bank TruPS CDO Default and Deferral Index," Structured Credit Special Report, FitchRatings, November 2010.

52 The Dodd-Frank Act required banking organizations with assets over $15 billion to phase out TruPS as a form of Tier 1 capital. For banking organizations with total assets between $500 million and $15 billion as of December 31, 2009, TruPS issued before May 19, 2010, may still be accepted as a form of Tier 1 capital. At the time of this study, bank holding companies under $500 million may continue to count TruPS toward Tier 1 capital under existing capital rules.

53 Emergency Economic Stabilization Act of 2008, P.L. 110-343, 10/3/2008, p. 2.

54 "Treasury, Capital Purchase Program, Program Purpose and Overview" http://www.treasury.gov/initiatives/financial-stability/TARP-Programs/bank-investment-programs/cap/Pages/default.aspx, and SIGTARP, Office of the Special Inspector General for the Troubled Asset Relief Program. *Quarterly Report to Congress*, April 25, 2012, Page 37 http://www.sigtarp.gov/Quarterly Reports/April_ 25_2012_Report_to_Congress.pdf.

Two other TARP programs provided capital to FDIC-insured banks. The Community Development Capital Initiative (CDCI) in early 2010 provided capital to viable certified Community Development Financial Institutions. Thirty-six banks received capital through the CDCI; 28 of these used the funds to convert existing CPP investments. Total outlays under the CDCI were $570 million. Also, under a program known as the Targeted Investment Program, Treasury provided to Citigroup and Bank of America Corporation $20 billion each in addition to earlier CPP investments.

55 Small Business Jobs Act, Public Law 111-240, September 27, 2010, p.1. http://www.gpo.gov/ fdsys/pkg/BILLS-111hr5297enr/pdf/BILLS-111hr5297enr.pdf.

56 "Treasury, Resource Center, Small Business Lending Fund" http://www.treasury.gov/resource-center/sb-programs/Pages/Small-Business-Lending-Fund.aspx and Treasury, *SBLF Transactions Report*, 9/28/2011 http://www.treasury.gov/resource-center/sb-programs/ DocumentsSBLFTransactions/ SBLF_Bi-Weekly_Transactions_Report_THRU_09272011. pdf.

57 Access to TruPS was determined by identifying bank or thrift holding companies with outstanding balances of TruPS at year end. Access to the TARP and SBLF programs was determined according to lists published by the U.S. Department of Treasury. Because it was not possible to distinguish capital raised under these programs from other capital raised, the totals discussed in this section include all capital raised by institutions with access to TruPS and all capital raised by institutions with access to the TARP or SBLF programs. The categories are not mutually exclusive, and a bank may appear on both lists.

58 In order to observe two full years of growth and acquisitions, the time series stops with capital raises made in 2009.

59 At year-end 2011, 1,039 institutions (14 percent of all FDIC-insured charters) reported under multi-bank holding companies, while another 4,319 institutions (59 percent) reported under single-bank holding companies and 1,999 (27 percent) operated independently of any holding company.

[60] Credit card banks are defined as institutions with credit card loans plus securitized receivables in excess of 50 percent of total assets plus securitized receivables. A consumer nonbank bank is a financial institution with a limited-purpose charter that can make commercial loans or take deposits, but not both. Industrial loan companies can be owned by commercial firms that are not regulated by a federal banking agency. A trust company is a corporation whose function is to act as a trustee, fiduciary, or agent for individuals or firms. A bankers' bank is a financial institution that provides financial services to other banks.

[61] Core deposits are defined as domestic deposits less brokered deposits. Historically, core deposits have been defined for analytical and examination purposes as the sum of demand deposits, all NOW and automatic transfer service accounts, money market deposit accounts, other savings deposits, and time deposits under $100,000. On March 31, 2011, this definition was revised to reflect the permanent increase in FDIC deposit insurance coverage from $100,000 to $250,000 and to exclude insured brokered deposits from core deposits. The definition used in the study provides consistency over time, since core deposits as defined before March 31, 2011, included some brokered deposits.

[62] Office data are obtained from the FDIC Summary of Deposits (SOD) and have been collected annually each June since 1987. These data are merger-adjusted to the end of the year for purposes of defining a community bank. In some cases, a bank with year-end data may have come into existence or obtained deposit insurance after SOD data were collected for that year. If no SOD data are available, data are used from the following year when possible. For banks in years prior to 1987, SOD data and thresholds for 1987 are used to determine whether banks are community banks. If 1987 SOD data are not available, as in the case of a bank failing or being acquired by another bank before 1987, office totals as reported in Call Reports and TFRs filed by banks are used to verify the minimum and maximum office criteria. The definition of an office as reported in the Call Reports and TFRs is slightly more expansive than the definition in SOD; so, for Call Report and TFR data, office thresholds are adjusted upward to 45. Banks in years prior to 1987 for which 1987 SOD data are not available are evaluated based on the loan-to-asset ratio, core-deposit-to-asset ratio, and minimum and maximum office criteria, since data are not available to evaluate the number of states, large metropolitan area, or the deposits in a single office criteria.

[63] As defined by the Office of Management and Budget, a metropolitan statistical area (MSA) contains a core urban area of 50,000 or more in population. For purposes of the study, a large MSA is defined as one with a population of more than 500,000.

[64] When filing the SOD, FDIC-insured institutions may follow different procedures when assigning deposits to branches, such as the proximity to the account holder's address, the office where the deposit account is most active, the office where the account originated, or the office assignment used when determining employee compensation. Conceivably, the methodology used by an institution could affect whether it exceeds this threshold.

[65] The minimum office requirement is effectively waived for institutions that fall under the asset size threshold. As described in Step 4, this requirement is intended to ensure that large institutions primarily gather deposits locally and do not rely excessively on the Internet or other automated means to obtain funding.

[66] A compound annual growth rate of 5.7 percent is applied to the asset size threshold in every year, making the size threshold $250 million in 1985, $1 billion in 2010. Approximately 90 percent of all banking organizations fall within these asset-size thresholds in both 1985 and 2010, our base years for arriving at this calculation.

[67] For purposes of these interviews, regulatory compliance costs are viewed as a decrease in income or an increase in expenses related to obtaining or maintaining compliance or conformance with banking rules and regulations and supervisory guidelines.

[68] See for example, Grant Thornton, "Bank Executive Survey: Bankers' Optimism Rebounds Amid Concerns Over Dodd-Frank," Third Quarter 2011. This survey indicated that compliance with regulatory reform was cited as a key concern by 91 percent of respondents. Respondents were not segregated according to community banker status, but were broken down by asset size, with 62 percent having more than $500 million in assets and 38 percent with less than $500 million.

[69] The selection criteria employed to determine the interview participants included a diverse set of factors, such as asset size, geographic location, business line, Minority Depository Institution status, and ownership structure, and participant banks met minimum supervisory ratings and other supervisory factors. All interview participants were state nonmember banks that had been informed that their responses would remain anonymous to promote candidness.

[70] Service providers assist community banks with processing financial transactions, automating business processes, managing mission-critical information, implementing regulatory requirements, and other essential business processes.

In: Community Banks
Editor: Christopher B. Joseph

ISBN: 978-1-62618-906-5

Chapter 2

COMMUNITY BANK EFFICIENCY AND ECONOMIES OF SCALE*

Stefan Jacewitz and Paul Kupiec

INTRODUCTION

A bank's efficiency ratio is defined as the ratio of a bank's non-interest expense to revenues. Higher efficiency ratios indicate less efficient banks. While there are many slightly modified definitions of the efficiency ratio, this basic ratio measures a bank's ability to generate revenues from its non-funding-related expense base.

The FDIC Community Banking Study finds that the efficiency ratios of community and noncommunity banks have diverged over time, especially since the late 1990s.[1] The analysis in the FDIC Community Bank Study compares asset-weighted average efficiency ratios for community banks (CBs) and noncommunity banks (NCBs) over the period 1984-2011. Over this period, the banking system experienced a substantial wave of consolidation, including the formation of very large NCB institutions over the second half of the 1990s and again more recently during the financial crisis. The consolidation among NCBs has led to a high concentration of banking system assets in relatively few large institutions.

An implication of the consolidation trend is that NCB asset-weighted average efficiency ratios are heavily influenced by the efficiency ratios of the very largest NCBs, especially since the late 1990s. The largest NCBs often have very different business models compared with smaller institutions (both CBs and NCBs). These business models include wholesale banking, capital markets, and derivative market making, which are often only conducted in the largest financial institutions. These activities may give rise to a very different efficiency ratio profile compared with smaller CB and NCB institutions, making it important to control for the shift in asset concentration toward the largest NCBs when analyzing the trends in the efficiency ratios of CBs and NCBs.

* This is an edited, reformatted and augmented version of the Federal Deposit Insurance Corporation, dated December 2012.

In the first section of this paper, we control for this consolidation trend by examining the median efficiency ratios of CBs and NCBs over time. Our analysis shows that asset concentration in the largest NCBs does affect the efficiency performance comparison between CBs and NCBs.

Still, after correcting for the increase in asset concentration among the largest NCBs, the overall conclusions of the FDIC Community Banking Study remain; CB efficiency ratios have increased relative to NCBs over the 1984-2011 time period.

In the second section of this paper, we provide additional detail regarding the estimates on CB economies of scale reported in the FDIC Community Banking Study. Economies of scale are often thought to be an important factor that encourages consolidation among smaller financial institutions. There is a large literature on measuring cost economies of scale in banking, but the literature that relates to community bank-sized institutions mostly uses data from the 1980s and early 1990s. We revisit the important issue of cost economies of scale using more recent CB data and newer estimation techniques than are typically found in the existing literature. Still, our findings are broadly consistent with historical literature that focuses on banks in the size range of modern community banks. While our specific results on economies of scale depend on a CB's lending specialization, our estimates provide no indication of any significant scale benefits beyond $500 million in asset size for most lending specializations. Further, our estimates suggest that, in many cases, most of the cost benefits from scale appear to be achieved for CBs as small as $100 million. While economies of scale are important for community banks, historical trends in the size distribution of community banks that have survived over the last quarter century do not suggest that economies of scale require a community bank to grow or merge to asset sizes larger than $1 billion. Of the community banks that have survived the last quarter century, 60 percent remain under $200 million and many remain under $100 million in asset size.

TRENDS IN MEDIAN EFFICIENCY RATIOS FOR CBS AND NCBS

Figure 1 shows the historical median efficiency ratios for CBs and NCBs.[2] Our analysis focuses on median efficiency ratios because these statistics provide the best representation of the typical CB and NCB. The inset box "Why Use Median Values?" discusses the calculation of median sample statistics and the advantages of using medians for this analysis. Figure 1 shows that the asset-weighted average efficiency ratio divergence reported in the FDIC Community Banking Study carries over when the median efficiency ratios for CBs and NCBs are compared over the same period.

After controlling for the effects of industry consolidation, it is still possible that because banks enjoy economies of scale benefits, we might expect larger institutions to exhibit higher efficiency (a lower efficiency ratio). Efficiency ratios for larger institutions would improve because a dollar of non-interest cost could support higher revenue if scale economies are present. The inset box "What Are Economies of Scale?" provides more detail on measuring economies of scale in banking. Before we analyze the components of median bank efficiency ratios, it is useful to consider whether the observed trends in CB and NCB efficiency ratios could be driven by economies of scale and a change in the relative size of CB and NCB institutions over the sample period.

Figure 2 compares the size of the median CBs and NCBs over time after adjusting for the effects of inflation and shows that the median size of a CB almost doubled over the period of analysis whereas the median size of an NCB increased by about 10 percent. If the efficiency benefits from growing in size are strongest for smaller institutions (a pattern suggested by our subsequent economies of scale estimates), a typical CB should have gained efficiency relative to typical NCBs. This prediction is inconsistent with observed trends in efficiency ratios. While not a formal test, the analysis suggests that economies of scale have probably not been an important factor causing the observed divergence in CB and NCB efficiency ratios.

WHY USE MEDIAN VALUES?

We choose to analyze median values rather than averages weighted by assets or simple average values in order to portray the experience of the typical CB and NCB. Especially for NCBs, the size distribution of institutions is very heavily skewed, with a very few extremely large institutions, so the use of weighted average statistics may give a misleading characterization of the changes that a typical institution has experienced.

The median value of a distribution is the value that is halfway between the smallest and the largest value when the data are ranked by magnitude. Unlike simple and weighted average values, median values are not influenced by a distribution's skewness, for example, when a distribution has a very small number of very large-valued observations.

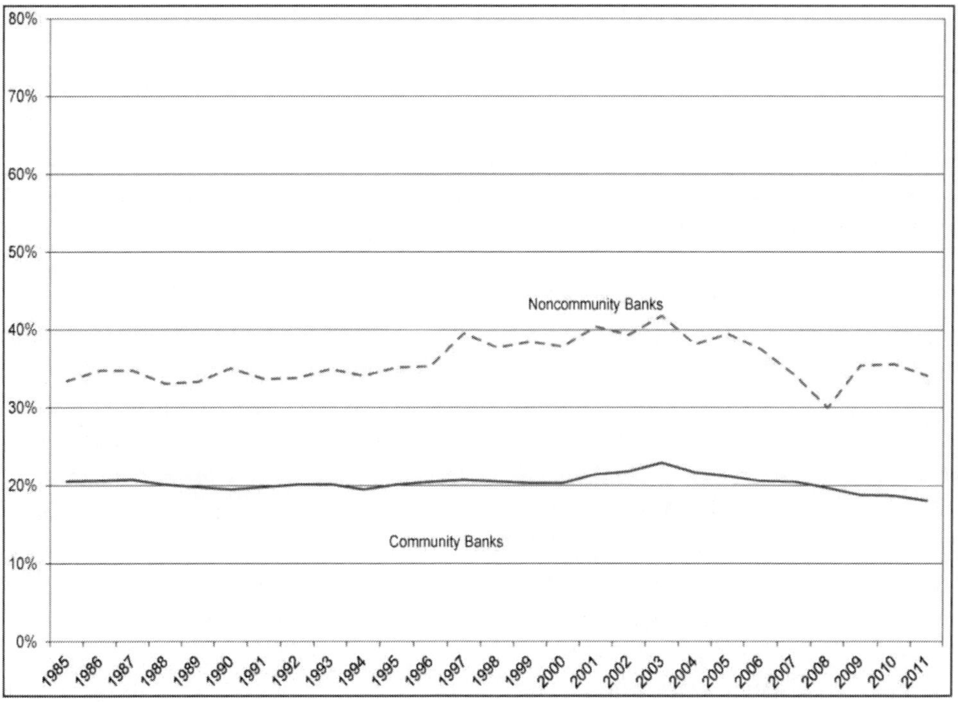

Source: FDIC.

Exhibit 1. Median Non-Interest Income to Non-Interest Expense Ratios.

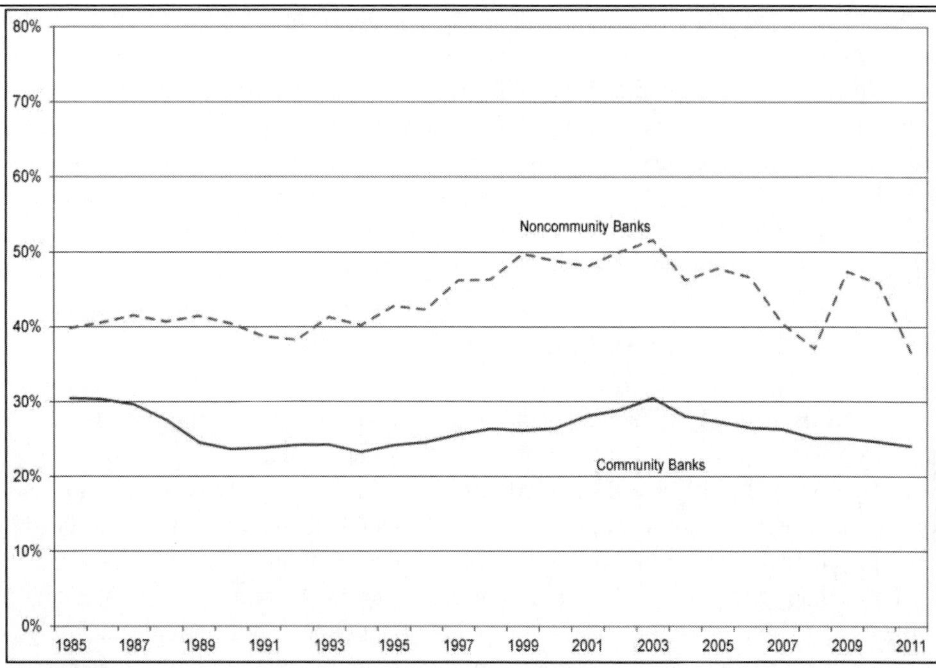

Source: FDIC.

Exhibit 2. Weighted Averages Non-Interest Income to Non-Interest Expense Ratios (Excluding Banks > $500B).

Given the extremely skewed distribution of assets among the population of banks, weighted averages generate statistics that are driven by the top few banks alone. In 2011, the median bank of the CB sample has about $160 million in assets. The largest CB has $14.66 billion (90 times larger than the median CB). In contrast, in the same year, the largest NCB in the sample has $1.6 trillion in assets, which is more than 300 times larger than the median NCB (at $5.5 billion).

When we plot a time series of median values, the plot represents the trend experienced by a typical CB and NCB. The analysis is little changed if we compare trends using simple average statistics, but it is very different if we compare trends using asset-weighted average statistics. When asset-weighted averages are used, NCB data trends follow the experiences of only a very small number of very large institutions with extensive capital market activities and other unique characteristics. Such comparisons contrast CB efficiency trends with the efficiency trends experienced by the very largest NCBs and not NCBs that are closer in size and scope to CBs.

For this sample data, medians generate very similar results to weighted averages provided that the largest banks (outliers) are removed from the sample. Exhibits 1 and 2 show median and asset-weighted average values for the sample banks' noninterest income to noninterest expense, where the asset-weighted average statistics are calculated after excluding the very largest banks. Exhibit 3 plots the asset-weighted average statistics for all banks in the sample. A comparison of Exhibits 1, 2 and 3 show that, for these data, using the median is roughly equivalent to using the average or the asset-weighted average, provided outliers are removed.

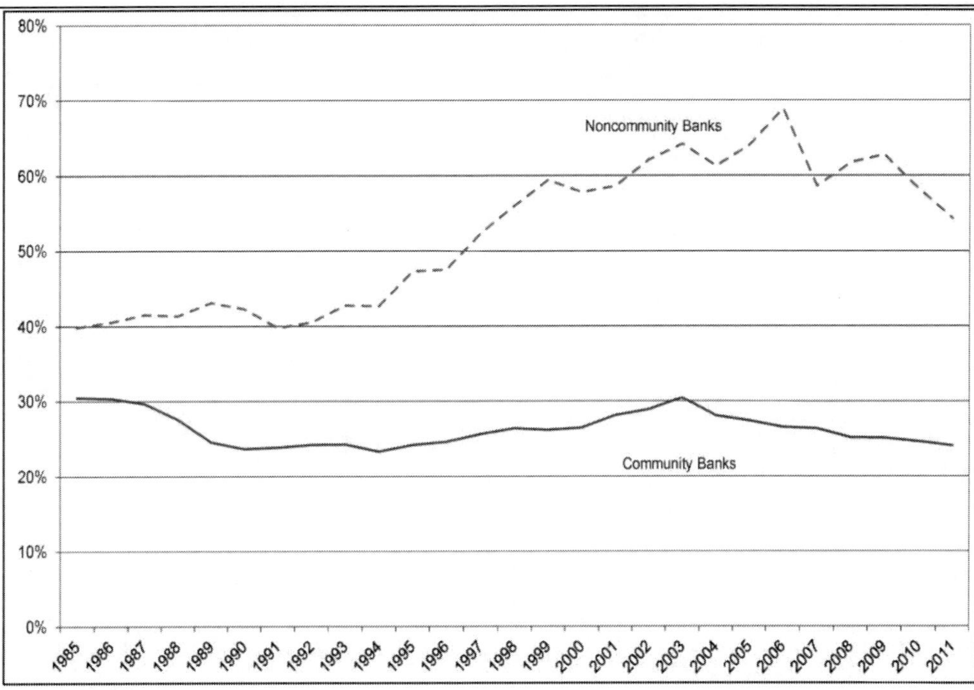

Source: FDIC.

Exhibit 3. Weighted Averages Non-Interest Income to Non-Interest Expense Ratios (All Banks Included).

In the analysis that follows, we show that the divergence in median efficiency ratios between CBs and NCBs can be attributed to a decline in the spread between the yields on loans and the costs of deposits at CBs. CBs once enjoyed a large advantage over NCBs in this important spread, but the advantage has dissipated over time. CBs now earn less on their loan portfolios and pay slightly more than NCBs for funding. The importance of the decline in this spread has been magnified because CBs have also increased their loan-to-asset ratios over time. In addition to the decline in the loan-to-deposit spread, CBs also experienced a sizable decline in the ratio of their non-interest income to non-interest expense. In contrast, NCBs' non-interest income to non-interest expense ratio was fairly steady over the period from 1985 through the second quarter 2012.

Expense patterns also explain some of the changes in the relative efficiency of CBs and NCBs. CBs have experienced slower productivity gains (in terms of assets per employee) compared with NCBs. Employee-related expenses increased at both CBs and NCBs, but the increase in employee expenses at NCBs was offset by higher productivity gains while the increase at CBs was not. Since employee-related expense is the largest non-interest expense for both groups, this factor explains a significant amount of the relative increase in non-interest expense at CBs.

Source: FDIC.

Figure 1. Median Efficiency Ratio at Community Banks and Other Depository Institutions.

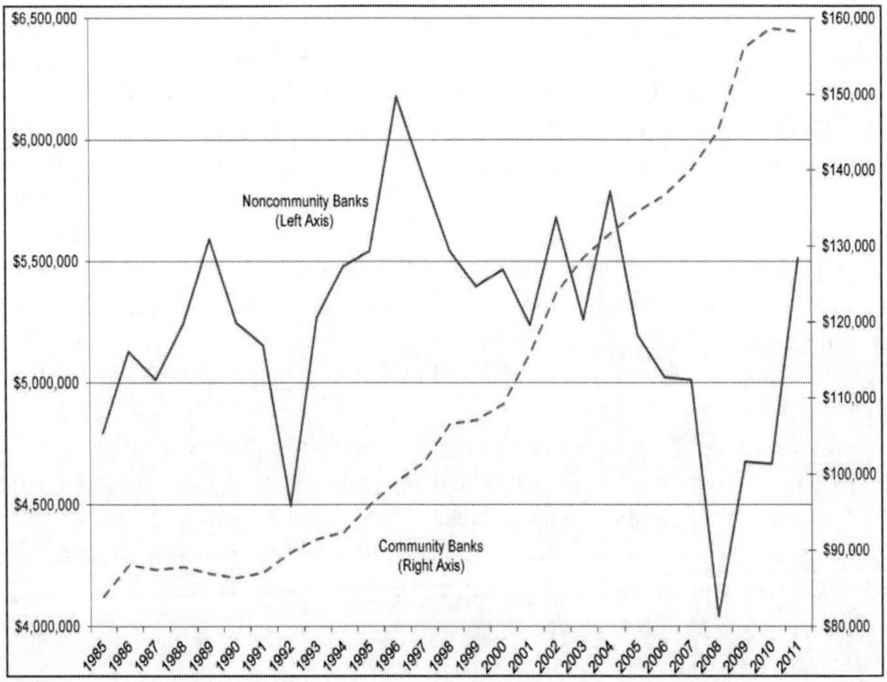

Source: FDIC.

Figure 2. Median Asset Size at Community Banks and Other Depository Institutions.

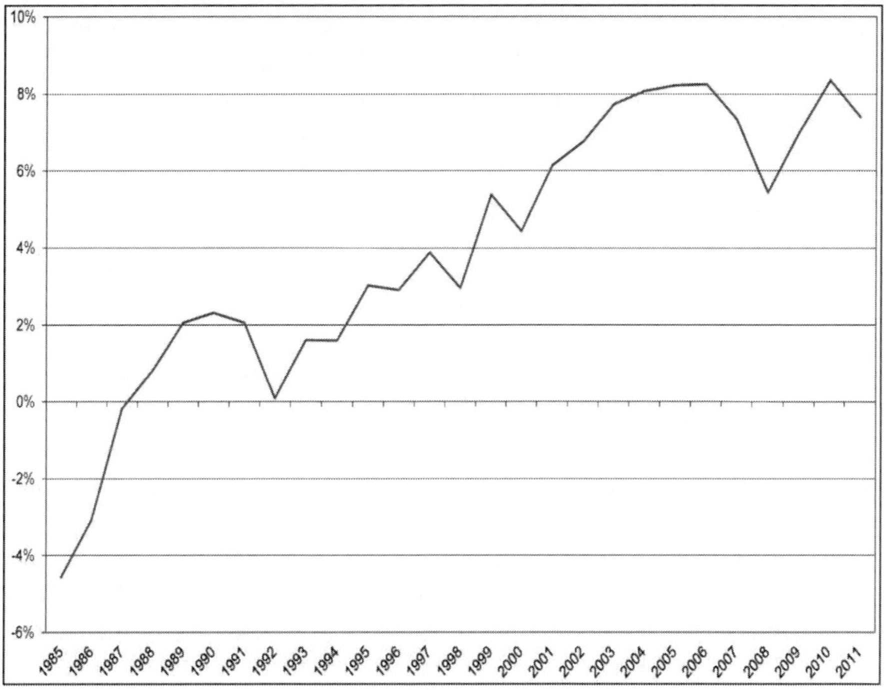

Figure 3. Noncommunity Bank Efficiency Ratio Advantage.

WHAT ARE ECONOMIES OF SCALE?

Economies of scale measure the relationship between the cost of producing a unit of output and the level of output. When the average cost of producing a unit of output declines as output increases, the activity is said to have (increasing) economies of scale. Economies of scale can be "local," meaning that average costs may decline for some levels of output and then stabilize or increase, or economies of scale can be "global" meaning that average costs continue to decline as output increases.

In manufacturing and agriculture, measuring outputs and inputs is conceptually straightforward. However, when measuring scale economies for service firms, the appropriate measure of output is often less clear. Consider, for example, health care. Should output be measured by the number office visits, the number of prescriptions written, or the number of illnesses cured? Or perhaps it should be measured by some combination of these and other observable measures? The problem of measuring output is also difficult in the case of banking due to difficulties in measuring output and distinguishing outputs from inputs. For example, banks provide loans, take deposits, and provide other services. Deposits are also used to fund bank activities. Are bank deposits a bank output or an input? Banks also provide cash management services. Should the services provided be measured by the dollar volume or the number of transactions processed? A similar question arises with bank loans and loan commitments. Is output measured by the number of loans or the dollar volume of lending? And how does one add up all these different service outputs?

There is no consensus as to the best measure of bank output. Bank output has been measured in many ways in the academic literature (e.g., loans, deposits, assets, loans plus deposits). In this study, we measure bank output using total bank balance sheet assets. That is, we measure banks' average cost of producing output as total bank costs divided by bank balance sheet assets. We define total costs as the sum of interest expenses, provisions for loan and lease losses, and non-interest expenses. Our measure accounts for all expenses, with the exception of extraordinary items and income taxes.

Using average bank cost per dollar of bank assets is a simplification that sidesteps the complex issue of defining a bank's output. If the average cost ratio declines as bank size increases, then economies of scale exist.

Using the average cost per dollar of assets implicitly assumes that banks' "true" output is a constant fraction of assets, regardless of a bank's size. If, however, a bank's output mix changes as it grows larger or it can use different technologies that allow the bank to produce more services per dollar of bank assets without a decline in total cost, then using the implicit assumption that all banks' output is a constant fraction of assets will give misleading results. In our analysis, we focus on estimating economies of scale separately for each CB specialty lending group because the mix of services provided by a CB specialty lender probably does not change in a systematic way as CBs grow in size.

WHAT EXPLAINS THE INCREASE IN COMMUNITY BANK EFFICIENCY RATIOS?

Figure 3 shows the difference in median efficiency ratios of CBs and NCBs between 1985 and 2012. CBs had an advantage in the beginning of the period, but by the early 1990s, CB efficiency began to deteriorate relative to the efficiency ratio of NCBs. While both groups have lost efficiency since the financial crisis, NCBs maintained their efficiency advantage throughout the crisis.

To explain the divergence in CBs' efficiency, we analyze the behavior of the inverse of the efficiency ratio, or the ratio of bank revenues to non-interest expense. This approach enables us to begin to understand the reasons for changes in the efficiency ratio by separating changes into those related to trends in non-interest income and those related to net interest income. Figure 4 plots the median of the inverse efficiency ratios for CBs and NCBs. When looking at the inverse of the efficiency ratio, higher values imply more favorable bank efficiency.

The inverse of the efficiency ratio is the sum of two component ratios: the net interest income to non-interest expense ratio and the non-interest income to non-interest expense ratio.[3] Figure 5 plots the median ratio of non-interest income to non-interest expense (NonII-NIE ratio) for CBs and NCBs. Over the historical period, the CB median NonII-NIE ratio declined from about 21 percent to about 18 percent in 2011. The comparable ratio for NCBs was roughly unchanged in 2011 versus 1985. So, while a decline in the NonII-NIE ratio contributed to the deterioration in CBs' relative efficiency over the past decades, it is not the most important cause of the observed decline.

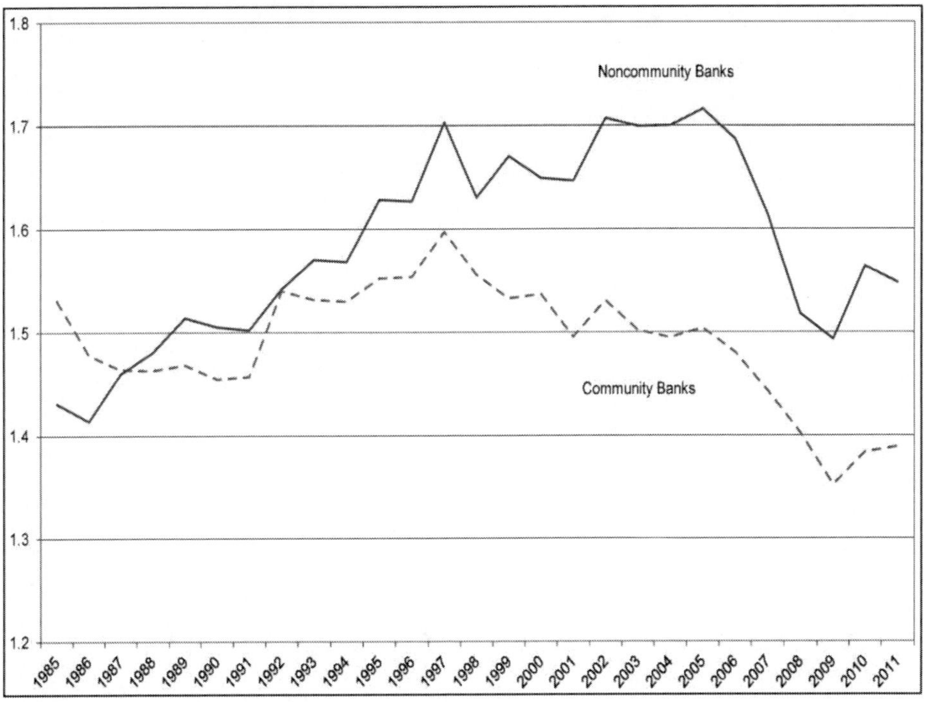

Source: FDIC.

Figure 4. Median of the Inverse Efficiency Ratio of Community and Noncommunity Banks.

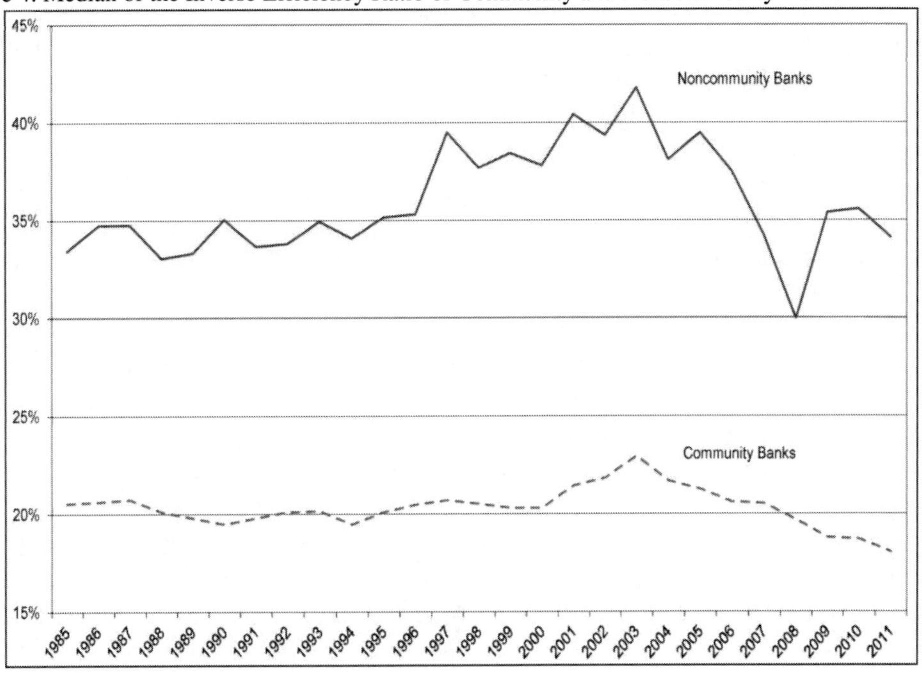

Source: FDIC.

Figure 5. Median Ratio of Non-Interest Income to Non-Interest Expense for Community and Noncommunity Banks.

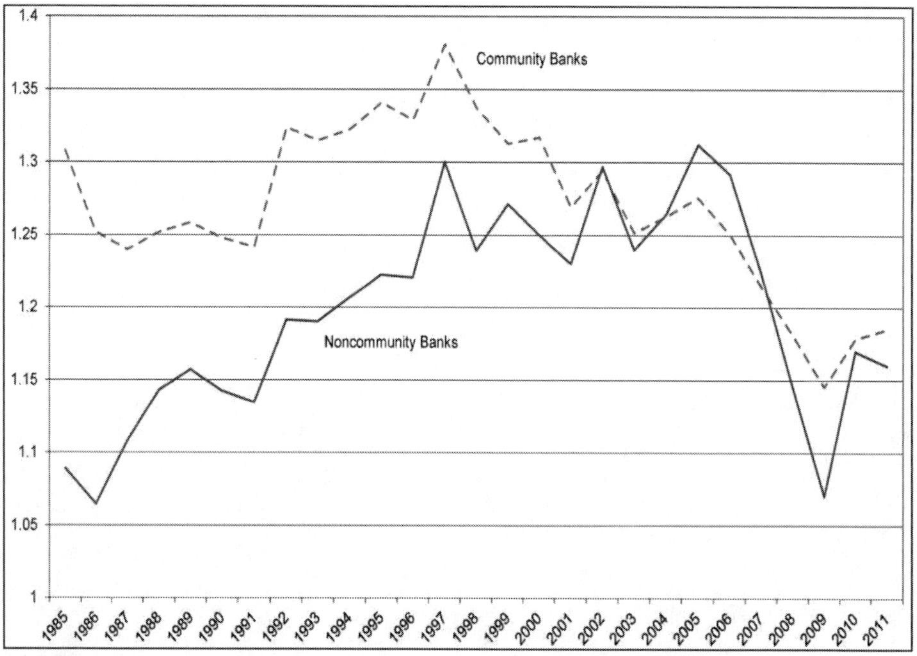

Source: FDIC.

Figure 6. Median Ratio of Net Interest Income to Non-Interest Expense for Community and Noncommunity Banks.

Much of the relative change in efficiency between the two groups can be attributed to trends in these respective institutions' net interest income (NII). Figure 6 shows the median ratios of NII to non-interest expense (NII-NIE ratio) for CBs and NCBs over time. CBs had a substantial advantage in this component of the efficiency ratio early in the sample period, but this advantage disappeared steadily over time. Meanwhile, the median value of the NII-NIE ratio among NCBs posted sizable gains, catching up to CBs and even surpassing them during the mid-2000s. By 2011, there was no significant difference between the median NII-NIE ratio for CBs and NCBs.

NII can be decomposed into interest income and interest expense. Figure 7 shows the interest income from loans as a fraction of non-interest expense. This ratio behaves similarly for CBs and NCBs over time; interest income from loans has become substantially smaller relative to non-interest expense for both CBs and NCBs.

A large part of the net interest income difference between CBs and NCBs can be explained by differences in these institutions' cost of funds (interest expense over liabilities), shown in Figure 8. For much of the sample period, CBs enjoyed a funding cost advantage over NCBs, although there were times when funding costs for CBs and NCBs converged. In some periods, the CB funding cost advantage was as large as 1 percentage point. From 2007, the cost of funds advantage enjoyed by CBs dissipated and now CBs fund themselves at a slight cost disadvantage compared to NCBs.

A Closer Examination of the Trends in CB Net Interest Margins

CBs' lending margins closely track the decline in the level of short-term interest rates, but other important and related determinants may also have changed over the sample period. In the lending process, banks provide maturity transformation by borrowing demandable deposits and funding longer maturity loans, so their lending rates should be related to the slope of the risk-free term structure of interest rates. Lending also involves exposure to credit risk for which CBs must be compensated. A typical market-based measure of credit risk used in many studies is the yield spread between BAA-rated corporate bonds and 10-year U.S. Treasury bonds.

In addition to financial factors, we expect CBs' net interest margins to be related to loan demand conditions in these banks' local markets. We expect net interest margin at CBs to be higher when there is strong loan demand from their local lending market, and lower when local market demand conditions are weak. A final factor we consider is the degree of concentration in the local banking market.

When banks operate in a concentrated market, they may be able to exercise market power, paying depositors slightly less for their deposits and charging borrowers slightly more for loans. If this is true, trends toward increased competition in local markets might result in lower CB interest margins as competition forces CBs to raise deposit rates and reduce the interest rates they charge for their loans.

We use panel regression analysis to explore what factors might have influenced the decline in CBs' net interest margins over time. We estimate our model using a sample of institutions that operate in a specific geographic market for which we can measure bank concentration and also control for local economic effects. We use FDIC Summary Deposit data to identify banks that collect 100 percent of their deposits in a single county. Our data sample period begins in the second quarter of 1994, when SOD data are first available, and ends at the end of 2011.

We measure banks' local competitive conditions in each quarter in each county using the Herfendahl-Hirshman index (HHI) for bank deposit concentration.[1] We include separate dummy variables for moderately and highly concentrated counties. The assumption that high HHI deposit concentration values may be an indication of monopoly power is common in the bank market structure antitrust banking literature.

We estimate separate models for the components of CBs' net interest income, average cost of funds (cost of funds to total liabilities), and average interest earned on loans (interest on loans to total loans). We control for market conditions in a CB's local county market by including county-level unemployment rates, the share of credit card accounts within a county that are 60-days past due, the county-level home price index, and bank fixed effects in our estimations.[2]

Exhibit 4 shows the estimation results for our sample. Generally, the Federal Funds rate, the slope of the term structure, and the credit risk yield have the largest impacts on the two components of CBs' net interest margin, the average cost of funds, and the average interest on loans. While there is some evidence that CBs can benefit in concentrated markets (markets with high HHIs), changes in HHIs do not appear to explain very much of the overall trend in CBs' net interest margin over this time period. The inclusion of time-invariant bank fixed effects explains a large share of the observed variation in net interet margins, suggesting that some banks have more profitable customer relationships that are not explained by the competitive nature of the banks' local markets as measured by a HHI deposit index.

Exhibit 4. OLS Estimates, Community Banks with 100% of Deposits in One County

Outcome	Cost of Funds to Liabilities (in percentage points)	Interest on Loans to Loans (in percentage points)
Federal Funds Rate	0.17*** (0.00)	0.61*** (0.00)
10Y T-Bond vs. 3M T-Bill Spread	0.09*** (0.00)	0.45*** (0.01)
BAA Bond Yield vs. 10Y T-Bond	0.13*** (0.00)	0.35*** (0.01)
=1 if Moderately Concentrated	0.00 (0.00)	0.05** (0.02)
=1 if Concentrated	-0.01*** (0.00)	0.03 (0.03)
County Unemployment Rate (Pct)	0.00*** (0.00)	0.01*** (0.00)
County Credit Card 60 Days DQ Rate (Pct)	0.03*** (0.00)	0.25*** (0.00)
County HPI Growth Rate (Pct)	0.00 (0.00)	0.00 (0.00)
Constant	-0.40*** (0.00)	3.34*** (0.04)
Quarterly Fixed Effects	N	N
County Fixed Effects	N	N
Bank Fixed Effects	Y	Y
N	246614	64843
R-sq	0.87	0.72

Source: FDIC.

[1] The Herfindahl-Hirschman (HHI) Index is a commonly accepted measure of market concentration calculated by squaring the market share of each firm competing in the market and then summing the resulting numbers. The HHI measures the relative size distribution of the firms in a market and takes a value close to zero when a market has a large number of approximately equal-sized firms and a maximum value of 10,000 when a market is controlled by a single firm.

[2] Our county-level unemployment rate is from the U.S. Bureau of Labor Statistics. House price growth rates are based on Case Schiller indexes adjusted for inflation using the consumer price index for consumers less shelter. For counties without reported house price index (HPI) values, we substitute the state HPI. County-level data on percentage of credit card accounts more than 60 days past due are from Trendata.

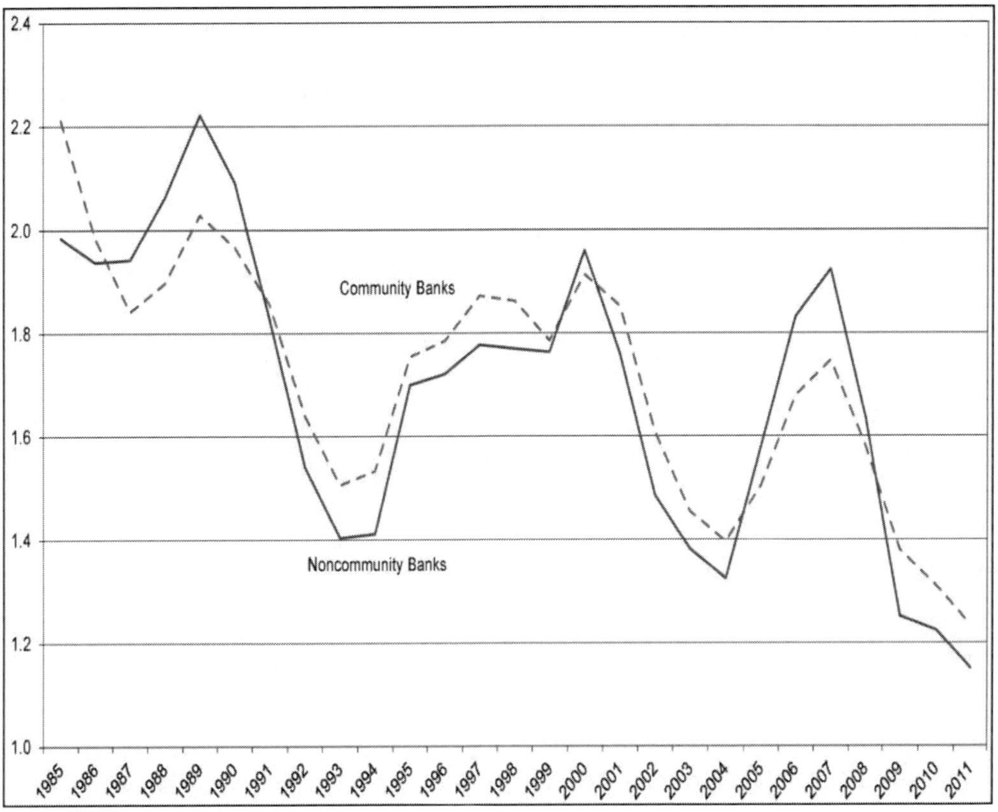

Source: FDIC.

Figure 7. Interest Income From Loans versus Non-Interest Expense.

The difference between the CB and NCB NII-NIE ratio medians over time is linked to changes in the loan-to-asset ratios and the yields these groups of institutions earn on their loans. Figure 9 is a time-series plot of the median loan-to-asset ratio for CBs and NCBs. Early in the sample period, the median loan-to-asset ratio for CBs was about 4 percentage points lower than the median for NCBs. Generally, until the recent crisis, both groups of banks increased their lending exposure over the sample period, but CBs increased their loan exposure at a faster pace. From 1985 to 2011, the median loan-to-asset ratio for CBs increased by over 7 percentage points, to within 1 percentage point of the median loan-to-asset ratio for NCBs.

Both CBs and NCBs increased their loan exposure while the average returns they earned on their loans declined. Figure 10 shows the median of average yields earned by CBs and NCBs on their loan portfolios. Both CBs and NCBs experienced large declines in the yield they earned on their loans. While CBs continue to have an advantage in the yield on loans, the differential they once enjoyed declined from 130 basis points in 1985 to about 60 basis points in 2011.

Figure 11 shows the difference between CBs and NCBs in terms of the spread between loan yields and deposit costs. CBs initially, and through much of the sample period, had a greater than 100 basis point spread advantage over NCBs, but this advantage declined to about 35 basis points by 2011. Figure 11 also shows that the decline in CBs' loan-to-deposit spread advantage over NCBs roughly tracks the path of the Federal Funds rate since late

1999, suggesting that lending margin compression may in part be related to the level of interest rates over this period. Inset box "A Closer Examination of the Trends in CB Net Interest Margins," provides a deeper analysis of factors that may have affected CBs' average borrowing and lending rates over this sample period.

The relative decrease in CBs loan–to-deposit spread tells only part of the comparative efficiency story. Non-interest expense trends are also a factor. Employee salaries are the largest single contributor to non-interest expenses at both CBs and NCBs (see Figure 12). However, unlike NCBs, the majority of CB non-interest expense is derived from employee-related expenses.

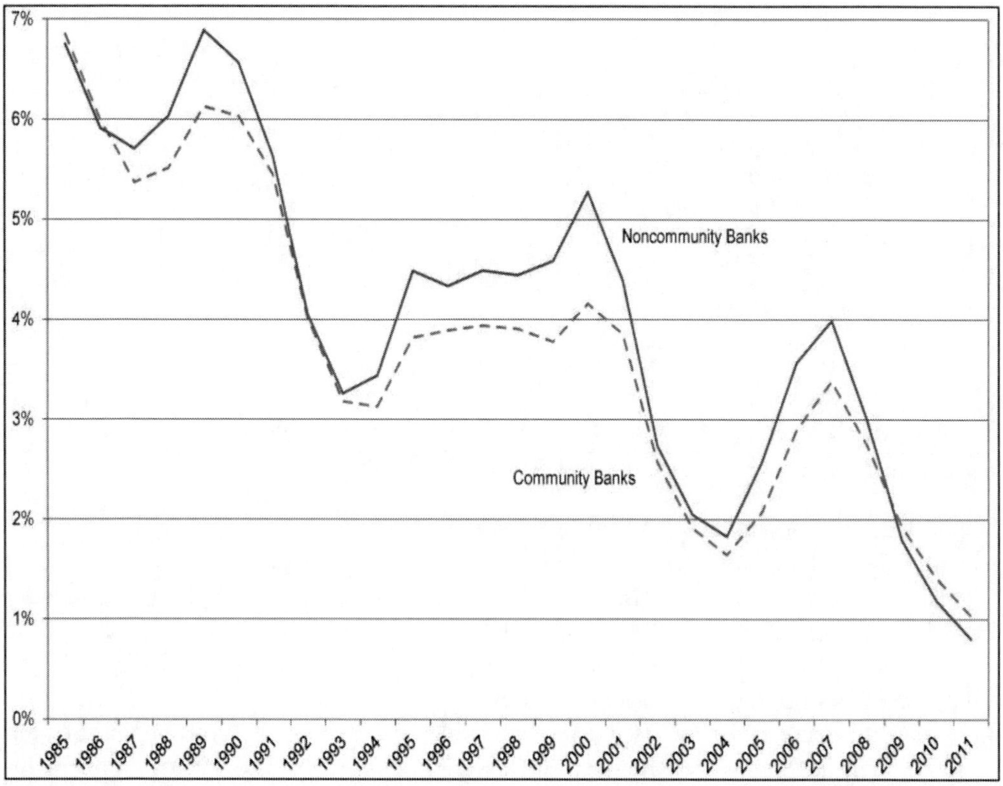

Source: FDIC.

Figure 8. Median Cost of Funds at Community and Noncommunity Banks.

The amount of assets managed per bank employee is a measure of labor productivity efficiency. This measure has also changed substantially over the last two and a half decades, after adjusting for inflation. Figure 13 shows that, in 1985, the amount of assets per employee was similar at CBs and NCBs. In 1985, NCBs managed around $3.25 million in assets (in 2011 dollars) per employee, or about 8 percent more assets per employee than CBs. In 2011, NCBs experienced significant efficiency gains in this respect, managing just under $5.5 million in assets per employee, an increase of almost 70 percent. Over the same period, growth in assets per employee at CBs was more modest, moving from around $3 million to just over $4 million, or a 30 percent increase. This implies that NCBs are now able to manage more than 35 percent more assets per employee than CBs.

Even though a greater portion of CBs' expenses is derived from employee compensation, CBs tend to pay less per employee. Using Call Report data on employee expenses (which include the cost of benefits), after adjusting for inflation, median compensation at NCBs was around \$50,000 per employee in 1985 (see Figure 14). Median compensation at NCBs increased to around \$80,000 in 2011, a 60 percent increase. The median compensation at CBs, in contrast, increased from \$45,000 in 1985 to around \$60,000 in 2011, an increase of 33 percent.

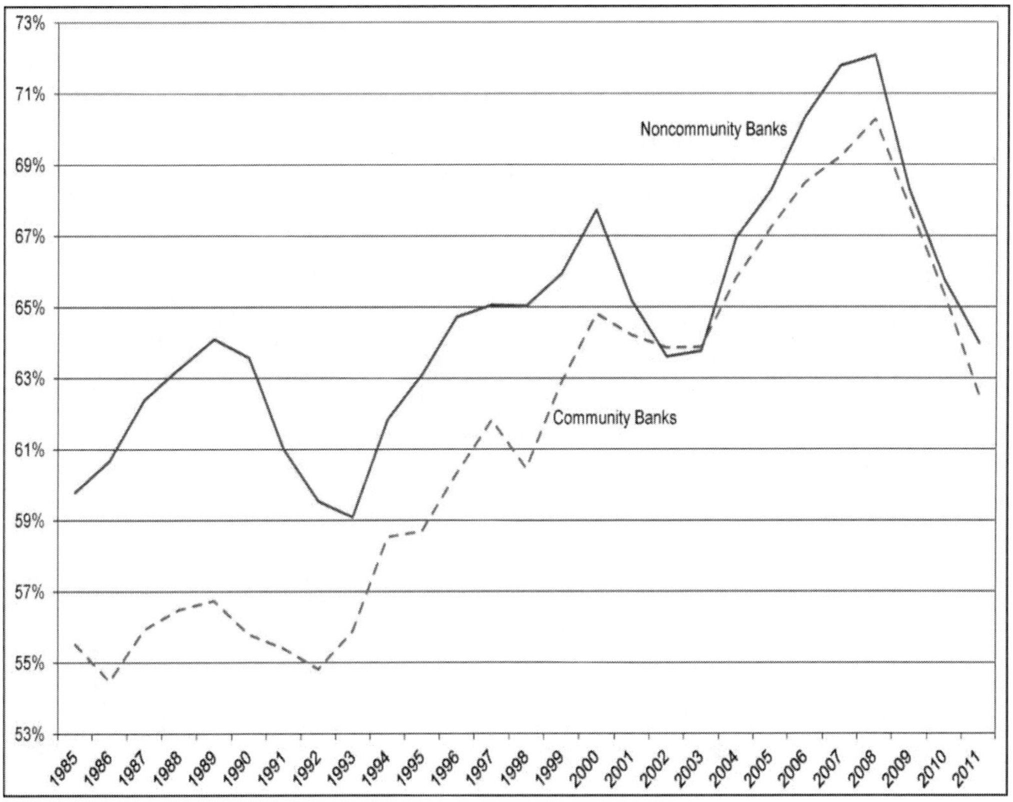

Source: FDIC.

Figure 9. Median Loans-to-Assets Ratio for Community and Noncommunity Banks.

Figure 15 shows the historical behavior of another ratio that can help explain trends in labor efficiency at CBs relative to NCBs. This figure shows the median ratio of total employee expenses to total assets at CBs and NCBs. The labor cost per dollar of assets at CBs has increased over the past decades, while it has decreased slightly for NCBs. In 1985, CBs had a slight advantage according to this measure, with CBs paying \$1.42 in employee expenses per \$100 in assets and NCBs paying \$1.47. In contrast, by 2011, NCBs' labor expenses per \$100 of assets declined to \$1.37, while CBs labor expenses per \$100 of assets rose to \$1.54. Over the sample period, CBs have not matched NCBs in managing labor cost per dollar of assets.

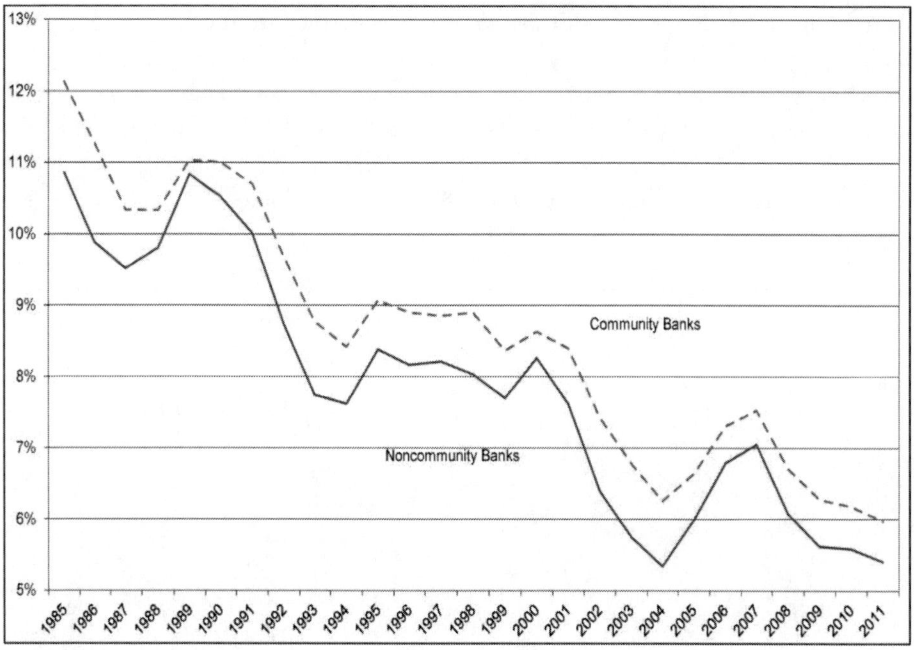

Source: FDIC.

Figure 10. Median Average Yield on Loans at Community and Noncommunity Banks.

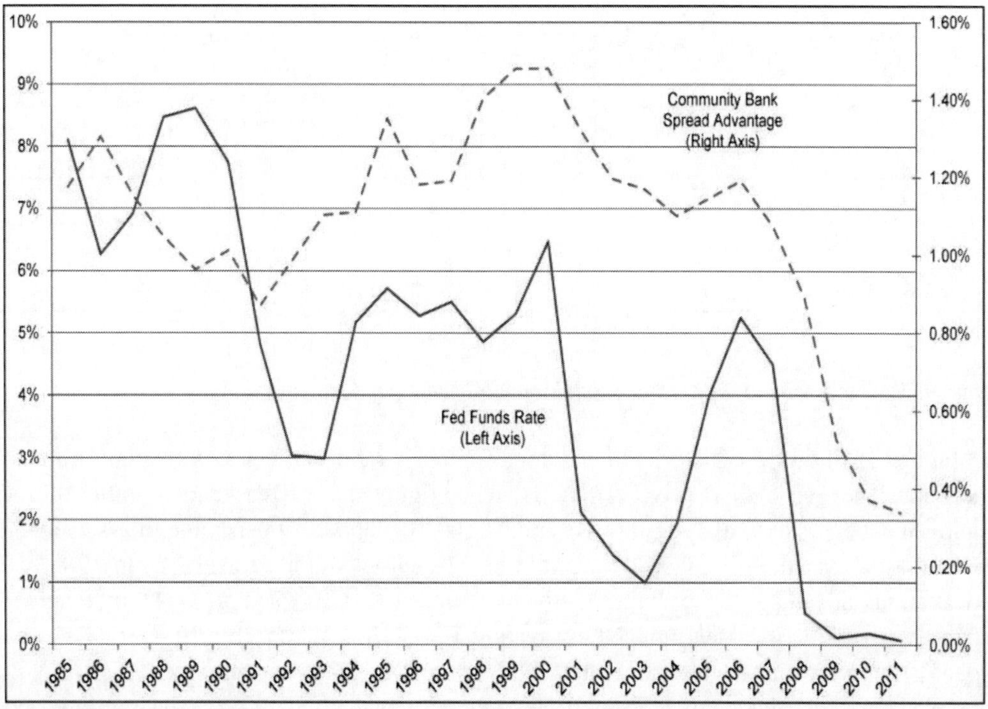

Source: FDIC.

Figure 11. Difference in Median Loan/Deposit Interest Spread between Community and Noncommunity Banks.

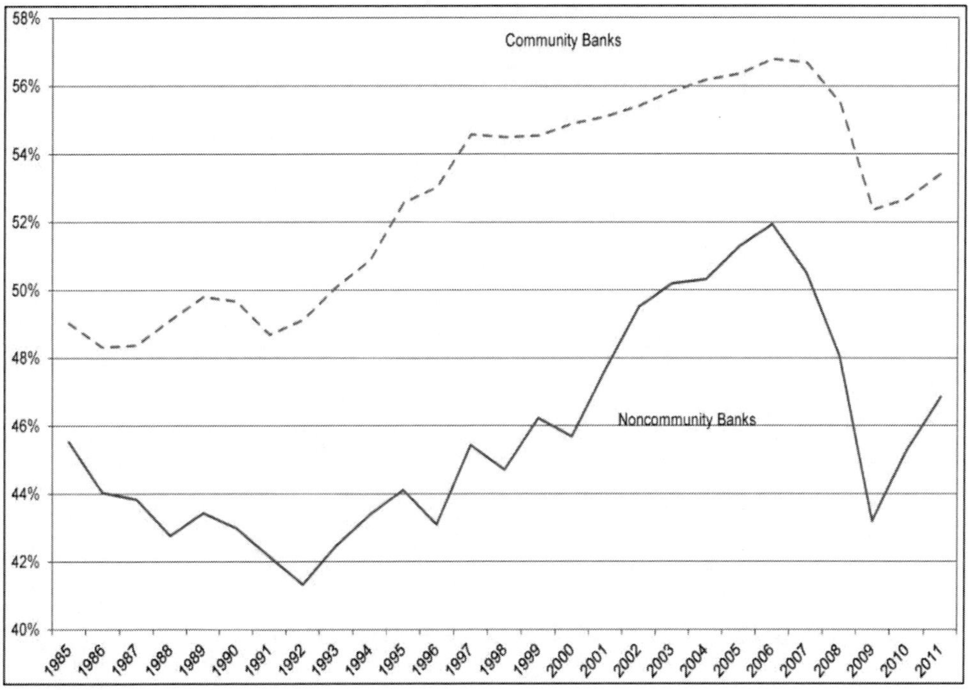

Source: FDIC.

Figure 12. Median Employee Related Expense to Total Non-Interest Expense Ratios for Community and Noncommunity Banks.

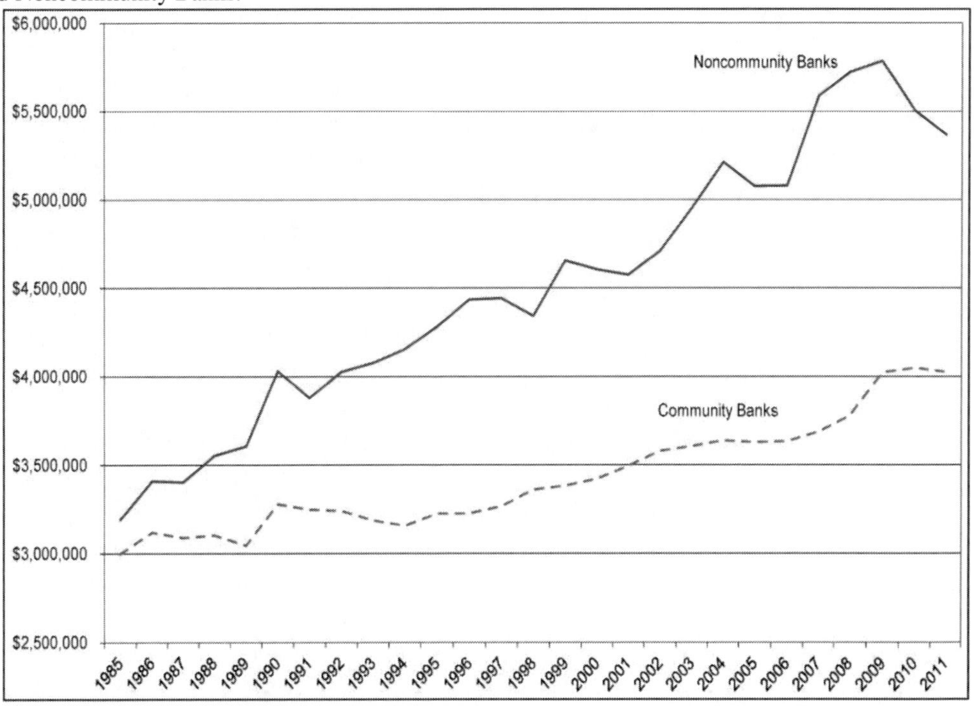

Source: FDIC.

Figure 13. Median Assets per Employee (Deflated by CPI) for Community and Noncommunity Banks.

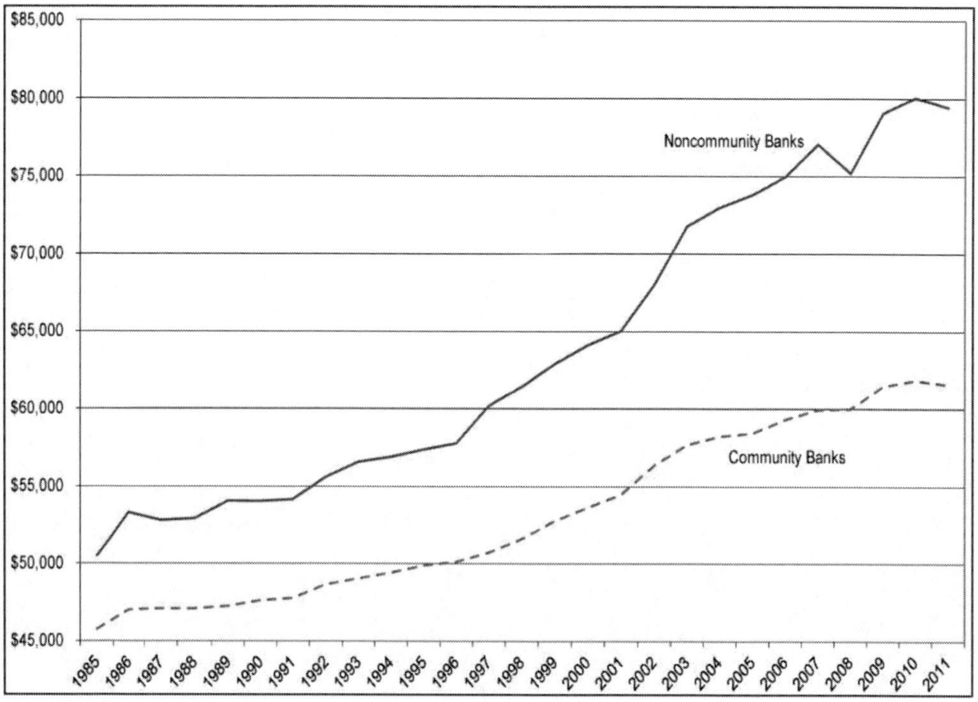

Source: FDIC.

Figure 14. Median Salary per Employee (Deflated by CPI) for Community and Noncommunity Banks.

DIFFERENCE IN COSTS AND ECONOMIES OF SCALE

Economies of scale describe the relationship between average costs and the output of a firm (see inset box "What Are Economies of Scale?"). A firm exhibits economies of scale if its average cost of producing output declines as output increases. An extensive literature from the 1980s and 1990s finds that there is potential for generating cost saving from economies of scale in banking. Typical findings suggest banks face a relatively shallow U-shaped average cost curve, with a minimum average cost estimate occurring for banks somewhere between $75 million and $300 million in asset value (Berger, Hunter, Timme (1993)). Numerous early studies find evidence of diseconomies of scale (increasing average costs) for the largest institutions in their sample time frame.

Many early studies use a translog cost function specification to estimate economies of scale. This methodology subsequently has been shown to have important shortcomings. McAllister and McManus (1993) find that the translog function does not work well unless all the banks analyzed have a nearly homogeneous product mix and do not differ greatly in size. Therefore, the evidence of bank diseconomies found in early studies may have been a consequence of the translog methodology and large banks may not be as inefficient as these early studies have suggested.

After these shortcomings were identified, researchers developed alternative approaches for estimating bank efficiency. Newer approaches shift from models in which banks were assumed to simply minimize costs to models that assumed banks maximized profits or even the bank manager's utility.[4] Many of these newer approaches retain a translog cost model but modify other model assumptions to improve performance. Some researchers have abandoned the translog model entirely in favor of using nonparametric methods with more flexible cost curve shape specifications to estimate banking sector efficiencies. In the analysis that follows, we estimate an average cost model for banks using a nonparametric approach that does not suffer the methodological shortcomings of the translog approach.

We measure bank output as total assets and bank total costs as the sum of interest expenses, provisions for loan and lease losses, and non-interest expenses. Our measure accounts for all expenses with the exceptions of extraordinary items and income taxes. Because both the numerator and the denominator of the average cost ratio (bank total costs divided by bank total assets) are expressed in nominal dollars, the ratio is unaffected by changes in the price level over the sample period.

To avoid making overly restrictive assumptions on the form and shape of the average cost curve, we employ a nonparametric method called kernel regression to estimate the relationship between bank size and average cost. Kernel regression is discussed in more detail in inset box "How re Kernel Regression Estimates Calculated?" We provide separate estimates for specialty lender designations (mortgage specialists, commercial real estate (CRE) specialists, agriculture specialists, etc.) because each form of specialty lending may have unique cost and technologies that lead to different scale economy characteristics.[5]

We estimate the relationship between size and average cost for two years, 2006 and 2009 (where size is measured in 2011 dollars). The first year is among the most profitable years for the banking industry while 2009 is a year of crisis and industry losses.[6] To eliminate outlier observations, this analysis is restricted to CBs with a cost of less than one dollar per dollar of bank assets. Further, technical considerations associated with the kernel regression method lead us to examine only specialty groups with more than 500 observations.

HOW ARE KERNEL REGRESSION ESTIMATES CALCULATED?

Kernel regression can be thought of as a simple histogram that has been "smoothed." The kernel regression approach we use assumes that the average cost is a constant in a local region for a given bank size, and estimates the constant average cost value using a Gaussian kernel. The kernel function defines the weight given to observations in the local region that are used to calculate the average cost estimate for that region.

To provide some intuition for kernel regression, we present a simplified example. Consider the relationship between bank size and observed bank average costs. If we arrange banks according to size from smallest to largest and plot these banks' average costs, we would have a plot that looks something like the points in Exhibit 5. While there appears to be a general pattern of declining average costs as size increases, there is a lot of "noise" and some banks close to each other in size have widely varying average costs. The kernel regression technique defines a local region of adjacent points, then takes a weighted average of the cost observations within this region to arrive at an estimate that smoothes out the "noise" in the data.

To simplify, our kernel regression example will use a band width of 2 units and a "triangle kernel" to calculate weights. So, for example, for a bank of size 10, our kernel estimate will use data from adjacent banks as well; that is, it will use the cost data for banks with sizes 9 through 11. The kernel regression estimate for a bank of size 10 is calculated by taking the weighted average of the costs of banks 9, 10, and 11. The estimate weights bank 9 and bank 11 costs by 25 percent (each), and the cost observation for bank 10 receives a weight of 50 percent. This simple triangle kernel regression estimate is illustrated by the dashed line in Exhibit 1. Notice that kernel estimator uses the observed data to produce a smoother function for the average cost-bank size relationship in the data.

In the actual estimation we perform, the size of the local region over which we average observations is called "the bandwidth," and for this we use a statistical rule of thumb suggested by Silverman (1986). Instead of using a "triangle distribution" to weight observations within the bandwidth, we use weights determined by a normal (or Gaussian) distribution. The results do not depend on the specific choices we made in applying this estimation technique. The same analysis was performed using a generalized additive model using splines for the nonlinear components of the scale economy estimates, and the results are very similar.

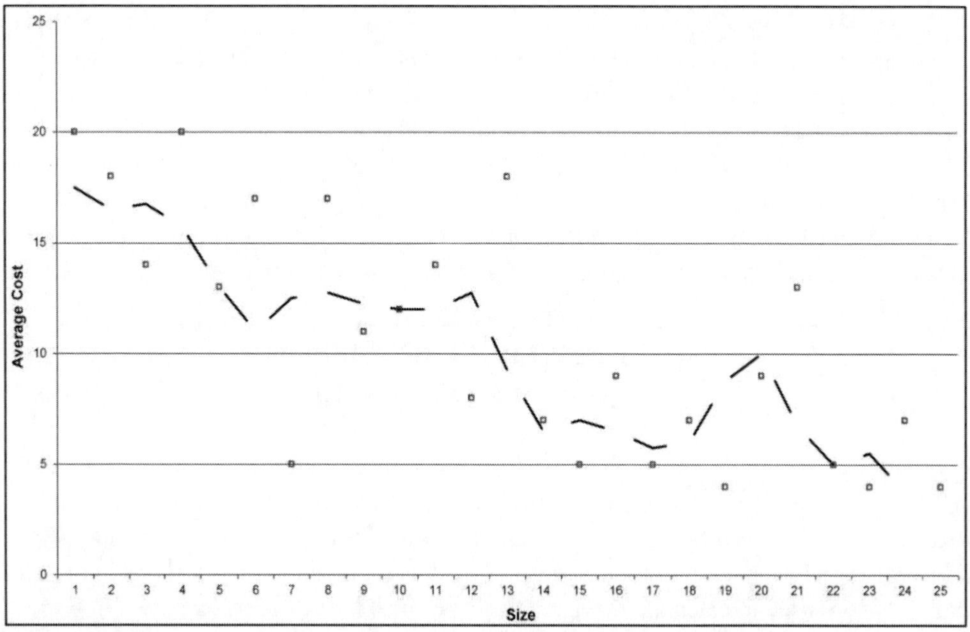

Source: FDIC.

Exhibit 5. Simplified Kernal Regression Example.

Figure 16a shows the estimated average cost as a function of bank asset size for CB mortgage lending specialists in 2006. The outer lines show the 95 percent confidence interval around the estimated conditional mean average cost. For mortgage lending specialists, these estimates provide evidence for economies of scale up to around $500 million in assets. The conditional mean average cost curve drops by about 150 basis points (bps) from the 6.25 percent average costs estimate for the smallest banks to around 4.75 percent for the large institutions. Even accounting for a 95 percent confidence level, the estimates show at least a small drop in average costs for larger institutions. Significant gains in efficiency (as measured by average cost) are exhausted by around $500 million in assets. Figure 16b shows a similar shape for the average cost curve in 2009 for CB mortgage specialists, but the estimated level of average costs declines somewhat more in 2009 for the largest banks. Still, accounting for the confidence bands around the average cost estimates, statistically significant benefits from scale economies for CB mortgage specialists are exhausted by about $500 million in assets.

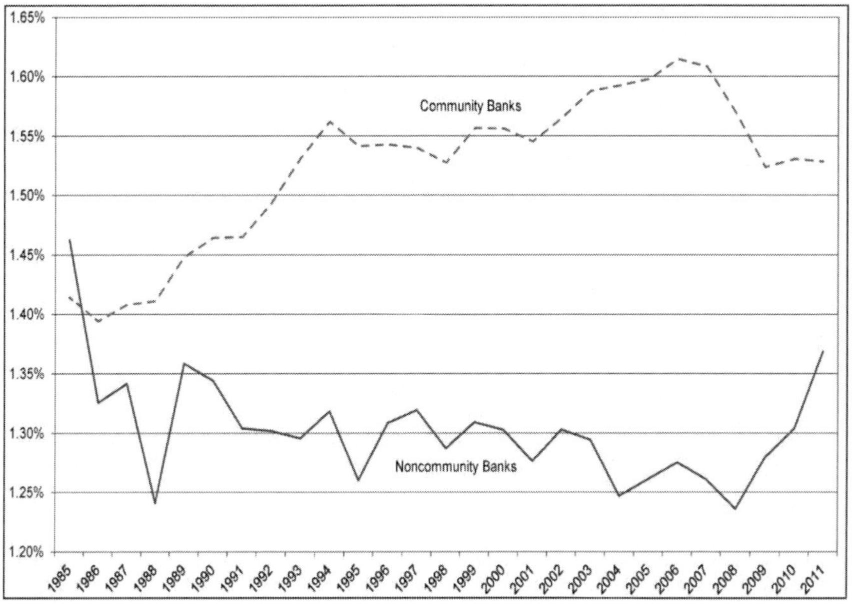

Source: FDIC.

Figure 15. Median Employee Expense-to-Asset Ratio at Community and Noncommunity Banks.

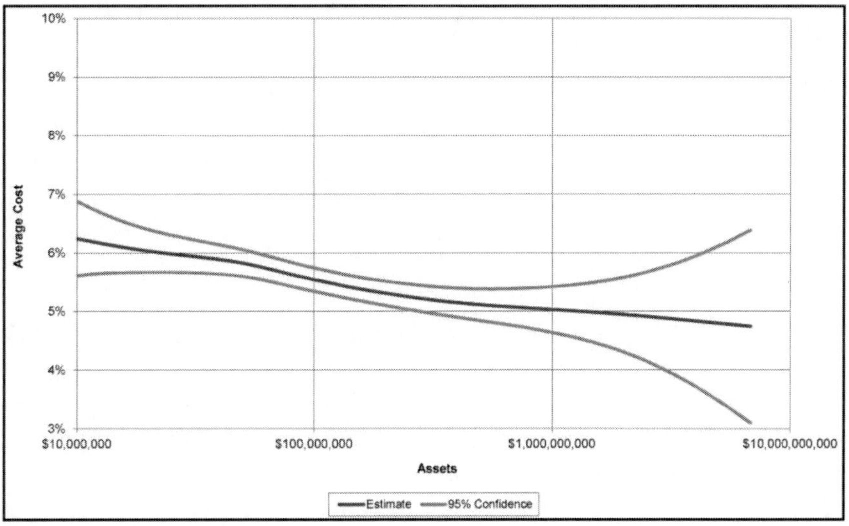

Source: FDIC.

Figure 16a. "Mortgage Lending Specialization" Estimated Average Cost Curve 2006.

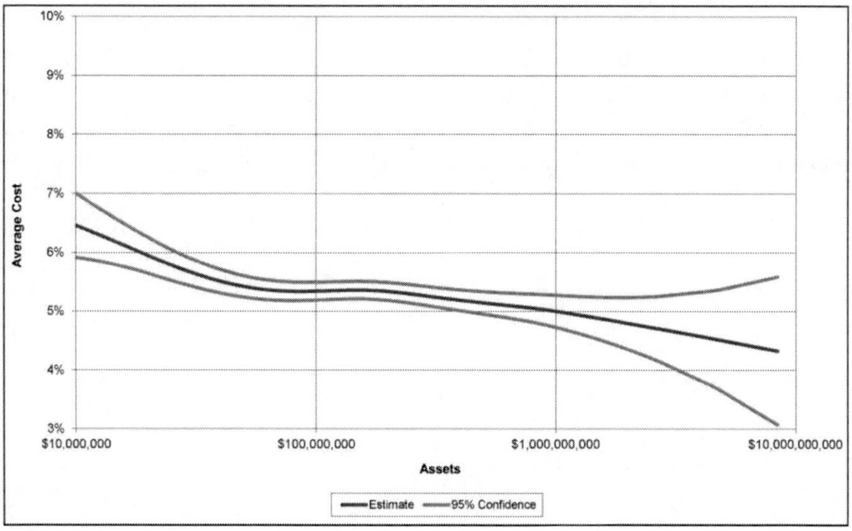

Source: FDIC.

Figure 16b. "Mortgage Lending Specialization" Estimated Average Cost Curve 2009.

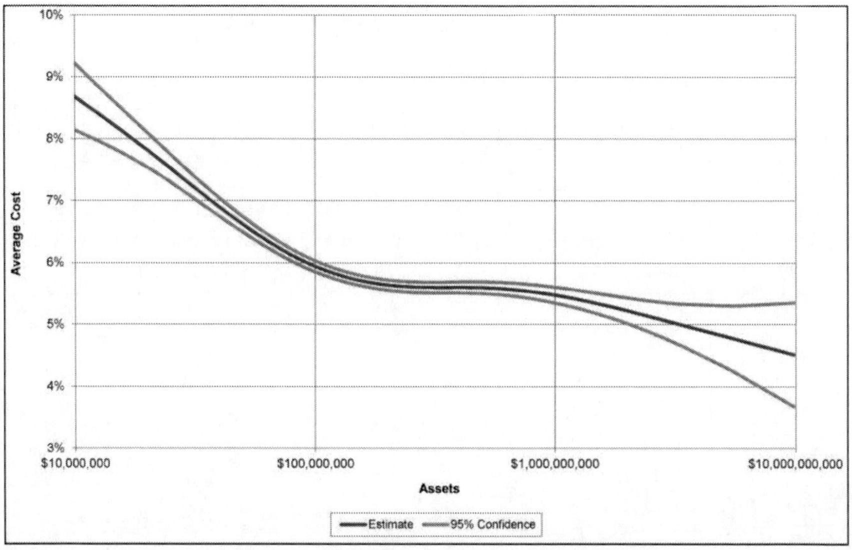

Source: FDIC.

Figure 17a. "Commercial Real Estate Lending" Specialization Estimated Average Cost Curves 2006.

In Figures 17 through 19, we show the results of the average cost curve kernel regression estimates for three other CB specialty groups. Among the specialist groups we examine, CRE specialists (Figure 17a and 17b) appear to have the largest potential benefit from economies of scale. Average cost estimates decline by about 400 bps between the smallest and largest lenders. Our estimates suggest little difference in average costs among banks between $100 million and $1 billion and only small additional economies of scale benefits beyond $1 billion. Overall, the estimates show that the majority of efficiency gains to scale are achieved by $100 million, with little significant average cost advantages above that level. Figure 17b shows crisis estimates for CRE specialists. Compared to 2006 estimates, CRE lending specialists had a substantially different cost structure in 2009. These changes are not surprising as the characteristics of CRE lenders were themselves altered by the crisis. The average cost estimate is flat above $500 million, suggesting no significant difference in the scale efficiencies among banks beyond $500 million in asset size.

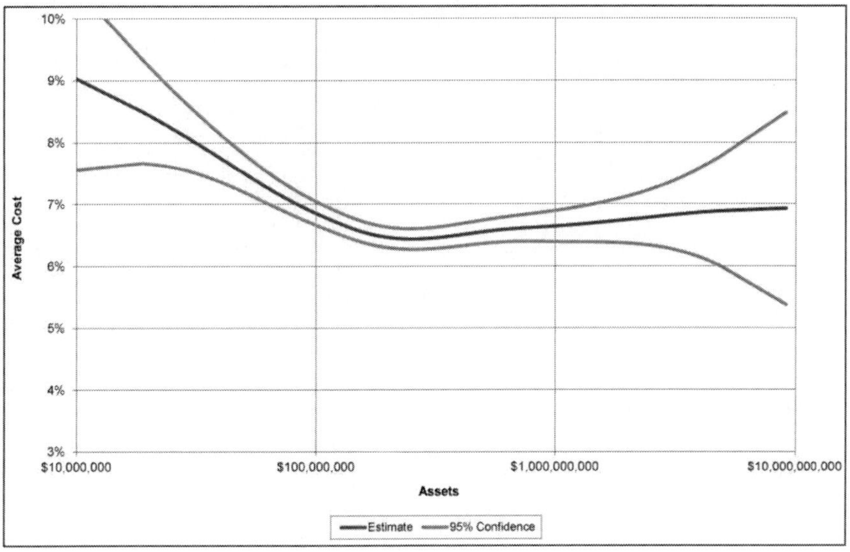

Source: FDIC.

Figure 17b. “Commercial Real Estate Lending” Specialization Estimated Average Cost Curves 2009.

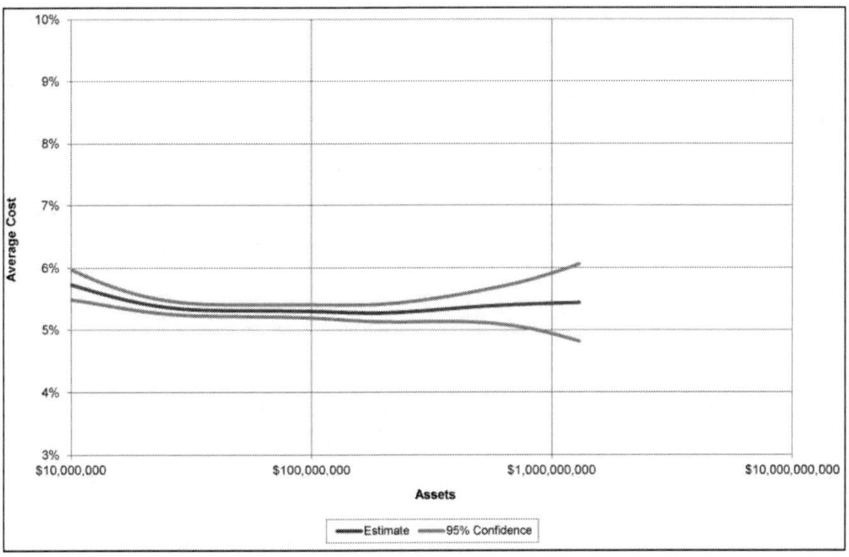

Source: FDIC.

Figure 18a. “Agricultural Lending” Specialization Estimated Average Cost Curves 2006.

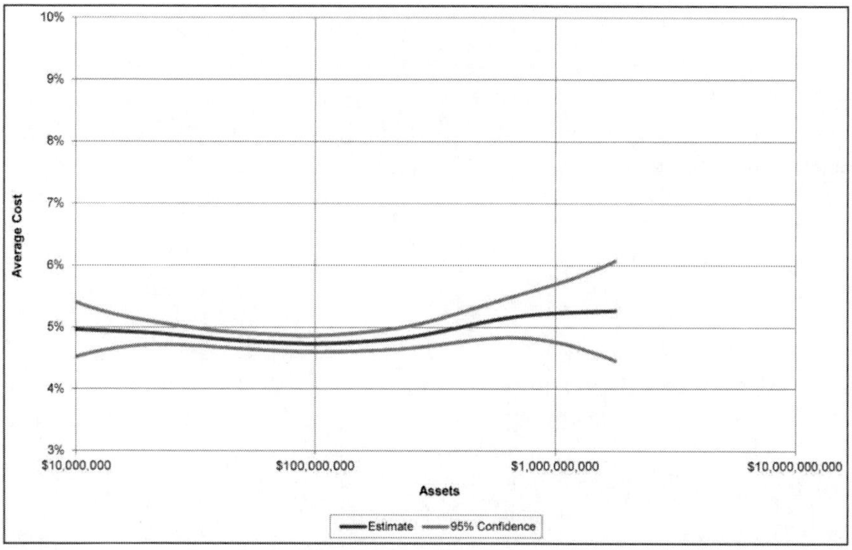

Source: FDIC.

Figure 18b. "Agricutural Lending" Specialization Estimated Average Cost Curves 2009.

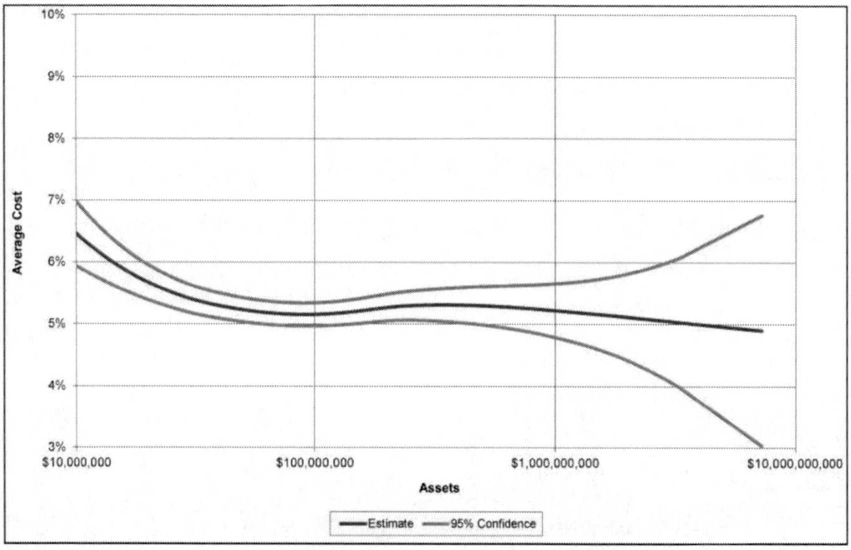

Source: FDIC.

Figure 19a. "No Specialty" Group Estimated Average Cost Curves 2006.

Figures 18a and 18b show the economies of scale estimates for CB agricultural lending specialists. For this group, there is little evidence of economies of scale. Figure 18a shows that estimated mean average costs differ very little from the smallest agricultural lenders to the largest. Further, the results indicate no statistically significant cost advantages beyond $100 million. Since the estimated cost curve is flat, agricultural specialists appear to have a smaller cost incentive to grow in terms of assets. Figure 18b shows estimates from 2009. The general shape of the average cost curve is similar to 2006, but the level of average cost decreases slightly at lower asset levels.

Figures 19a and 19b plot kernel regression estimates for the CB no specialty lending group. Figure 19a shows that the no specialty lending group had some statistically significant evidence of economies of scale in 2006. The estimated mean average cost drops by almost 150 bps at the largest banks compared with the smallest banks within this group. Taking statistical confidence into account, our estimates suggest that significant economies of scale are exhausted when an institution reaches about $100 million in assets.

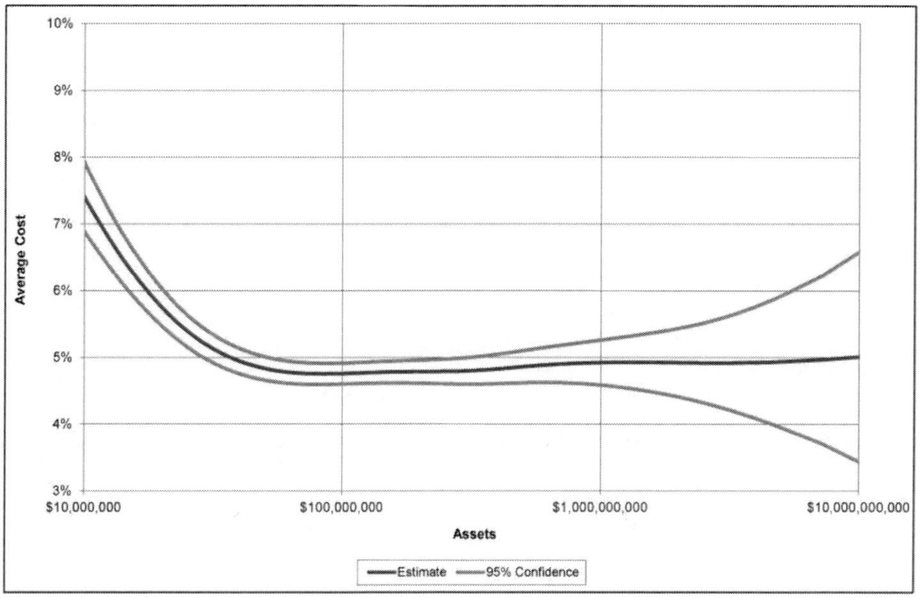

Source: FDIC.

Figure 19b. "No Specialty" Group Estimated Average Cost Curves 2009.

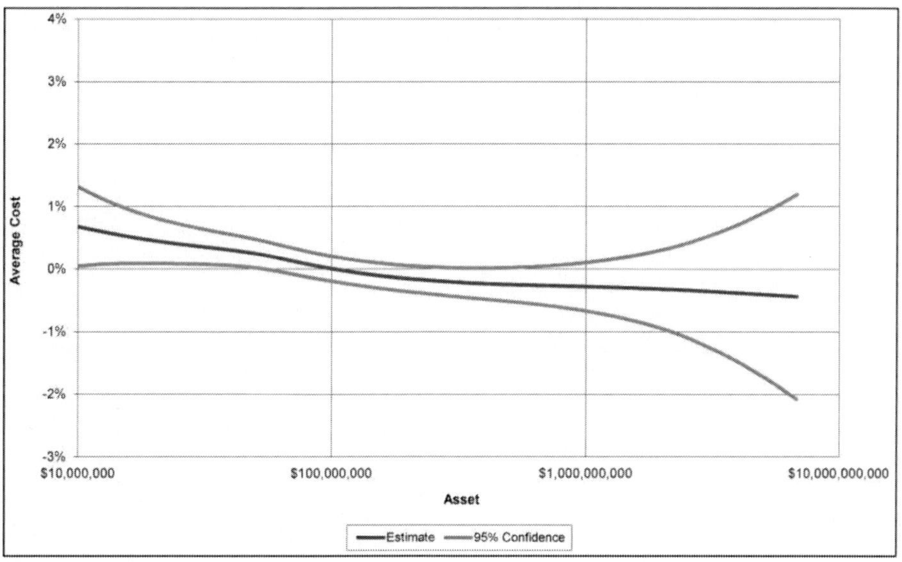

Source: FDIC.

Figure 20a. Average Costs Relative to the Regional Mean (2006) at Mortgage Lending Specialists.

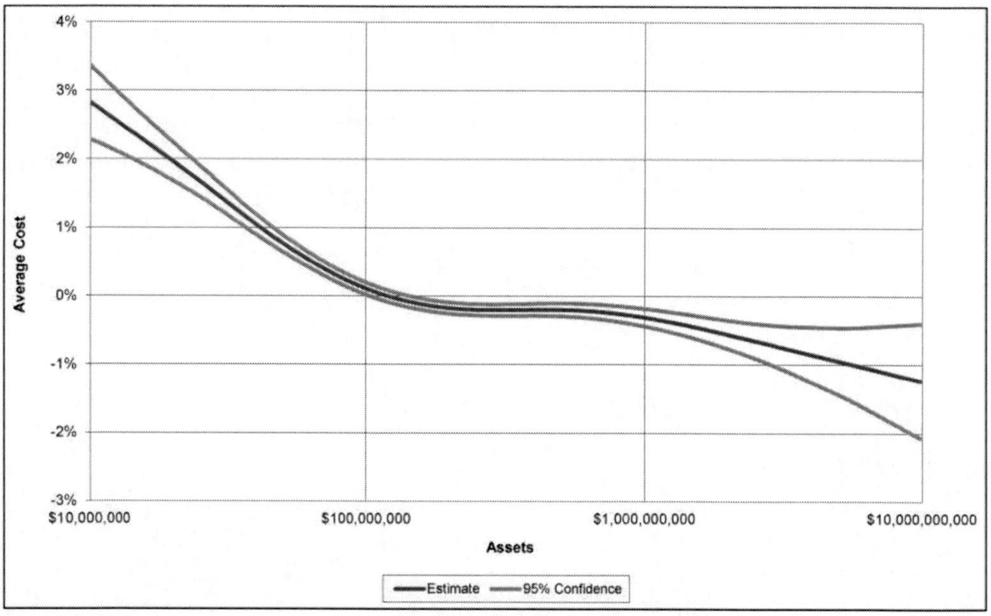

Source: FDIC.

Figure 20b. Average Costs Relative to the Regional Mean (2006) at Commercial Real Estate Lending Specialists.

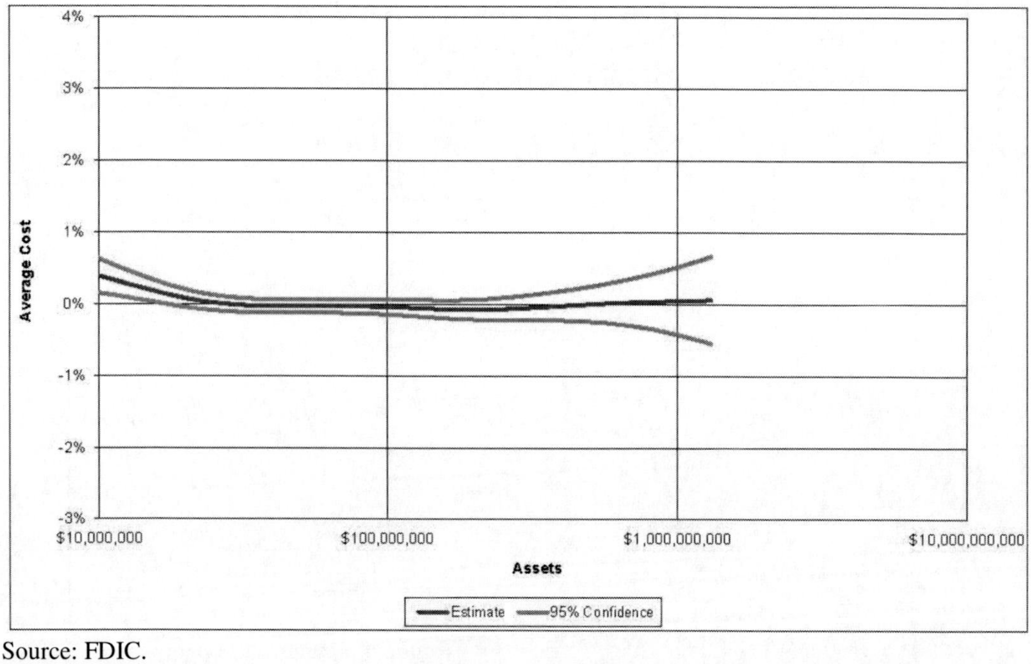

Source: FDIC.

Figure 21a. Average Costs Relative to the Regional Mean (2006) at Agricultural Lending Specialists.

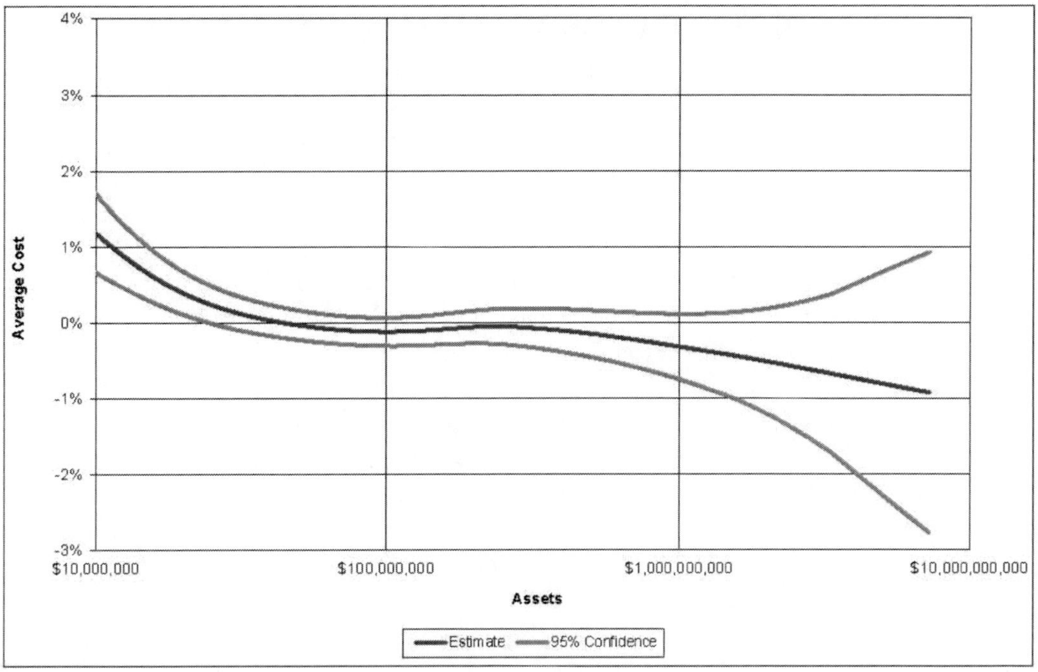

Source: FDIC.

Figure 21b. Average Costs Relative to the Regional Mean (2006) at the "No Specialty" Group.

DOES LOCATION AFFECT COST DIFFERENCES?

Just as costs of living vary across the nation, banks may have inherently higher operating costs in some regions of the country than in others. If operational costs vary by region in a systematic way, it may cause us to misestimate the potential for economies of scale in the prior analysis. For example, if smaller banks are more often located in more expensive areas of the country, they may appear to have higher average costs irrespective of any economies of scale and the previous analysis would overstate the importance of scale economies. In contrast, if large banks are more likely to be located in expensive regions, the importance of their true scale economies will be understated by the prior analysis.

We control for differences in the level of regional costs by subtracting the appropriate regional mean average cost from each observation. Figure 20 and Figure 21 show the relationship between size and average cost relative to regional average costs for different CB specialty lender categories in 2006 and 2009 respectively. These figures show economies of scale characteristics that are similar to those calculated in the prior analysis, even after we adjust for regional difference in costs. These results provide a check on our earlier analysis and show that our results for economies of scale are not distorted by the existence of a systematic relationship between bank size and location-specific costs characteristics.

Is There a Minimum Viable Size for a Community Bank?

The viability of small banks is an important issue within the community banking industry. Are there important economies of scale that push the smallest institutions to merge or exit the industry? While the estimates suggest that community banks do experience reductions in average cost as they grow in size, the importance of these economies of scale should not be overstated. The estimates indicate that most scale benefits are exhausted at asset levels far smaller than $1 billion, and for many specialty lender groups, much of the benefit can be achieved at a scale as small as $100 million.

While economies of scale may create incentives for community banks to grow toward $100 million in assets and beyond, economies of scale are probably not the most important factor that determines the viability of smaller institutions. Consider the size and growth history of all the CBs that have survived the last quarter century. Figure 22 plots the evolution of the size distribution of all CBs that existed in 1985 and survive through 2011; more than 60 percent of CBs (3,212) have weathered two banking crises and finished 2011 with less than $200 million in assets. Therefore, community banks of relatively modest size appear to be not only viable, but resilient. While a very few CBs grew to over $1 billion in asset size, about 85 percent of CBs (4,419 banks) that survived have less than $500 million in assets at year-end 2011.

Conclusion

This analysis has identified factors that help to explain why NCB and CB efficiency ratios have changed over time. Overall, a large part of the change in the relative efficiency of CBs versus NCBs can be explained by two general trends. First, CBs once held a distinct advantage in net interest income over community banks, which has since evaporated. On the expense side of the efficiency ratio, NCBs have been able to increase the amount of assets they manage per employee relative to CBs. While both CBs and NCBs have increased their salary expenses per employee, CBs have lost ground on employee expenses after accounting for productivity trends.

Finally, we estimate the average cost curve as a function of bank size for various CB specialty lender groups for two separate years: 2006, a very profitable year; and 2009, a crisis year. The results show that the average cost structure of banks varies across specialization groups. CRE specialists, in particular, exhibit potentially important economies of scale. In contrast, the agricultural lending group displays little potential for economies of scale. Further analysis shows that the estimates of relationship between size and average cost among lending specialties is not driven by regional differences in costs. Importantly, while the results show that community banks may benefit from economies of scale, there is no indication of any significant benefit beyond $500 million in asset size, and much of the benefits from scale appear to be achieved for CBs as small as $100 million. Large size and economies of scale are unlikely to be the most important factor in determining bank viability as analysis of the last quarter century of community bank data reveals that more than 60 percent of community banks that survived the last 25 years have less than $200 million in assets.

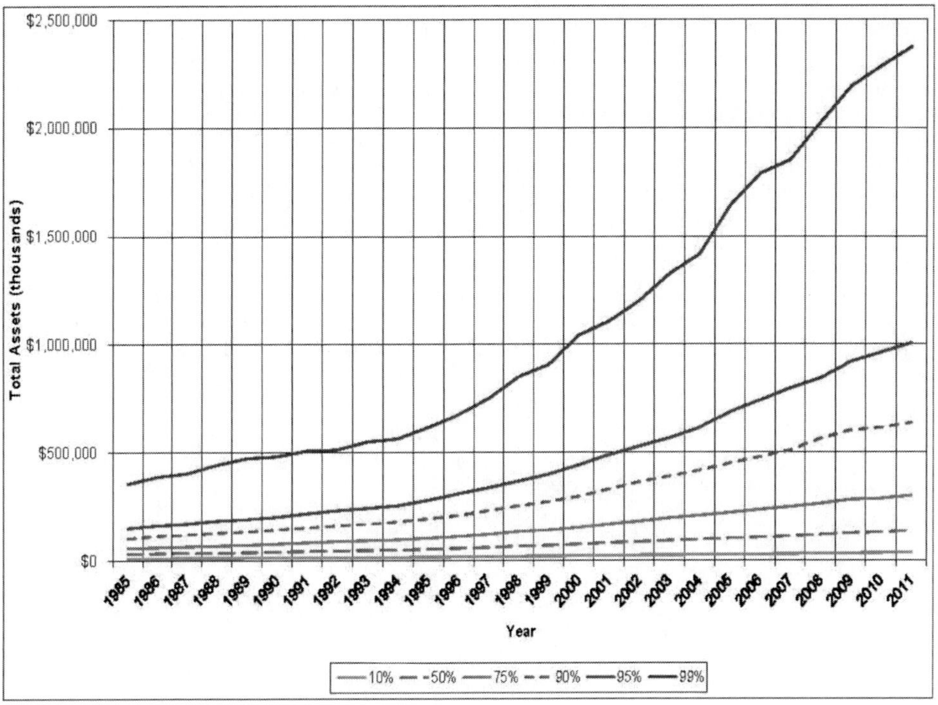

Source: FDIC.

Figure 22. Evolution of the Size Distribution of Surviving Community Banks.

REFERENCES

Berger, Allen, William Hunter & Stephen Timme. (1993). "The efficiency of financial institutions: A review and preview of research past, present, and future." *Journal of Banking and Finance*, *17*, 221-249.

Davidson, Russell & Emmanuel Flachaire. (2008). "The wild bootstrap, tamed at last." *Journal of Econometrics*, *146*, no. 1, 162-169.

Hughes, Joseph P. (2011). "*The elusive scale economies of the largest banks and their implications for global competitiveness*." Paper presented at the fourteenth annual banking conference, Federal Reserve Bank of Chicago, October.

Hughes, Joseph P. & Mester, Loretta J. (2011). "*Who Said Large Banks Don't Experience Scale Economies? Evidence from a Risk-Return-Driven Cost Function*," Federal Reserve Bank of Philadelphia Working Paper No. 11-27, July.

McAllister, P. H. & McManus, D. (1993). "Resolving the scale efficiency puzzle in banking." *Journal of Banking and Finance*, *17*, 389-405.

Silverman, Bernard W. (1986). *Density Estimation for Statistics and Data Analysis*. Vol. *26*. Chapman & Hall/CRC.

Wheelock, David C. & Wilson, Paul W. (2009). "*Are U.S. Banks Too Large?*" Federal Reserve Bank of St. Louis, Working Paper 2009-054B, revised December.

End Notes

[1] FDIC Community Banking Study, December 2012, http://www.fdic.gov/regulations.

[2] This figure and those that follow use the FDIC Community Banking Study research definition of CBs and NCBs.

[3] The median of a sum is not generally the sum of the medians. A similar analysis using means, after we remove outliers, produces results that are very similar to the results based on median values.

[4] See, for example, Hughes and Mester (2011), Hughes (2011), Wheelock and Wilson (2009) and references therein.

[5] Definitions of lending specialties can be found in the FDIC Community Banking Study.

[6] Confidence intervals for the average cost estimates are estimated using a bootstrap technique (with 1,000 bootstraps) described in David- son and Flachaire (2001). A bootstrap process estimates confidence intervals by re-sampling the actual data many times, at each stage producing a new random sample. For each new sample, the model's parameters are re-estimated. The distribution of the parameter values from these re-sampling estimates is used to construct confidence intervals for the model's parameter estimates.

In: Community Banks
Editor: Christopher B. Joseph

ISBN: 978-1-62618-906-5

Chapter 3

WHAT FACTORS EXPLAIN DIFFERENCES IN RETURN ON ASSETS AMONG COMMUNITY BANKS?*

Paul Kupiec and Yan Lee

INTRODUCTION

An important measure of bank profitability is return on assets (ROA). For banks with similar business risk profiles, pretax ROA is a useful statistic for comparing the profitability of banks because it avoids distortions that are introduced by differences in financial leverage and complications in the tax laws. We control for the differences in economic conditions among bank markets by focusing our analysis on community banks (CBs) that primarily operate in a single county.[1] Even among this select group of CBs, ROA displays wide variation both across banks within a quarter and among banks over time. Figure 1 plots average and median ROAs, and the difference between the 90th percentile and the 10th percentile of the ROA distribution for community banks that primarily operate within a single individual county for each year between 1994 and 2011.[2] NBER-designated recession periods are indicated by gray shading. Figure 1 shows substantial variation in average CB ROAs over time, as well as large and variable differences between strong and weak performing CBs in each year of the sample.

Figure 1 suggests that economic conditions in local and national banking markets are certainly important determinants of CBs' ROAs. To explore this further, we examine performance in both benign and crisis periods. Figure 2 is a map of the 2000Q2 average bank ROA by county, where the county averages are for banks that raised at least 75 percent of their deposits in a single county in that quarter. On average, 2000Q2 was a profitable quarter for many community banks; only a few counties have average ROAs that are negative.

Figure 3 is a map of average bank ROA by county from the population of banks that raised at least 75 percent of their deposits in a single county in 2009Q2. In contrast to

* This is an edited, reformatted and augmented version of the Federal Deposit Insurance Corporation, dated December 2012.

2000Q2, 2009Q2 was a period of earnings stress for many community banks and a significant share of counties had negative average CB ROAs. Compared with 2000Q2, far fewer counties have average ROAs higher than 60 basis points. Among counties with positive average ROAs in 2009, relatively few were located near the coasts where local market conditions deteriorated the most sharply. Figures 2 and 3 illustrate clear macro and regional economic patterns across time in banks' ROA data that must be accounted for when analyzing differences among CB bank ROA performance.

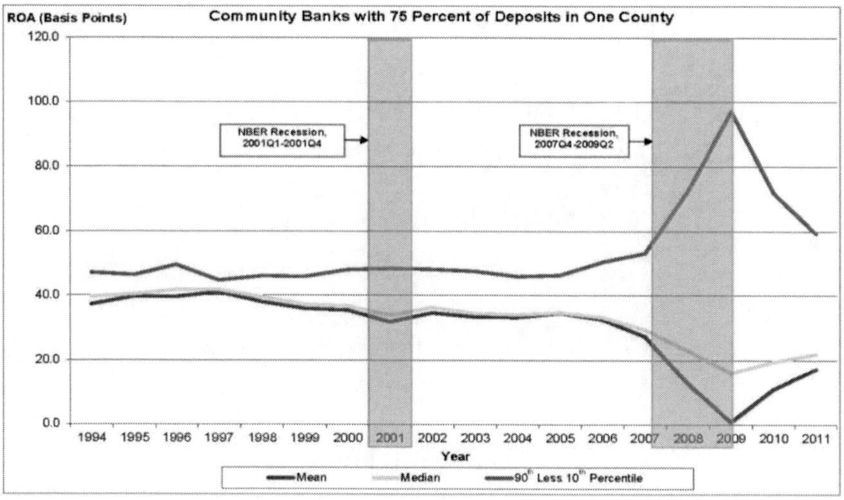

Source: FDIC.

Figure 1. Before Tax Return on Assets, by Year.

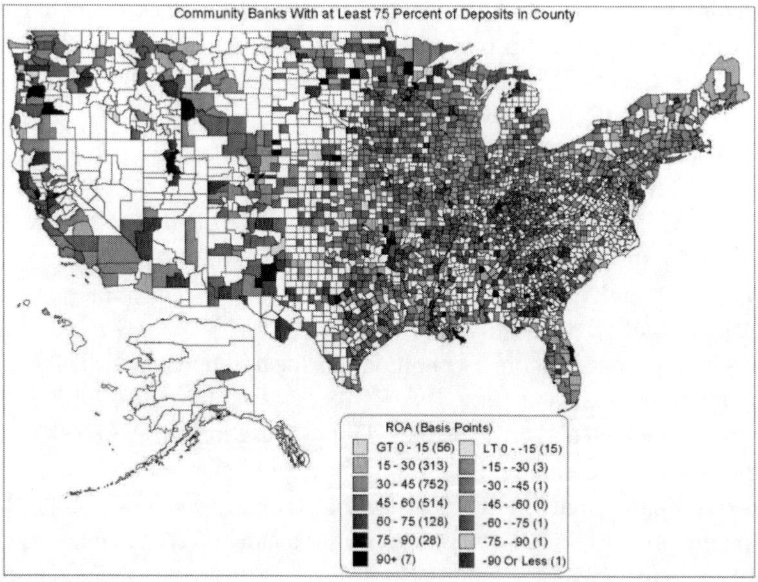

Source: FDIC.

Note: White indicates county not in sample.

Figure 2. Average ROA by County, 2000Q2.

IDENTIFYING FACTORS THAT EXPLAIN ROA

Many studies that investigate bank profitability are concerned with distinguishing between the effects of market concentration and bank efficiency on profitability (see for example, Smirlock [1985] and Berger [1995]). A standard economic paradigm argues that concentration leads to market power, which then allows banks to set prices and increase profits. An alternative explanation for a positive relationship between profits and market concentration is that concentration is a consequence of superior efficiency, which is the true cause of increased profitability. Typically, these studies measure concentration using a Herfindahl-Hirschman Index (HHI) of bank deposits, and the market is defined as a Metropolitan Statistical Area (MSA).[3] Overall, these studies find that market concentration is associated with increased profitability; however, the underlying causality (market power or efficiency) is in dispute. Other studies focus on the macroeconomic and institutional forces that determine bank returns across countries (see for example, Demirguc-Kunt and Huizinga [1999]). These studies find a positive association between concentration, measured at the country level, and bank profitability.

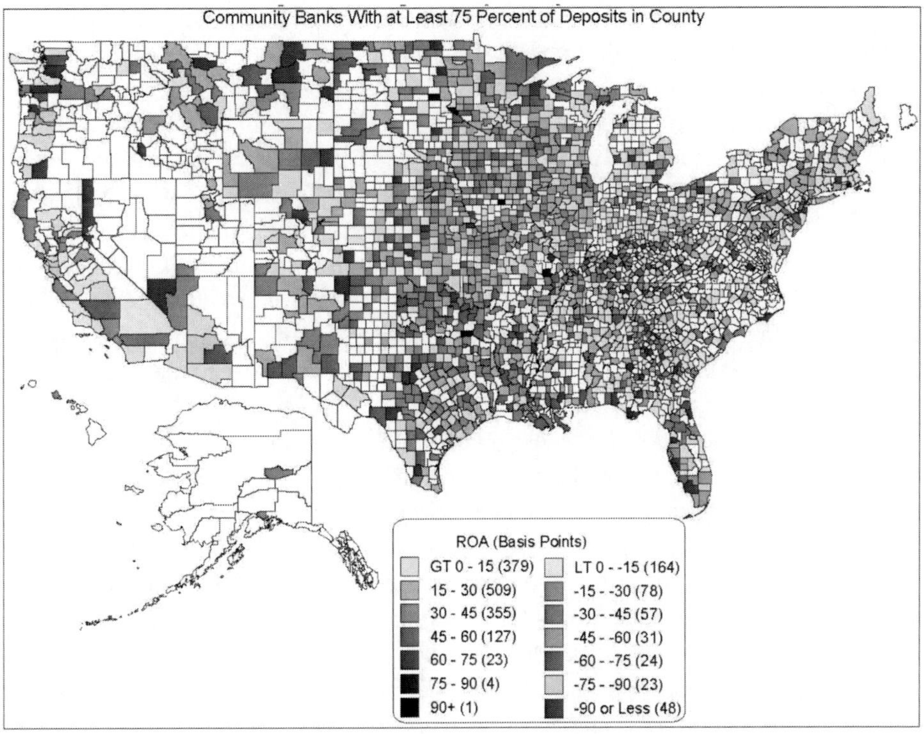

Source: FDIC.
Note: White indicates county not in sample.

Figure 3. Average ROA by County, 2009Q2.

In addition to the studies that focus on bank market power and profitability, Whalen (2001) and Hannan and Prager (2009) investigate whether the profitability of small community banks is affected by the presence of large multimarket financial institutions.

Whalen studies these effects using a sample of banks with total assets of $500 million or less that have at least 67 percent of their deposits in an MSA, in the 1995 to 1999 period. Hannan and Prager (2009) study the issue using a sample of banks with assets of less than $1 billion that derive at least 90 percent of their deposits from one MSA or non-MSA county, from 1996 to 2003. These studies find that the presence of multimarket financial institutions often lowers the profitability of community banks, but Hannan and Prager argue that this effect is only apparent in rural markets. Berger et al (2007) also finds this effect and posits that technological progress might be the driver of the multimarket bank effect.

While our methods are similar in some respects to Whalen (2001), Hannan and Prager (2009), and Berger et al (2007), we are primarily interested in distinguishing between the effects of management decisions and local economic conditions on the profitability of community banks. In order to identify true CB performance differences, we differentiate between factors that are within the control of a CB's management and factors that are mostly exogenous to the bank. For example, once a CB decides to locate in a particular area, for the most part, the economic conditions within its market area are exogenous factors that affect bank profitability. That is, in most situations it is probably reasonable to assume that a CB's operating behavior does not determine the economic conditions in its local market. While this scenario is possible in some unusual circumstances, we consider such cases to be exceptional, as our methodology necessarily assumes local market economic conditions are exogenous and not determined by the behavior of individual CBs.

To the extent that ROAs are generated by exogenous economic conditions, CBs' returns are attributable to the good luck of "being in the right place at the right time," and not to exceptional managerial skill. Still, among banks that face a favorable economic environment, some will perform better than others as a consequence of operational differences that are fully under the control of the CB's management. The ability to separate the component of bank returns that owe to good management decisions from those that are attributable to "luck" of location requires that we are able to identify the geographic market in which a CB operates and find variables that collectively provide good controls for the economic conditions that CBs face in their local markets.

In the analysis that follows, we use panel data regression techniques to identify the determinants of individual CB's ROAs. To control for macro economic conditions and demand for bank services in a CB's local market, we include in our analysis only community banks that undertake a majority of their business in a single market, which we define as a single county. While this sample selection criterion may not permit us to include some banks that operate primarily in large metropolitan areas that span multiple counties, it is necessary because we control for economic conditions using county-level economic statistics on the unemployment rate, the county house price growth rate, and the county delinquency rate on credit cards. We also control for quarterly time fixed effects.[4]

In addition to time variation in the economic environment, differences in bank ROA may also be attributed to differences in operational and business management choices, which may include bank underwriting standards, loan administration practices, loan growth, capital base, funding mix (including the use of noncore deposit funding), lending specializations, security investments, staffing and perhaps other factors that affect bank profitability. A bank's supervisory rating may also be correlated with its ROA. Over the longer term, ROA in the supervisory context is likely endogenous, meaning that the ratings take into account a bank's ROA along with other operating statistics and many other factors. In the short run, however, a bank's poor existing supervisory rating may be indicative of a limited ability to generate ROA, because these banks must take steps—which can often be costly— to improve the bank's condition, and may face operating restrictions or other requirements to implement remedial safety and soundness measures.

In order to control for local economic conditions that are assumed to be outside the control of bank managers, we select a sample of CBs whose markets are concentrated within a single county, within each quarter, and then control for quarterly measures of county and national level economic activity in a regression framework. We do so by estimating the share of deposits each CB raises in a county. County deposit shares are derived from annual FDIC SOD data, and county-level deposit share estimates for intervening quarters are estimated by merger-adjusting the prior June's SOD data over the following three quarters. Our data sample period begins when SOD data become available, 1994Q2, and ends in 2011Q4.

As a check of the robustness of our method for controlling for economic conditions, we select our CB sample using four different deposit share thresholds. In our largest sample, we select all CBs that raise at least 50 percent of their deposits within a single county. Three additional CB samples are pulled that increasingly focus on a single geographical area. In the second sample, a CB must raise at least 75 percent of its deposits within a single county to be included and identified with that county. The third and fourth samples use at least 90 percent and 100 percent as the respective county deposit share thresholds. The same estimation process is used for each of the four samples.

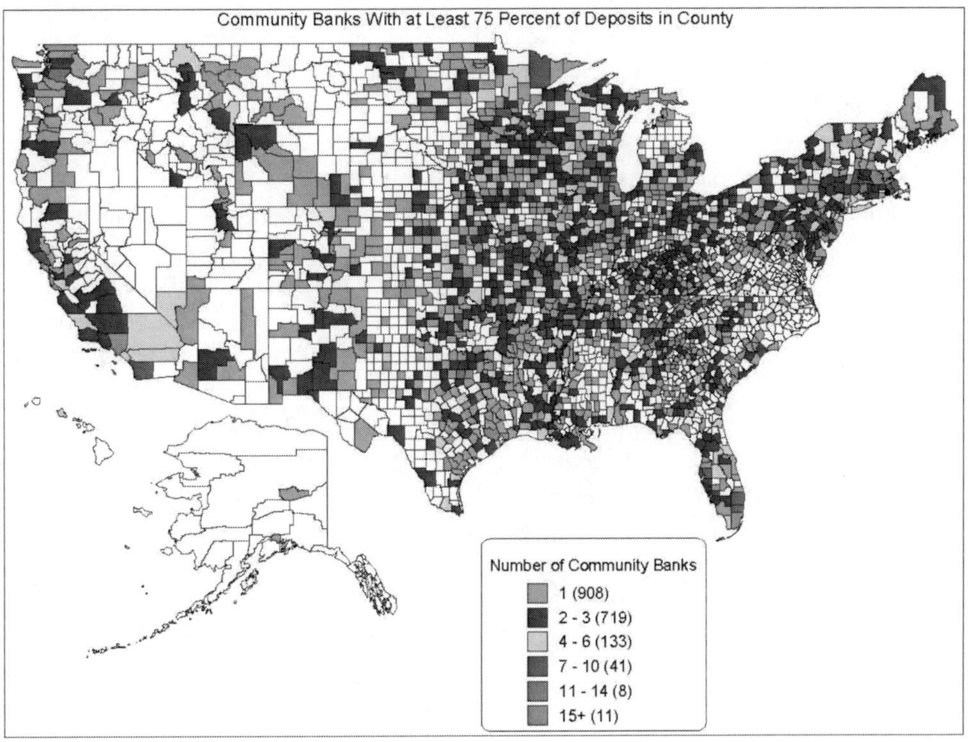

Source: FDIC.

Note: White indicates county not in sample.

Figure 4. Number of Sample Banks by County, 2000Q2.

As our deposit share threshold for sample inclusion increases from 50 percent to 100 percent, we trade off reduced sample size for a collection of banks with a more focused geographical market that will better enable us to control for the economic conditions CBs face in their local markets. The sample size associated with a 50 percent deposit threshold is more than 414,000 CB-quarter observations, whereas a 100 percent deposit threshold reduces the sample size to about 238,000 CB-quarter observations (see Table 1, Summary Statistics).

For illustration, Figure 4 is a map of the number of CBs in each county that meet the 75 percent deposit share threshold using 2000 SOD data. Counties that include multiple banks that satisfy the threshold requirement tend to be concentrated in the Midwest, Northeast and mid-Atlantic, California, Florida, eastern Texas, and Washington. While the geographic characteristics of the sample changes with each annual SOD report, the geographic location of sample banks remains broadly consistent with the pattern in the 2000Q2 SOD data.

EXPLANATORY VARIABLES AND REGRESSION MODEL SPECIFICATION

To control for market conditions in a CB's county, we include county-level unemployment rates, the share of credit card accounts within a county that are 60-days past due, the county-level home price index, the county-level HHI for bank deposits as a measure of local competition among banks for deposits, and quarterly time fixed effects to account for national variation in macroeconomic factors.[5] We expect unemployment and credit card delinquency rates to have negative effects on CB ROA and house price appreciation to have a positive effect. To the extent that concentration in deposit taking markets leads to market power in setting deposit rates and loan pricing, we expect the HHI concentration index to be positively related to bank ROA.[6]

In addition to county-level controls for local bank market conditions, we include bank-specific characteristics that may also in part determine CB ROA outcomes. We group our discussion of bank-specific controls according to whether the control variables are related to past loan growth, supervision, scale properties that may be associated with bank efficiency, bank asset quality, bank funding characteristics, and the bank's investment portfolio characteristics.

To control for differences in historical growth rates, we include lagged loan growth as a bank-specific control. However, the expected sign of the lagged loan growth coefficient is not tightly predicted by theory. Banks should expand lending when they identify positive net present value lending projects, and so high loan growth might be expected to generate high future bank ROAs as new loans season. Nevertheless, some historical experience suggests that above-average loan growth can be a leading indicator of elevated bank risk. For example, loan growth may be facilitated by relaxed underwriting standards, new lending product offerings, or new loans to customers without established bank relationships. To the extent that above average loan growth is facilitated by such practices, high loan growth may lead to high future loan losses and reduced bank ROA. A third possibility is a negative relationship between high prior loan growth and ROA if banks expanded by growing low-margin, low-risk loans. The upshot is that links between loan growth and subsequent ROA performance can arise for any number of reasons, and further analysis is required to understand the underlying transmission mechanism.

We include CBs' leverage capital ratios in the ROA regression. While the Modigliani and Miller (1958) theorem suggests that ROA should be independent of bank capital structure, a bank's capital structure may affect its measured ROA in a number of ways. The first reason for including leverage in the regression is that a bank's measured ROA is typically defined as net earnings before tax, which includes a deduction for interest expenses, divided by average assets. This way of measurement means that ROA will be positively related to the bank regulatory leverage ratio.[7] In addition to this measurement issue, bank leverage may be related to ROA for theoretical reasons. Because banks benefit from public safety nets, a large literature argues that weakly capitalized banks face incentives to magnify their risk-taking. In particular, weakly capitalized banks may enhance their profit by undertaking risky investments that offer high payoffs under the best of circumstances, but may generate losses under a wide variety of less positive economic conditions. To the extent that risk and return are positively related, this argument might suggest that banks with high leverage capital ratios (high equity-to-asset ratios) will invest in safer assets and have smaller ROAs on average. On the other hand, banks may maintain high equity buffers to protect profitable franchises and maintain lending capacity. Banks with high ROAs and potentially many profitable investment opportunities may decide to maintain high leverage ratios to maintain the capacity for profitable future growth. To summarize, economic theory does not uniquely predict the sign of the relationship between ROA and a CB's leverage ratio.

In addition to a bank's leverage ratio, we include dummy variables that indicate whether a bank is entering the period with a poor supervisory CAMELS rating.[8] At the conclusion of an on-site examination, supervisors assign a bank a CAMELS grade of 1 to 5, where 1 represents an exceptionally well-run institution (from a supervisory perspective) while 5 identifies an institution with serious safety and soundness deficiencies. By statute, small community banks must be examined at least every 18 months, and so CAMELS ratings may be up to 18 months old for some banks in some data quarters.[9] To account for potential ROA implications of a poor supervisory rating, we include separate dummy variables that indicate whether a bank's CAMELS rating was 3, or 4 or 5 in quarters prior to the quarter in which we measure ROA. Because of the related costs that may be required to remedy problem assets and other operational problems, to upgrade risk management systems and practices, and to implement other remedial measures, and because of the constraints that may be placed on banks experiencing problems, we expect poor CAMELS ratings to be associated with lower bank ROA.

We include the ratios of loans 30-89 days past due to bank assets and noncurrent loans (those 90 days or more past due or on nonaccrual) to bank assets as measures of bank asset quality. We expect these two variables to have a negative effect on bank ROA. We also include the standard deviation of a bank's charge-off rate over the lagging eight quarters as a sample-based measure of the riskiness of a bank's loan portfolio. If risk and expected return are positively related, and this variable is a proxy for bank loan portfolio risk, we might expect this variable to have a positive sign in the regression.

We also include a bank's average cost of funds (specifically the cost of funds-to-liabilities ratio), the ratio of its brokered deposits-to-assets, and its ratio of noncore funds-to-assets, to control for a bank's liability structure. We expect all these funding variables to be negatively related to a bank's ROA. In addition to controlling for CBs' cost of funds, we also control for banks' efficiency ratios. The efficiency ratio is defined as the ratio of noninterest expenses to revenues. High efficiency ratios suggest that a bank may be having difficulties controlling its noninterest costs and so we expect ROA to be negatively associated with bank efficiency ratios.

To control for potential economies of scale in community banks, we include the average value of deposits per bank branch, the average number of employees needed to manage a dollar of assets, bank size, size squared, size cubed and size to the fourth power, where bank size is measured by bank assets.[10] If community banks have important economies of scale, potentially we might find a positive coefficient on average deposits per branch, a negative coefficient of the number of employees used to manage a dollar of bank assets, and a positive coefficient on bank size, with a negative coefficient on the square of bank size under the anticipation that the marginal benefits of scale decline as the size of the bank increases.[11]

Finally, we include a number of bank-specific variables to measure the importance of a bank's mix of loans and other investments in determining its ROA. We control for a bank's total security-to-assets ratio and its total loans-to-assets ratio. We expect both of these variables to have a positive effect on bank ROA. Differences in a bank's lending concentrations are measured by including the CBs' commercial and industrial (C&I) loans-to-assets ratio, consumer loans-to-assets ratio, commercial real estate (CRE) loans-to-assets ratio, construction and land development (C&D) loans-to-assets ratio, and residential real estate loans-to-assets ratio. Because the banks' overall loans-to-assets ratio is included in the regression, the specialty loan concentration coefficients measure the differences between the ROA on a specific loan specialization relative to the ROA effect for nonspecialized lending.

FIXED EFFECT ESTIMATION AND CB ECONOMIES OF SCALE

Important estimation bias may be created when an important causal factor is omitted from a regression model. When the explanatory variables in the model are correlated with the omitted variable, the coefficient estimate of the variable included in the model will reflect both its own effect and the effects of the omitted factor. This bias is called "omitted variable bias."

The omitted variable problem is common in situations where the data set is repeated observations on cross-sections of individuals (e.g., families, firms, banks) over time—so called panel data. In this paper, we use data on individual CBs followed over time. One possible way to remove omitted variable bias in panel data is to change the regression model so that it allows each CB to have its own intercept term. The bank-specific intercept will measure differences across banks' ROA that do not vary over time. Since this method controls for "time-invariant" differences among banks, it is called a "fixed effect estimator," and it controls for omitted explanatory variables that are not expected to change over the sample period, such as a CB's management risk-taking preferences or its credit underwriting culture.

The use of bank fixed effects, while fully appropriate for our CB ROA analysis, creates an interpretation issue when we measure the importance of economies of scale. To better understand this issue, recall that in a simple regression model, the model coefficient estimates ensure that the regression line goes through the sample mean values. For example, if y is the dependent variable, X is the vector of independent variables, β is the vector of the independent variable coefficients, α is the model intercept, and ε is a vector of residuals, the regression model is,

$$y = \alpha + \beta X + \varepsilon.$$

The regression model coefficient estimates $(\hat{\alpha},\hat{\beta})$ will always ensure that the regression line goes through the sample mean values,

$$\bar{y} = \hat{\alpha} + \hat{\beta}\bar{X}.$$

From this relationship, it is easy to see the impact of a change in the independent variable values. If, for example, X takes on a value that is ΔX larger than the sample mean value X, then the dependent variable y will have a value that is $(\hat{\beta}\cdot\Delta X)$ larger than $\bar{y}$.

When bank fixed effects are introduced, the regression model coefficient estimates will ensure that the regression line goes through the sample averages for each bank. In other words, the regression model coefficient estimates will require

$$\bar{y}_i = \hat{\alpha}_i + \hat{\beta}\bar{X}_i$$

for bank i, and,

$$\bar{y}_j = \hat{\alpha}_j + \hat{\beta}\bar{X}_j$$

for bank j.

A consequence of this different restriction on the regression line is that the interpretation of the impact of a change in the value of the independent variables is now slightly different.

When the model includes fixed effects, if we increase each bank's independent variables by ΔX over its individual sample mean values of $\bar{X}_i$ and $\bar{X}_j$, then bank's respective dependent variables values are each expected to increase by $(\hat{\beta}\cdot\Delta X)$ relative to their individual mean values $\bar{y}_i$ and $\bar{y}_j$, which are generally different across banks when fixed effects are used to control for omitted unobserved factors. This difference of interpretation is important because we cannot use the coefficient estimates from the fixed effect estimator to establish an overall optimal bank size to maximize CB ROA. Instead, our estimates tell us how bank ROA will increase with bank size *relative to each bank's average sample size*. And so the fixed effects model estimates tell us whether a bank's ROA can be improved by growing larger than its own sample average size, but they do not tell us a single bank size that is optimal for all banks.

For example, the ROA effect of C&D lending is the sum of the coefficients on the bank's loans-to-assets ratio and its C&D loans-to-assets ratio.

The regression model is of the form:

$$\widetilde{ROA}_{it} = \alpha_i + \sum_{q=1}^{T} \varsigma_q Q_q + \sum_{h=1}^{H} \delta_h Markt_{iht} + \beta\, loan\, growth_{it-1}$$

$$+ \sum_{j=1}^{J} \gamma_j\, Sup_{jit-1} + \sum_{l=1}^{L} \eta_l AQual_{ilt-1}$$

$$+ \sum_{m=1}^{M} \kappa_m Fun_{imt-1} + \sum_{n=1}^{N} \lambda_n Scale_{int} + \sum_{p=1}^{P} \mu_p ACon_{pi-1t} + \tilde{\varepsilon}_{it}$$

where α_i is a bank-specific constant; Q_q ,$\{q=1,2,...,T\}$ are T quarterly fixed effect dummy variables; $Markt_{iht,}\{h=1,2,...,H\}$ are H factors that capture economic conditions in bank i's primary deposit-taking county at time t; $loangrowth_{it-i}$ is bank i's loan growth during period t-1; Sup_{ijt-1},$\{j=1,2,...,J\}$ are J supervisory factors for bank i at date t-1 (e.g., Tier 1 leverage ratio and CAMELS dummies); $AQual_{ilt-1}$,$\{l=1,2,...,L\}$ are L factors that measure bank i's asset quality at time t; Fun_{imt-1},$\{m=1,2,...,M\}$ are factors that measure bank i's funding characteristics at date t; $Scale_{int}$,$\{n=1,2,...,N\}$ are N factors associated with bank i's scale economies at date t; $ACon_{ipt-1}$,$\{p=1,2,...,P\}$ and are P factors that measure bank i's asset portfolio composition at date t. $\tilde{\varepsilon}_{it}$ is the regression error term for bank i at time t.

The regression model includes bank fixed effects to control for important time-invariant bank-specific omitted variables that may determine ROA. One example of an important omitted variable is the bank management's preferences for risk and return. The fixed effect estimation methodology corrects for this omission provided banks' risk preferences are unchanging over time. Time-varying bank-specific factors are lagged one quarter to minimize endogeniety.

SAMPLE CHARACTERISTICS AND EMPIRICAL RESULTS

Before selecting our four samples using the share of deposit thresholds in a single county, the data are adjusted to remove uncharacteristic institutions and outlier observations. We excluded institutions with no lending, and credit card banks, de novo and foreign banks.[12] We also excluded observations with missing data and observations with outlier or implausible values.[13] Sample summary statistics for each of the four samples, by county deposit threshold, appear in Table 1.

Table 1. Summary Statistics

Variable	50% of Deposits in County				75% of Deposits in County				90% of Deposits in County				100% of Deposits in County			
	Mean	Std. Dev.	Min	Max	Mean	Std. Dev.	Min	Max	Mean	Std. Dev.	Min	Max	Mean	Std. Dev.	Min	Max
Before Tax Return-on-Assets, 1-Qtr Lag (Basis Points)	29.4	36.3	-1,817	1,346.7	29.7	36.3	-1,817	1,346.7	29.9	36.2	-1,817	1,346.7	30.0	36.3	-1,817	1,164.9
Quarter-to-Quarter Loan Growth (Pct)	1.5	4.3	-11.3	18.8	1.5	4.4	-11.3	18.8	1.5	4.4	-11.3	18.8	1.5	4.5	-11.3	18.8
=1 if Composite Rating = 3, 1-Qtr Lag	0.07	0.26	0	1	0.07	0.25	0	1	0.06	0.25	0	1	0.06	0.25	0	1
=1 if Composite Rating = 4 or 5, 1-Qtr Lag	0.02	0.15	0	1	0.02	0.15	0	1	0.02	0.14	0	1	0.02	0.14	0	1
Leverage Capital Ratio, 1-Qtr Lag (Pct)	9.9	2.7	0.2	26.1	10.1	2.7	0.2	26.1	10.2	2.8	0.4	26.1	10.3	2.8	0.4	26.1
Past Due-to-Assets, 1-Qtr Lag (Pct)	0.9	1.0	0	59.9	1.0	1.0	0	59.9	1.0	1.0	0	59.9	1.0	1.0	0	59.9
Non-current-to-Assets, 1-Qtr Lag (Pct)	0.8	1.3	0	35.5	0.8	1.3	0	35.5	0.8	1.2	0	35.5	0.8	1.2	0	26.6
Charge-off Rate, 8-Quarter Standard Deviation, 1-Qtr Lag (Pct)	0.1	0.2	0	14.0	0.1	0.2	0	14.0	0.1	0.2	0	14.0	0.1	0.2	0	14.0
Cost of Funds-to-Liabilities, 1-Qtr Lag (Pct)	0.7	0.3	0	5.1	0.7	0.3	0	5.1	0.7	0.3	0	5.1	0.7	0.3	0	5.1
Brokered Deposits-to-Assets, 1-Qtr Lag (Pct)	1.5	4.8	0	88.2	1.5	4.9	0	88.2	1.5	4.9	0	88.2	1.4	4.8	0	88.2
Noncore Funds-to-Assets, 1-Qtr Lag (Pct)	18.3	10.2	0	92.5	18.0	10.3	0	92.5	17.7	10.3	0	92.5	17.4	10.2	0	92.5
Total Assets (2000 $Millions)	$178	$297	$1	$11,810	$154	$246	$1	$10,204	$131	$191	$1	$10,204	$111	$141	$1	$8,480

Table 1. (Continued)

Variable	50% of Deposits in County				75% of Deposits in County				90% of Deposits in County				100% of Deposits in County			
	Mean	Std. Dev.	Min	Max	Mean	Std. Dev.	Min	Max	Mean	Std. Dev.	Min	Max	Mean	Std. Dev.	Min	Max
Average Deposits Per Branch in County (2000 $Millions)	39.2	38.9	1.1	5,310.3	38.8	38.3	1.1	5,310.3	37.8	36.7	1.1	5,310.3	36.7	34.1	1.1	1,182.6
Number of Employees-to-Assets (2000 $Millions), 1-Qtr Lag	0.39	0.15	0.004	8.3	0.38	0.15	0.004	8.3	0.38	0.15	0.004	4.6	0.38	0.15	0.004	4.6
Efficiency Ratio, 1-Qtr Lag (Pct)	68.3	32.4	-3,432.4	12,454.6	68.1	33.6	-3,432.4	12,454.6	68.0	34.3	-3,432.4	12,454.6	68.0	35.6	-3,432.4	12,454.6
Securities-to-Assets, 1-Qtr Lag (Pct)	22.6	13.1	-44.4	93.4	23.1	13.3	-2.2	93.4	23.4	13.5	-2.2	93.4	23.5	13.6	-2.2	93.4
Total Loans-to-Assets, 1-Qtr Lag (Pct)	65.2	13.0	1.7	99.0	64.6	13.2	1.7	99.0	64.2	13.4	1.7	99.0	63.9	13.5	1.7	99.0
Consumer Loans-to-Assets, 1-Qtr Lag (Pct)	6.2	5.9	0	82.1	6.2	6.0	0	82.1	6.3	6.0	0	82.1	6.4	6.1	0	82.1
Commercial & Industrial Loans-to-Assets, 1-Qtr Lag (Pct)	9.0	7.2	0	83.7	9.0	7.2	0	83.7	9.0	7.3	0	83.7	8.9	7.3	0	83.7
Construction & Land Devel-opment Loans-to-Assets, 1-Qtr Lag (Pct)	4.5	6.3	0	95.7	4.3	6.2	0	95.7	4.2	6.1	0	95.7	4.0	6.0	0	95.7
Commercial Real Estate Loans-to-Assets, 1-Qtr Lag (Pct)	12.8	10.1	0	87.3	12.4	10.0	0	87.3	12.1	9.9	0	87.3	11.7	9.8	0	87.3
Residential Real Estate Loans-to-Assets, 1-Qtr Lag (Pct)	22.8	16.2	0	97.5	22.8	16.2	0	97.5	22.6	16.2	0	97.5	22.5	16.4	0	96.5

Variable	50% of Deposits in County				75% of Deposits in County				90% of Deposits in County				100% of Deposits in County			
	Mean	**Std. Dev.**	**Min**	**Max**	**Mean**	**Std. Dev.**	**Min**	**Max**	**Mean**	**Std. Dev.**	**Min**	**Max**	**Mean**	**Std. Dev.**	**Min**	**Max**
County Unemployment Rate (Pct)	5.7	2.5	0.6	37.5	5.7	2.5	0.6	37.5	5.6	2.5	0.7	37.5	5.6	2.5	0.7	37.5
County Credit Card 60 Days DQ Rate (Pct)	2.6	1.3	0	100	2.6	1.3	0	100	2.6	1.3	0	100	2.6	1.3	0	100
County HPI Growth Rate (Pct)	0.1	2.4	-21.3	19.0	0.1	2.4	-21.3	19.0	0.1	2.4	-21.3	19.0	0.1	2.4	-21.3	19.0
County Deposit Share HHI	0.21	0.13	0.03	1	0.21	0.13	0.03	1	0.20	0.13	0.03	1	0.20	0.13	0.03	1
Share of Total SOD Deposits in County, for Cert	0.90	0.15	0.50	1.00	0.96	0.07	0.75	1.00	0.99	0.02	0.90	1.00	1.00	0.00	1.00	1.00
Share of Branches in County, for Cert	0.82	0.23	0.06	1.00	0.90	0.17	0.07	1.00	0.97	0.10	0.07	1.00	1.00	0.02	0.33	1.00
Total Number of Branches, for Cert	4.2	4.4	1	160	3.5	3.5	1	68	3.0	2.7	1	47	2.6	2.1	1	31
N				414,843				333,148				270,598				238,122

The regression results appear in Table 2, where the coefficient estimates are separated using shaded or white groupings to identify control variables associated with similar function, i.e., those that measure local market economic conditions, supervisory effects, asset quality factors, etc. The columns in Table 2 report regression results for the four different bank samples. In the column labeled "50," the sample includes all CBs with 50 percent or more of their deposits raised in a single county. In the column labeled "75," estimates are for the sample of CBs that raised at least 75 percent of their deposits in a single county. The columns labeled "90" and "100" include estimates based on samples in which at least 90 percent or 100 percent of bank deposits were raised in a single county.

Table 2. OLS Estimates, Quarterly Before Tax Return on Assets (in Basis Points)

County Percent SOD Share	50	75	90	100
Qtr-to-Qtr Loan Growth, 1-Qtr Lag (Pct)	-0.11*** (0.02)	-0.10*** (0.02)	-0.11*** (0.03)	-0.10*** (0.03)
=1 if Composite Rating = 3, 1-Qtr Lag	-8.59*** (0.48)	-8.34*** (0.53)	-8.26*** (0.60)	-8.22*** (0.66)
=1 if Composite Rating = 4 or 5, 1-Qtr Lag	-24.83*** (1.34)	-24.08*** (1.54)	-22.80*** (1.69)	-22.61*** (1.83)
Leverage Capital Ratio, 1-Qtr Lag	-0.22*** (0.08)	-0.31*** (0.10)	-0.38*** (0.10)	-0.41*** (0.11)
Past Due Loans to Assets, 1-Qtr Lag (Pct)	-1.80*** (0.18)	-1.82*** (0.20)	-1.88*** (0.20)	-1.87*** (0.20)
Non-current Loans to Assets, 1-Qtr Lag (Pct)	-6.36*** (0.21)	-6.24*** (0.24)	-6.17*** (0.27)	-6.00*** (0.28)
Charge-off Rate Standard Deviation over 8-Qtrs (Pct)	-1.72** (0.84)	-0.98 (0.92)	-0.77 (1.00)	-0.34 (1.05)
Cost of Funds to Liabilities, 1-Qtr Lag (Pct)	-38.08*** (1.44)	-38.92*** (1.57)	-39.52*** (1.76)	-39.39*** (1.71)
Brokered Deposits to Assets, 1-Qtr Lag (Pct)	-0.33*** (0.04)	-0.31*** (0.05)	-0.32*** (0.06)	-0.26*** (0.06)
Noncore Funds to Assets, 1-Qtr Lag (Pct)	-0.02 (0.02)	-0.04 (0.02)	-0.05* (0.03)	-0.07** (0.03)
Efficiency Ratio, 1-Qtr Lag (Pct)	-0.06** (0.03)	-0.06* (0.03)	-0.05 (0.03)	-0.04 (0.03)
Assets (2000 $Mills)	0.00 (0.00)	0.01 (0.00)	0.01*** (0.00)	0.02*** (0.01)
Assets (2000 $Mills), 2nd Order	-0.00 (0.00)	-0.00 (0.00)	-0.00*** (0.00)	-0.00** (0.00)
Assets (2000 $Mills), 3rd Order	0.00* (0.00)	0.00 (0.00)	0.00** (0.00)	0.00* (0.00)
Assets (2000 $Mills), 4th Order	-0.00* (0.00)	-0.00 (0.00)	-0.00* (0.00)	-0.00 (0.00)
Avg Deposits Per Branch in County (2000 $Mills)	0.04*** (0.01)	0.04*** (0.01)	0.04*** (0.01)	0.04*** (0.01)
Number of Employees to Assets (2000 $Mills), 1-Qtr Lag (Pct)	-19.20*** (2.81)	-22.16*** (3.25)	-24.92*** (3.55)	-27.97*** (3.55)
Securities-to-Assets, 1-Qtr Lag (Pct)	0.43*** (0.02)	0.43*** (0.02)	0.43*** (0.03)	0.43*** (0.03)
Total Loans-to-Assets, 1-Qtr Lag (Pct)	0.78*** (0.03)	0.76*** (0.04)	0.76*** (0.04)	0.76*** (0.04)
Consumer Loans-to-Assets, 1-Qtr Lag (Pct)	-0.16*** (0.04)	-0.16*** (0.05)	-0.17*** (0.06)	-0.18*** (0.06)

County Percent SOD Share	50	75	90	100
Commercial and Industrial Loans-to-Assets, 1-Qtr Lag (Pct)	-0.09** (0.03)	-0.09** (0.04)	-0.08* (0.05)	-0.06 (0.05)
Construction and Land Develop. Loans-to-Assets, 1-Qtr Lag (Pct)	-0.13*** (0.04)	-0.09* (0.05)	-0.08 (0.06)	-0.07 (0.06)
Commercial Real Estate Loans-to-Assets, 1-Qtr Lag (Pct)	-0.06* (0.03)	-0.06* (0.03)	-0.04 (0.04)	-0.03 (0.04)
Residential Real Estate Loans-to-Assets, 1-Qtr Lag (Pct)	-0.09*** (0.03)	-0.09** (0.04)	-0.09** (0.04)	-0.08* (0.04)
County Unemployment Rate (Pct)	-0.69*** (0.07)	-0.72*** (0.08)	-0.74*** (0.09)	-0.73*** (0.09)
County Credit Card 60 Days DQ Rate (Pct)	-0.81*** (0.14)	-0.81*** (0.15)	-0.92*** (0.18)	-0.81*** (0.18)
County HPI Growth Rate (Pct)	0.38*** (0.05)	0.35*** (0.05)	0.31*** (0.06)	0.28*** (0.06)
County Deposit Share HHI	5.17*** (1.96)	3.72 (2.62)	4.84 (2.96)	4.89 (3.21)
Constant	-8.92** (3.84)	-6.45 (4.24)	-4.79 (4.53)	-4.90 (4.55)
Bank Fixed Effects	Y	Y	Y	Y
Quarterly Fixed Effects	Y	Y	Y	Y
Cluster By County	Y	Y	Y	Y
N	414843	333148	270598	238122
R-sq	0.44	0.44	0.45	0.45
County Percent SOD Share	50	75	90	100
F-Statistic for Test:	0.7	0.0	0.0	0.0
C&I = Construction & Land Dev (CLD)				
Prob > F =	0.39	0.96	0.91	0.90
Comm Real Estate (RE) = Res RE	0.9	1.0	1.7	1.0
Prob > F =	0.34	0.33	0.19	0.31
CLD = Res RE	0.9	0.0	0.1	0.0
Prob > F =	0.33	0.92	0.79	0.89

Note: Robust standard errors in parentheses; * p <0.10, ** p<0.05, ***p<0.01.
Source: FDIC.

The regression model estimates are, for the most part, very similar across the different county share deposit thresholds.[14] While the 100 percent sample ensures that banks face, as near as possible, identical local market conditions, banks in the 50 percent sample react similarly to the variables that control for county-level economic conditions. Across the samples, the county-level unemployment rate and credit card delinquency rate are both negative and statistically significant determinants of bank ROA. County-level house price appreciation is positive and statistically significant. The county's HHI index for bank deposits, however, while positive across samples, is significant for only the 50 percent sample.

Above-average bank loan growth in prior quarters is negatively associated with bank ROA. We have estimated specifications with additional loan growth lags up to one year (results not reported) with similar results. Above-average loan growth on average has negative implications for future bank ROA. The negative loan growth result could be consistent with a number of explanations. One possible explanation is that underwriting standards are relaxed to achieve higher growth. An alternative explanation might be that high-growth banks expand into lower margin lending businesses without taking on higher-risk loans. The panel regression analysis does not distinguish among these or other possible explanations.

Tier 1 leverage ratios are negative and statistically significant, indicating that higher leverage ratios are associated with smaller bank ROAs. This result is consistent with better capitalized banks on average investing in lower-risk assets. The regression results also show that an existing supervisory CAMELS composite rating of 3, or 4 or 5 is negative and statistically significant. An existing CAMELS composite rating of 4 or 5 is, on average, associated with an ROA that is more than 22 basis points smaller than a CAMELS 1 or 2 rated bank.

Asset quality is an important determinant of bank ROA. Two measures of asset quality, past-due and noncurrent loans, are both negative and statistically significant. This suggests that, controlling for economic factors, solid underwriting and loan administration practices favorably affect ROA. The standard deviation of bank charge-off rates over the past eight quarters is negative, but statistically significant for only the 50 percent sample. From this analysis, it is difficult to interpret the meaning of the charge-off volatility coefficient estimate. Since it is only significant for the 50 percent sample, it may be a proxy for omitted factors that measure economic conditions in the more geographically diverse markets in which these banks operate.

The variables that measure bank funding characteristics are negative and statistically significant. Not surprisingly, after controlling for other factors, on average, having a higher cost of funds-to-total liabilities ratio is associated with lower bank ROA. Other things equal, a 1 percentage point increase in a bank's average cost of funds is associated with almost a 40 basis point decline in bank ROA. The use of brokered deposits is statistically significant and associated with lower bank ROA across all the samples, while the coefficients on the noncore-funds-to-assets ratio are negative, but gain significance only for the more geographically concentrated sample banks.

The variables that measure the potential for scale economies suggest that larger scale is associated with improved ROA. Higher average deposits per branch result in small incremental increases in ROA and more assets per employee also improve ROA. Both of these effects are statistically significant. For the smaller, more geographically concentrated banks of the 90 percent and 100 percent deposit share samples, the coefficient estimates for bank assets and higher powers of bank assets are statistically significant. The coefficient on assets is positive while the squared term is negative, indicating positive economies of scale that diminish as bank size increases. We will examine the economies of scale relationship in more detail below. The coefficients on the efficiency ratio are negative, but statistically significant for only the two less geographically concentrated samples.

Variables that measure differences in CB investment portfolios are also statistically significant, indicating that they can help explain differences in CBs' ROA outcomes. On average, CB loans produced higher ROAs compared with CB security holdings. The coefficient on the loans-to-assets ratio is close to twice as large as the coefficient on the securities-to-assets ratio. Among the measures of loan specializations, on average over the entire sample period, controlling for local and national banking market conditions, all CB specialty lending categories experienced lower ROAs compared with uncategorized CB lending. Estimates suggest that the negative return component associated with C&I, C&D, and CRE lending diminishes as a bank's market is restricted to its headquarters county. Said differently, the negative effects of CRE and C&D lending on ROA are much more pronounced for the 50 percent sample, suggesting that banks with a more dispersed geographic market experienced poorer performance on their CRE and C&D lending activities, whereas this effect is not apparent for the other specialty lending categories. Among the loan specialization categories, estimates suggest that consumer loans offer the smallest ROAs. However, the bottom panel that presents F-statistics for tests of differences between coefficients shows that there does not appear to be statistically significant differences in the return offered by the different lending specialties.

Table 3. OLS Estimates, Quarterly Before Tax Return on Assets (in Basis Points) With Pre-Crisis and Crisis Interactions

	County Percent SOD Share			
	50	**75**	**90**	**100**
Total Loans-to-Assets, 1-Qtr Lag (Pct)	0.82*** (0.03)	0.81*** (0.04)	0.81*** (0.04)	0.81*** (0.04)
Consumer Loans-to-Assets, 1-Qtr Lag (Pct)	-0.19*** (0.04)	-0.20*** (0.05)	-0.22*** (0.06)	-0.22*** (0.06)
Commercial and Industrial Loans-to-Assets, 1-Qtr Lag (Pct)	-0.09*** (0.03)	-0.08** (0.04)	-0.09* (0.05)	-0.06 (0.05)
Construction and Land Develop. Loans-to-Assets, 1-Qtr Lag (Pct)	0.21*** (0.04)	0.22*** (0.05)	0.23*** (0.06)	0.24*** (0.06)
Commercial Real Estate Loans-to-Assets, 1-Qtr Lag (Pct)	-0.00 (0.03)	-0.01 (0.03)	0.01 (0.04)	0.03 (0.04)
Residential Real Estate Loans-to-Assets, 1-Qtr Lag (Pct)	-0.08** (0.03)	-0.10*** (0.04)	-0.10** (0.04)	-0.09** (0.04)
Consumer Loans-to-Assets, 1-Qtr Lag (Pct) *=1 if Year GE 2008	0.11* (0.06)	0.13* (0.07)	0.13** (0.07)	0.12* (0.07)
Commercial and Industrial Loans-to-Assets, 1-Qtr Lag (Pct) *=1 if Year GE 2008	-0.16*** (0.05)	-0.20*** (0.05)	-0.17*** (0.06)	-0.16*** (0.06)
Construction and Land Develop. Loans-to-Assets, 1-Qtr Lag (Pct) *=1 if Year GE 2008	-1.26*** (0.06)	-1.26*** (0.08)	-1.26*** (0.09)	-1.28*** (0.10)
Commercial Real Estate Loans-to-Assets, 1-Qtr Lag (Pct) *=1 if Year GE 2008	-0.13*** (0.03)	-0.11*** (0.04)	-0.11*** (0.04)	-0.13*** (0.05)
Residential Real Estate Loans-to-Assets, 1-Qtr Lag (Pct) *=1 if Year GE 2008	0.03* (0.01)	0.02 (0.02)	0.02 (0.02)	0.02 (0.02)
Other Baseline Controls	Y	Y	Y	Y
Bank Fixed Effects	Y	Y	Y	Y
Quarterly Fixed Effects	Y	Y	Y	Y
Cluster by County	Y	Y	Y	Y
N	414843	333148	270598	238122
R-sq	0.44	0.45	0.45	0.46

Note: Robust standard errors in parentheses; * p <0.10, ** p<0.05, ***p<0.01.
Source: FDIC.

Overall, the results in Table 2 suggest that higher bank ROAs are on average associated with traditional basic banking fundamentals: a business model based on lending (not security investments), with solid underwriting standards and loan administration practices that minimize nonperforming loans, and management attention focused on maximizing the use of core funding and minimizing overall funding costs. There appear to be some benefits from limited competition and economies of scale, and little evidence that specialization to any one particular type of lending increases bank ROA.

The ROA results regarding lending specialization may be unexpected since some of the specialization categories are often thought of as core CB businesses. For example, local C&D and CRE often are thought of as core business lines for community banks and it may be surprising that both of these categories yield ROAs that are less than generic (meaning no specialty designation) CB lending. We undertake additional analysis of the loan specialization ROAs by decomposing asset lending returns into a pre-crisis period (1994-2007) and a crisis period (2008-2011). The entire regression specification in Table 2 is repeated, with the addition of new variables that measure each lending specialization share interacted with a crisis period dummy variable. In Table 3 we report only the coefficient estimates associated with the lending specialty categories and suppress the coefficient estimates on the other control variables.

Table 3 reports the coefficient estimates for the lending specialization shares and the lending specialization shares interacted with the crisis period dummy variable. When the data are analyzed accounting for the crisis period, it is clear that C&D had larger expected ROAs than the other lending specializations in the period before the crisis. When the crisis hit, however, consumer and residential real estate lending at CBs performed better and produced higher ROAs compared with their pre-crisis averages, while CRE, C&I, and especially C&D loans performed much worse that their pre-crisis averages would have suggested. Among these specialization categories, C&D lending generates the greatest ROA variability between the pre-crisis and crisis periods. The characteristics of C&D lending suggest that it has been a high-risk, high-expected return lending specialty for CBs.

A Closer Look at CB Economies of Scale

The issue of economies of scale in community banking is important. If scale economies are only attained at substantial size, strong economic forces will encourage growth or continued consolidation among existing CBs. It is difficult to control for differences in CB market conditions, location, business model and operating characteristics and also accurately estimate the ROA effects associated with bank size alone. While the regression in Table 2 controls for many features that affect bank ROA, the equation also includes bank fixed effects to account for important time-invariant bank-specific factors that may affect bank ROA but are not measured or included in the regression. A fixed effect estimator removes the effect of omitted variables by removing the time series averages of each bank's ROA, and the averages of the CB's associated explanatory variables, before estimating the regression coefficients in Table 2. This procedure changes the interpretation of the size-related coefficient estimates in the regression. Using the fixed effects estimator, the coefficients on individual bank size indicate how much a CB's ROA changes as each bank's size is altered from its sample average size.

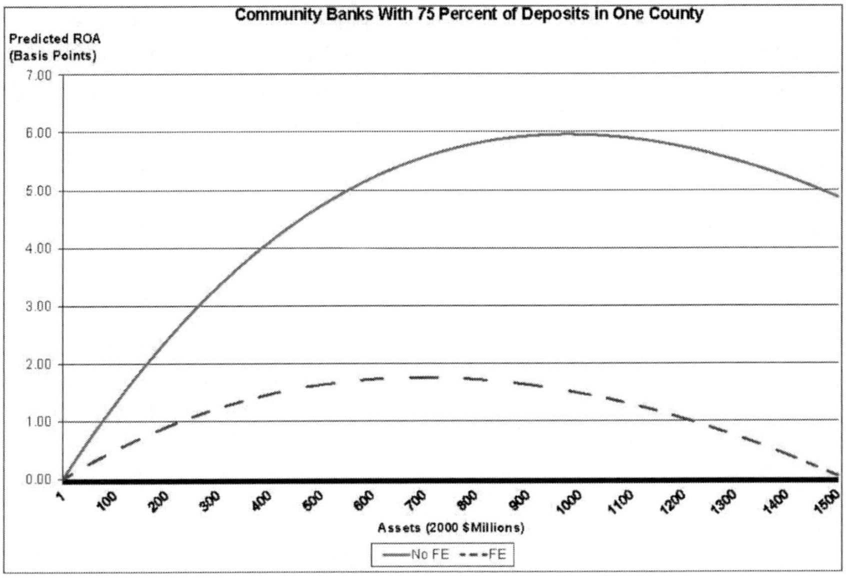

Source: FDIC.

Figure 5. No Fixed Effects versus FEs -Effect of Asset Size on ROA.

If the economies of scale potential for increasing asset size are very large when banks are very small and diminish as banks grow large, the fixed effects estimator cannot measure this phenomenon. Instead, the fixed effect estimator will measure the sample average effect of an increase in size relative to each bank's sample average size. If there are many very small banks in the sample and scale economies are important for very small banks, the fixed effect estimator is likely to show a large potential for ROA increase from an increase in bank size even if larger banks cannot accrue these benefits. The fixed effect estimator does not identify an overall average optimal bank size, but instead indicates a range over which each bank might increase (or decrease) its size (measured relative to its own sample average size) and experience positive (or negative) ROA effects.

An alternative method that can be used to estimate economies of scale is to run ordinary least squares (OLS) estimates without bank fixed effects while controlling for other important observable factors that affect bank ROA. This approach produces an estimate of the optimal size of the bank, but the estimate may be biased by omitting bank fixed effects. An underlying assumption is that the technology that generates ROA is fixed over the sample period. The resulting bank size-related coefficient estimates relate bank ROA to the actual asset size of a bank (and not to bank size measured as deviation from each bank's sample average size). If there are important bank-specific factors that are omitted from the regression but which are correlated with bank size and ROA, then the OLS estimator will give a biased estimate of the true size effect and attribute the combined effects of size and the omitted factors to size alone. As a consequence, omitted factors could impart a positive or negative bias to the size coefficient estimates. Still, given these caveats, the OLS estimator can provide a useful estimate of the economies of scale in CB ROA data.

Figure 5 plots the ROA-size relationship implied by the fixed effect and OLS estimator for the regression model specified in Table 2, for the 75 percent sample. The fixed effect, or "within" estimator, suggests that, on average, community banks in our sample could maximize their ROA by increasing their asset size above their sample average size by about $700 million; the mean size for this sample is $154 million. While the scale increase for achieving maximum ROA is large, the ROA effect—even at the optimum implied size—is less than 2 additional basis points (bps) over the bank's sample average ROA (about 30 bps per quarter over the sample period). In contrast, the OLS estimator suggests that the optimal size of a CB for maximizing ROA is roughly $1 billion, and the scale economies associated from going from a very small bank to a billion-dollar bank improve ROA by about 6 basis points. While 6 bps is large relative to the sample quarterly ROA average, our estimates suggest that 3bps of these efficiencies are achieved by about $300 million in assets, and about 5 bps are realized on average for CBs that reach $600 million. Overall, our results suggest that scale economies can improve CBs' ROAs up to about $1 billion in asset size, but a significant share of these benefits can be achieved at relatively modest scale.

CONCLUSION

Community banks exhibit substantial cross-sectional and time series variation in ROA. Much of the observed variation in CB ROA can be attributed to differences in the economic conditions CBs face in their local markets. We assume that economic conditions in a local banking market are exogenous, and use panel regression methods on a carefully selected sample of CBs to control for both variation in underlying economic conditions and in observable bank-specific characteristics. After controlling for economic conditions in CB local markets over time, we find that high ROAs are associated with above-average performance on operations and decisions that are basic to the banking intermediation process. Above-average ROAs are associated with higher loans-to-assets ratios, solid underwriting and loan administration practices that minimize delinquent and nonperforming loans, limited use of noncore deposit funding and lower overall funding costs. CB lending specializations do not generally improve ROAs over generalized lending. ROAs increase as bank size increases, but benefits likely diminish beyond about $1 billion in CB asset size, and CBs as small as $300 million appear able to secure half of the total available scale benefit. Above-average loan investment concentrations outside of a bank's primary market in commercial and industrial, construction and development, and commercial real estate loans are associated with lower ROAs during our sample period.

REFERENCES

Berger, Allen N. (1995). The Profit-Structure Relationship in Banking—Tests of Market-Power and Efficient Structure Hypotheses. *Journal of Money, Credit, and Banking*, *27*, no. 2, 404-431.

Berger, Allen N., Asli Demirguc-Kunt, Ross Levine & Haubrich, Joseph G. (2004). Bank Concentration and Competition: An Evolution in the Making. *Journal of Money, Credit, and Banking*, *36*, no. 3, 433-451.

Berger, Allen N., Dick, Astrid A., Goldberg, Lawrence G. & White, Lawrence J. (2007). Competition from Large, Multi-market Firms and the Performance of Small, Single-

Market Firms: Evidence from the Banking Industry. *Journal of Money, Credit, and Banking*, *39*, no. 2-3, 331-368.

Demirguc-Kunt, Asli & Harry Huizinga. (1999). Determinants of Commercial Bank Interest Margins and Profitability: Some International Evidence. *The World Bank Economic Review*, *13*, no. 2, 379-408.

Hannan, Timothy H. & Prager, Robin A. (2009). The Profitability of Small Single-market Banks in an Era of Multi-market Banking. *Journal of Banking & Finance*, *33*, no. 2, 263-271.

Modigliani, Franco & Merton Miller. (1958). The Cost of Capital, Corporation Finance and the Theory of Investment. *American Economic Review*, *48*, no. 3, 261-297.

Smirlock, Michael. (1985). Evidence of the (Non)Relationship between Concentration and Profitability in Banking. *Journal of Money, Credit, and Banking*, *17*, no. 1, 69-83.

Whalen, Gary. (2001). The Impact of the Growth of Large, Multistate Banking Organizations on Community Bank Profitability. Economic and Policy Analysis Working Paper 2001-5, Office of the Comptroller of the Currency.

End Notes

[1] Community banks are banks that satisfy the 2012 FDIC community bank research definition criteria. http://www.fdic.gov/regulationsresources.

[2] Banks are included in this sample if they raised at least 75 percent of their deposits in a single county in a quarter. County deposit shares are estimated from FDIC Summary of Deposits (SOD) data, which are collected annually in June. In quarters between SOD reporting dates, SOD data are adjusted to reflect mergers and acquisitions. SOD data are only available electronically from 1994. Throughout this paper, ROA references are on a pretax basis.

[3] The HHI is a commonly accepted measure of market concentration calculated by squaring the market share of each firm competing in the market and then summing the resulting numbers. The HHI measures the relative size distribution of the firms in a market and takes a value closer to zero when a market has a large number of approximately equal-sized firms and a maximum value of 10,000 when a market is controlled by a single firm.

[4] Quarterly time fixed effects allow the overall average bank ROA within a quarter to vary quarter by quarter. The variation in average bank ROA could be caused by macroeconomic factors that vary each quarter (for example, aggregate GDP growth) and affect all bank's ROAs in a similar direction.

[5] Our county-level unemployment rate is from the U.S. Bureau of Labor Statistics. House price growth rates are based on Case Schiller indices adjusted for inflation using the consumer price index for consumers less shelter. For counties without reported house price index (HPI) values, we substitute the state HPI. County-level data on percentage of credit card accounts more than 60 days past due are from Trendata. Among our county-level economic controls, for the 50 percent SOD sample, we have unique county-level data for 100 percent of observations on credit card delinquency rates, for 76.6 percent of observations on unemployment data, and for only 30.2 percent of observations on HPI values; the remaining values are filled with state-level values. The county-level HHI is based on all bank deposits in the county.

[6] This assumption that high HHI deposit concentration values may be an indication of monopoly powers is common in the bank market structure antitrust banking literature.

[7] This is because a higher bank leverage ratio implies less debt and lower interest expenses. While the text book definition of ROA is earnings before interest and taxes divided by assets, the convention is to use earnings before taxes, net of interest payments, divided by assets. This definition is used in the FDIC's *Quarterly Banking Profile*.

[8] Under the Uniform Financial Institutions Rating System (adopted by the Federal Financial Institutions Examination Council), each financial institution is assigned a composite rating based on an evaluation of six financial and operational components, which are also rated. These six components are: capital adequacy, asset quality, management capabilities, earnings sufficiency, liquidity position, and sensitivity to market risk. These component ratings are commonly referred to by their acronym, CAMELS. A bank's composite rating generally bears a close relationship to its component ratings. However, the composite rating is not derived by averaging the component rating. When assigning a composite rating, some components may be given more

weight than others depending on the situation at the institution. In general, assignment of a composite rating may incorporate any factor that bears significantly on the condition of the financial institution.

[9] We emphasize the temporal relationship between a CAMELS rating and the regression-dependent variable to stress that the bank's CAMELS rating is not endogenous in the ROA regression model specification.

[10] Each scale measure uses assets measured in millions of constant dollars (base year 2000).

[11] Size-cubed and the fourth power of size are included to allow for a flexible shape to the functional form that measures scale economies.

[12] We define de novo banks as banks newly chartered in the past seven years. It is well-known that de novo loan growth and earnings patterns are substantially different from mature institutions.

[13] The data quality filter excluded observations with: reported loans-to- assets ratios less than 0 or greater than 100 percent; negative reported cost of funds; negative reported capital ratios; negative reported employees or an extremely large number of employees relative to an institution's size; share of deposit data values that were grossly inconsistent with the institution's call report data and other similar screens. We also exclude institutions in the top 5 percent of capital ratios for the quarter, among all Call Report filers, to further eliminate banks that do not primarily focus on lending. Last, consistent with the methodology of the *Uniform Bank Performance Report*, we drop institutions in the bottom and top 5 percent in loan growth values, among all institutions, for each quarter.

[14] Standard errors are clustered at the county level to relax the assumption of independence across banks in the same county.

In: Community Banks
Editor: Christopher B. Joseph

ISBN: 978-1-62618-906-5

Chapter 4

STATEMENT OF DOREEN R. EBERLEY (DIRECTOR), BRET D. EDWARDS (DIRECTOR), RICHARD A. BROWN (CHIEF ECONOMIST), THE FEDERAL DEPOSIT INSURANCE CORPORATION. HEARING ON "STATE OF COMMUNITY BANKING: IS THE CURRENT REGULATORY ENVIRONMENT ADVERSELY AFFECTING COMMUNITY FINANCIAL INSTITUTIONS?"*

Chairwoman Capito, Ranking Member Meeks, and members of the Subcommittee, we appreciate the opportunity to testify on behalf of the Federal Deposit Insurance Corporation (FDIC) regarding the state of community banking and to describe the findings of the *FDIC Community Banking Study*, a comprehensive review based on 27 years of data on community banks.[1] We also welcome the opportunity to discuss the reviews by the Government Accountability Office (GAO) and the FDIC Office of Inspector General (OIG) of the causes of the recent financial crisis and the FDIC's supervision and resolution-related responses.

As the Subcommittee is well aware, the recent financial crisis has proved challenging for all financial institutions. The FDIC's problem bank list peaked at 888 institutions in 2011. Since January 2008, 469 insured depository institutions have failed, with banks under $1 billion making up 407 of those failures. Fortunately, the pace of failures has declined significantly since 2010, a trend we expect to continue.

The failure of a bank has the potential to be a highly disruptive event. While the FDIC protects insured depositors and resolves each institution in the least costly and least disruptive manner possible, the customers of a failed bank may still face the need to establish a new banking relationship that meets their financial needs. A bank failure also may be disruptive to a local community if the failure results in an adverse impact on the availability of credit or if distress sales of the failed bank's assets adversely affect local real estate prices.

* This is an edited, reformatted and augmented version of the testimony given on March 20, 2013 before the House Financial Services Committee, Subcommittee on Financial Institutions and Consumer Credit.

Given the challenges that community banks, in particular, have faced in recent years, the FDIC last year launched a "Community Banking Initiative" to refocus our efforts to communicate with community banks and to better understand their concerns. The knowledge gathered through this Initiative will help to ensure that our supervisory actions are grounded in the recognition of the important role that community banks play in our economy. A key product of the Initiative was the recently published *FDIC Community Banking Study*, which is discussed in more detail below.

Congress also enacted P.L. 112-88, which mandates comprehensive reviews by the GAO and by the FDIC OIG of the causes of the recent crisis, the supervisory response, and the resolution of failed institutions. Consistent with the *FDIC Community Banking Study*, the GAO and OIG reviews identify three primary factors that contributed to bank failures in the recent crisis, namely: 1) rapid growth; 2) excessive concentrations in commercial real estate lending (especially acquisition and development lending); and 3) funding through highly volatile deposits. By contrast, community banks that followed a traditional business plan of prudent growth, careful underwriting and stable deposit funding were much more likely to survive the recent crisis.

Our testimony discusses the findings of the *FDIC Community Banking Study*, as well as our assessment and response to the reviews by the FDIC OIG and the GAO.

FDIC Community Banking Study

In December 2012, the FDIC released the *FDIC Community Banking Study*, our comprehensive review of the U.S. community banking sector covering 27 years of data. The Study set out to explore some of the important trends that have shaped the operating environment for community banks over this period, including: long-term industry consolidation; the geographic footprint of community banks; their comparative financial performance overall and by lending specialty group; efficiency and economies of scale; and access to capital. This research was based on a new definition of community bank that goes beyond size to also account for the types of lending and deposit gathering activities and limited geographic scope that are characteristic of community banks.

Specifically, where most previous studies have defined community banks strictly in terms of asset size (typically including banks with assets less than $1 billion), our study introduced a definition that takes into account a focus on lending, reliance on core deposit funding, and a limited geographic scope of operations. Applying these criteria for the baseline year of 2010 has the effect of excluding 92 banking organizations with assets less than $1 billion while including 330 banking organizations with assets greater than $1 billion. Importantly, the 330 community banks over $1 billion in size held $623 billion in total assets – approximately one-third of the community bank total. While these institutions would have been excluded under many size- based definitions, we found that they operated in a similar fashion to smaller community banks. It is important to note that the purpose of this definition is research and analysis; it is not intended to substitute for size-based thresholds that are currently embedded in statute, regulation, and supervisory practice.

Our research confirms the crucial role that community banks play in the American financial system. As defined by the Study, community banks represented 95 percent of all

U.S. banking organizations in 2011. These institutions accounted for just 14 percent of the U.S. banking assets in our nation, but held 46 percent of all the small loans to businesses and farms made by FDIC-insured institutions. While their share of total deposits has declined over time, community banks still hold the majority of bank deposits in rural and micropolitan counties.[2] The Study showed that in 629 U.S. counties (or almost one-fifth of all U.S. counties), the only banking offices operated by FDIC-insured institutions at year-end 2011 were those operated by community banks. Without community banks, many rural areas, small towns and urban neighborhoods would have little or no physical access to mainstream banking services.

Our Study took an in-depth look at the long-term trend of banking industry consolidation that has reduced the number of federally insured banks and thrifts from 17,901 in 1984 to 7,357 in 2011. All of this net consolidation can be accounted for by an even larger decline in the number of institutions with assets less than $100 million. But a closer look casts significant doubt on the notion that future consolidation will continue at this same pace, or that the community banking model is in any way obsolete.

More than 2,500 institutions have failed since 1984, with the vast majority failing in the crisis periods of the 1980s, early 1990s, and the period since 2007. To the extent that future crises can be avoided or mitigated, bank failures should contribute much less to future consolidation. In addition, about one third of the consolidation that has taken place since 1984 is the result of charter consolidation within bank holding companies, while just under half is the result of voluntary mergers. But both of these trends were greatly facilitated by the gradual relaxation of restrictions on intrastate branching at the state level in the 1980s and early 1990s, as well as the rising trend of interstate branching that followed enactment of the Riegle-Neal Interstate Banking and Branching Efficiency Act of 1994. The pace of voluntary consolidation has indeed slowed over the past 15 years as the effects of these one-time changes were realized. Finally, the Study questions whether the rapid pre-crisis growth of some of the nation's largest banks, which occurred largely as a result of mergers and acquisitions and growth in retail lending, can continue at the same pace going forward. Some of the pre-crisis cost savings realized by large banks have proven to be unsustainable in the post-crisis period, and a return to pre-crisis rates of growth in consumer and mortgage lending appears, for now anyway, to be a questionable assumption.

The Study finds that community banks that grew prudently and that maintained diversified portfolios or otherwise stuck to their core lending competencies during the study period exhibited relatively strong and stable performance over time. Other institutions that pursued higher-growth strategies – frequently through commercial real estate or construction and development lending – encountered severe problems during real estate downturns and generally underperformed over the long run. Moreover, the Study finds that economies of scale play a limited role in the viability of community banks. While average costs are found to be higher for very small community banks, most economies of scale are largely realized by the time an institution reaches $100 million to $300 million in size, depending on the lending specialty.

These results comport well with the experience of banking industry consolidation since 1984, in which the number of bank and thrift charters with assets less than $25 million has declined by 96 percent, while the number of charters with assets between $100 million and $1 billion has grown by 19 percent.

With regard to measuring the costs associated with regulatory compliance, the Study noted that the financial data collected by regulators does not identify regulatory costs as a distinct category of noninterest expenses. In light of the limitations of the data and the importance of this topic in our discussions with community bankers, the FDIC conducted interviews with a group of community banks as part of our Study to try to learn more about regulatory costs. As described in Appendix B of the Study, most interview participants stated that no single regulation or practice had a significant effect on their institution. Instead, most stated that the strain on their organization came from the cumulative effects of all the regulatory requirements that have built up over time. Many of the interview participants indicated that they have increased staff over the past ten years to support the enhanced responsibility associated with regulatory compliance. Still, none of the interview participants indicated that they actively track the various costs associated with regulatory compliance, because it is too time-consuming, too costly, and so interwoven into their operations that it would be difficult to break out these specific costs. These responses point to the challenges of achieving a greater degree of quantification in studying this important topic.

In summary, the Study finds that, despite the challenges of the current operating environment, the community banking sector remains a viable and vital component of the overall U.S. financial system. It identifies a number of issues for future research, including the role of commercial real estate lending at community banks, their use of new technologies, and how additional information might be obtained on regulatory compliance costs.

Examination and Rulemaking Review

In addition to the comprehensive study on community banks, the FDIC also reviewed its examination, rulemaking, and guidance processes during 2012 with a goal of identifying ways to make the supervisory process more efficient, consistent, and transparent – while maintaining safe and sound banking practices. This review was informed by a February 2012 FDIC conference on the challenges and opportunities facing community banks, a series of six roundtable discussions with community bankers around the nation, and ongoing discussions with the FDIC's Advisory Committee on Community Banking.

Based on concerns raised in these discussions, the FDIC has implemented a number of enhancements to our supervisory and rulemaking processes. First, the FDIC has restructured the pre-exam process to better scope examinations, define expectations and improve efficiency. Second, the FDIC is taking steps to improve communication with banks under our supervision by using web-based tools to provide critical information about changes in regulations, including deadlines for submitting comments on proposed new rules. Finally, the FDIC has instituted a number of outreach and technical assistance efforts, including increased direct communication between examinations, increased opportunities to attend training workshops and symposiums, and conference calls and training videos on complex topics of interest to community bankers.

The FDIC plans to continue its review of examination and rulemaking processes, and is developing new initiatives to provide technical assistance to community banks, which we expect to introduce later this year.

REVIEWS REQUIRED BY P.L. 112-88

Under P.L. 112-88, the GAO was tasked with analyzing the causes and impact of a number of elements of the crisis, including: 1) the causes of high levels of bank failures in states with 10 or more failures since 2008; 2) the procyclical impact of fair value accounting standards; 3) the causes and potential solutions for the "vicious cycle" of loan write downs, raising capital, and failures; 4) an analysis of the community impact of bank failures; and 5) the feasibility and overall impact of loss share agreements.

P.L. 112-88 also tasked the FDIC's OIG with reviewing eight specific issue areas: 1) loss share agreements, otherwise known as shared-loss agreements (SLAs); 2) losses at failed banks; 3) examiner implementation of appraisal guidelines; 4) examiner assessment of capital adequacy and private capital investment in failing institutions; 5) examiner implementation of loan workout guidance; 6) the application and impact of formal enforcement orders; 7) the impact of FDIC policies on investments in institutions; and 8) the FDIC's handling of private equity company investments in institutions. The OIG subsequently reviewed and described FDIC compliance with applicable regulatory and supervisory standards in each of the eight areas.

The resulting GAO and OIG reviews were detailed and comprehensive, providing a wealth of information and data regarding the causes of the recent crisis and the FDIC's response. Although the GAO review did not include any recommendations, the OIG made several useful recommendations that are highly relevant to the FDIC's efforts to address the many issues arising from the crisis. The FDIC concurs with all of the OIG's recommendations and is now in the process of implementing them. Detailed descriptions of the FDIC's assessment of the issues identified by P.L. 112-88, the OIG's recommendations and the FDIC's implementation efforts are provided as an Appendix to this testimony.

CONCLUSION

The recent financial crisis has proved challenging for financial institutions in general and for community banks in particular. Analyses of bank failures during the crisis by the FDIC, its OIG and the GAO point to some common risk factors, including rapid growth, concentrations in high-risk loans, and funding through volatile deposits. In contrast, community banks that followed more conservative business models were much more likely to survive the crisis. The FDIC's extensive study of community banking over a 27-year period shows that while these institutions face a number of challenges, they will remain a viable and vital component of the overall U.S. financial system in the years ahead.

As mandated by statute, the GAO and the FDIC OIG conducted reviews that provided valuable information regarding the causes of the recent crisis and the FDIC's response. The FDIC welcomes the insights provided by the GAO and the OIG regarding the causes of the recent crisis. As described in the Appendix to this testimony, the review by the FDIC OIG also made a number of useful recommendations that the FDIC is now in the process of implementing. We believe that this type of analysis and policy review is an important element of our long-term efforts to maintain a safe and sound financial system and to effectively and appropriately respond when FDIC-insured institutions encounter financial distress.

APPENDIX

The discussions below correspond to the eight issue areas identified in P.L. 112-88 for review by the FDIC's Office of Inspector General (OIG). Each section includes a discussion of the key policy issues, any recommendations by the OIG and actions being undertaken by the FDIC to implement the recommendations.

Issue 1 -- Shared-Loss Agreements

When the Office of the Comptroller of the Currency (OCC) or a state banking regulator closes an FDIC-insured institution, federal law requires the FDIC to use the least costly method to resolve the failing institution. During the savings and loan and banking crisis of the late 1980s and early 1990s, the FDIC in most cases took control of the troubled assets of failed banks and managed them for eventual liquidation. Although the management of troubled assets in receivership met our statutory responsibilities in resolving failed banks, this strategy was found to have some serious shortcomings. Liquidating assets in receivership can result in significant disruptions for borrowers and surrounding communities, a diminution in the value of assets held under government control, and high losses to the insurance fund. In addition, the FDIC and the Resolution Trust Corporation had to employ over 20,000 people to manage and sell the assets from those bank failures.

An innovation introduced in the early 1990s was the shared loss agreement (SLA), in which the acquiring institution would assume all of the assets of the failed bank in exchange for a partial indemnification against future losses on troubled assets. Under a typical SLA structure, the FDIC would assume 80 percent of future losses on troubled assets, with the acquiring institution assuming the remaining 20 percent. While this partial indemnification against loss would induce risk averse acquirers to take on these troubled assets under private management, and thus keep them out of a government-controlled receivership, it also provided an incentive for the acquirer to maximize net recoveries on those assets – consistent with the fiduciary responsibility of the FDIC.

In the recent financial crisis, the FDIC has made much more extensive use of SLAs to facilitate the prompt transfer of failed bank assets to private management. SLAs were an essential tool to overcome the extreme uncertainty and risk aversion with regard to future loan performance and collateral values, especially early in the crisis. Almost 65 percent of the bank failures since the beginning of 2008 through 2012 were resolved through whole-bank purchase and assumption transactions with SLAs. As of December 31, 2012, the cost savings obtained through using whole-bank purchase and assumption transactions with SLAs, as opposed to more costly resolution alternatives, were projected to be approximately $41.1 billion

The goals of SLAs are to allow as many assets as possible to be kept in the private sector with a lending institution and to have the acquiring institution manage those assets under incentives that closely align the interests of the bank with the interests of the FDIC. Because an acquiring institution has financial exposure to the losses on assets purchased under this arrangement, it has an incentive to utilize a "least loss" strategy in managing and disposing of these assets.

SLAs also address the effect of bank failures on the local market by keeping more of the failed bank's borrowers in a banking environment. The acquiring institution can more easily work with the borrowers to restructure problem loans or to advance additional funding when prudent, helping to avoid a further decline in collateral values in the failed bank's market. Most importantly for the borrowers, the provisions of the SLAs entered into by the FDIC during this crisis require the acquiring institution to consider modifications for nonperforming loans in order to minimize unnecessary foreclosures.

Prospective bidders for failed institutions have the option to bid with or without an SLA. As expected, the number of failing bank resolution transactions conducted with SLAs has begun to decrease as the economy has recovered and as real estate markets have stabilized. In 2010, 130 of 157 bank failures, or 83 percent, were resolved using SLAs. Since then, both the number and percent of failed bank resolutions involving SLAs has declined steadily. In 2011, 58 out of 92 failed bank resolutions, or 63 percent, involved an SLA, as did 20 of 51 resolutions, or 39 percent, in 2012. None of the four failures so far this year was resolved using an SLA.

Term of Shared-loss Agreements

There are two primary types of SLAs, those applied to single family mortgage loans and those applied to non-single family loans. Single family SLAs have a term of ten years. Non-single family loan SLAs have a term of eight years, consisting of five years of shared-loss coverage followed by three years to allow for recovery payments to the FDIC on the assets for which a shared-loss claim was paid. The long term nature of the agreements is intended to allow for the acquiring institution to maximize the value of the failed bank's assets. As part of that process, banks work with distressed borrowers, attempting to reach a mutually beneficial resolution. The expiration of these agreements does not change the underlying incentives for the acquiring institution to develop new customer relationships and maximize net recoveries.

Management of Acquired Assets

The SLA requires the acquiring institution's best efforts to maximize recoveries. In satisfying this requirement, the acquiring institution is expected to consider every resolution alternative, including loan modifications. As such, acquiring institutions must undertake loss mitigation efforts prior to taking any foreclosure action. Additionally, the acquiring institution is required to manage and administer each loan covered under an SLA in accordance with prudent business and banking practices and in accordance with the acquiring institution's written internal credit policies and established practices.

The requirement for acquiring institutions to undertake loan modifications is subject to a financial analysis designed to ensure that qualifying borrowers are approved for modification and that such a strategy will maximize long-term recoveries. Because acquiring institutions generally share a portion of any losses, they share the FDIC's interest in pursuing modification in cases where it can be shown to maximize recoveries. Loss mitigation alternatives that increase the value of the loans will likely improve the affordability of the loan to the borrower and thereby lower the probability of default. Loan modifications can help borrowers preserve their stake in their homes and businesses. Collectively, these efforts to avoid foreclosures can help to preserve the viability of the community as a whole, which is also clearly in the best interest of an acquiring bank doing business in that community. All of these considerations point to a strong incentive on the part of the acquiring bank to avoid foreclosure or short sale and pursue a loan modification or restructuring whenever that alternative proves feasible.

Commercial Real Estate Loan Restructuring Requirements

On December 17, 2010, the FDIC issued *Commercial Loss Mitigation Guidance on Commercial Real Estate (CRE) Loans,* requiring acquiring institutions to pursue a disposition strategy other than foreclosure on a covered asset when an alternative strategy is projected to result in the least loss. For commercial loans that are restructured by an acquiring institution, the loss share reimbursement is based on the portion of a restructured loan that is categorized as a loss. Therefore, an acquiring institution may file a shared-loss claim on a commercial loan based on the market value of the underlying collateral without the need to foreclose.

Residential Mortgage Modification Requirements

SLAs also require the acquiring institution to implement a comprehensive loan modification program, such as HAMP or the FDIC Loan Modification Program, for single-family mortgages covered under the agreement. Modifications improve borrower affordability, increase the probability of performance, and allow borrowers to remain in their homes. Prior to any foreclosure action, the acquiring institution is required to perform and document a simple financial analysis to assess the feasibility of modifying a single family mortgage loan. If a qualified borrower accepts the modification offer, the bank can submit a shared-loss claim to the FDIC. One clear advantage for acquiring institutions to pursue modification is the ability to be paid sooner than might be the case in a foreclosure. Not only must the institution exhaust all loss mitigation options before foreclosure can proceed, but foreclosure and the sale of foreclosed property is a process that can take up to two years or more, depending on the state in which the property is located. Hence, the acquiring institution has a strong incentive to consider and engage in single family mortgage loan modifications where viable.

Monitoring of Shared-loss Agreements

The FDIC monitors compliance with the SLAs through quarterly reporting by the acquiring institution and through periodic reviews of the acquiring institution's adherence to the agreement terms. If the FDIC determines that an acquiring institution has not complied with the terms of the SLA, including the requirement to consider and engage in loan modifications, the FDIC will delay payment of shared-loss claims until compliance problems are corrected. The FDIC can deny payment of a claim altogether or indefinitely suspend payments for as long as the acquiring institution remains out of compliance with the agreement. The periodic reviews of the acquiring institution are completed onsite, and include: verifying the accuracy of shared-loss claims; ensuring compliance with loss mitigation efforts; testing the acquiring institution's policies and procedures to ensure uniform criteria are being applied to both shared-loss assets and the bank's own legacy assets; reviewing internal audit reports and the external independent public accountant reports to ensure that internal controls are in place; and verifying that adequate accounting, reporting, and recordkeeping systems are in place. Thus far, we have found that the overwhelming majority of acquiring institutions are diligent in their efforts to comply with all the terms of the SLAs.

OIG Recommendation

The OIG recommended that the FDIC develop a strategy for mitigating the impact of impending portfolio sales and SLA terminations on the Deposit Insurance Fund, and that it ensure that procedures, processes, and resources are sufficient to address the volume of terminations and potential requests for asset sales.

The FDIC agrees with this recommendation, and steps are being taken to meet its stated goals. At the same time, we believe that a number of factors, including the provisions of the SLAs themselves, will help to avoid the unnecessary sale of distressed assets and mitigate the market impact once the SLAs are terminated.

For example, the FDIC policy for portfolio note sales provides that: 1) the acquiring institution's right to conduct a portfolio sale is conditional and requires FDIC consent; 2) the evaluation of portfolio sales by the FDIC will include an analysis of alternative collection and modification strategies and a review to determine whether collections would be maximized on an asset-by-asset basis; 3) the FDIC's Loan Sale Advisory Review Committee will review all request for portfolio sales and large individual loan sales to ensure a consistent approach to the approval process; and 4) an acquiring institution is not to rely on portfolio sales as a primary resolution strategy for shared-loss assets.[3]

The FDIC has closely monitored and diligently enforced compliance with the SLAs. We believe that, as a result of our efforts in this regard combined with the aging of the portfolios, a relatively small portion of the original principal balance of non-single family assets covered under SLAs will remain outstanding when the shared-loss coverage periods on those agreements terminate. Since the inception of the program in 2008 through year-end 2012, the total covered principal balance for non-single family assets has already shrunk by over 60 percent, from approximately $139 billion to $54 billion. We project the total covered principal balance to shrink further to approximately $25 billion by the time the shared-loss coverage periods for the remaining non-single family SLAs expire. Furthermore, the majority of the shared-loss coverage periods on the outstanding non-single family SLAs are scheduled to expire over a four-year period (from 2014 to 2017) and over a wide geographic area. To the extent that the balances of covered assets have already declined, and that the expiration of the non-single family SLAs that cover these remaining balances will be spread out over a period of years and across different geographical regions, we do not expect the scheduled expiration of non-single family SLAs to have severe effects on local asset markets.

Some also have expressed the concern that, after the shared-loss coverage periods end, acquiring institutions will sell or otherwise dispose of non-single family assets at distressed prices. However, SLAs do not provide incentives for the acquiring institutions to engage in the "fire sale" of covered assets at the end of the shared-loss coverage period. As these agreements expire, the acquiring institutions will absorb 100 percent of all losses from below market sales or other dispositions, resulting in a hit to capital for these institutions. Further, the FDIC retains rights to recoveries on assets during the recovery period and, as a result, the acquiring institutions remain bound by the requirements of the SLA, including the requirement to maximize recoveries.

The FDIC has committed to conducting a full assessment of the sufficiency of its procedures, processes, and resources for the anticipated volume of portfolio sales and SLA terminations. The FDIC will complete the assessment and deliver its conclusions to the OIG by September 30, 2013.

OIG Recommendation

The second OIG recommendation was that the FDIC research the risks presented by commercial loan extension decisions and determine whether additional controls should be introduced to monitor the efforts of acquiring institutions to extend the terms of commercial loans. We agree with this recommendation.

The FDIC has established an internal national task force that is composed of staff from the Division of Resolutions and Receiverships and the Division of Risk Management Supervision to share information and proactively collaborate on topics such as concerns about shared-loss agreements. In addition, regular collaboration with regulators at the Federal Reserve Board (FRB), the OCC, and the Canadian Office of Superintendent of Financial Institutions has been established to ensure consistency and to facilitate open communication and information sharing throughout the term of the SLAs.

The FDIC is in the process of enhancing its Compliance Review Program to require the evaluation of loan amendments, including maturity date extensions, to ensure that they comply with the SLA provisions governing loan modifications. The goal of this effort is to ensure that any loan modification or refusal to modify a loan is consistent with maximizing recoveries and with the acquiring institution's policies and procedures with regard to legacy loans. Violations of the SLA will not be tolerated. If found, such violations could result in loans being removed from loss sharing and, when appropriate, the clawback of any claims paid by the FDIC. In addition, the Compliance Review Program will target high risk areas, such as sales of real estate owned, where assets could be liquidated in a manner that is inconsistent with prudent management standards and that fails to maximize collections.

The FDIC conducts targeted Loss Mitigation Reviews, which are undertaken in addition to our regularly scheduled compliance monitoring reviews and serve as a mechanism to directly communicate with acquiring institutions as to the requirements of the program. The acquiring institutions are reminded of the contractual obligations of the agreements and expectations for loan modification efforts, as well as the potential penalties for violations of the terms of the SLA. The reviews include, but are not limited to, inconsistent policies on commercial loan term extensions, violations of management standards and permitted amendment provisions, violations of internal bank policy and procedures, and actions that are inconsistent with maximizing collections.

In response to the OIG report, the FDIC has committed to reinforcing previous communications, requiring FDIC compliance monitoring contractors to review a sample of loan modification decisions for maturing loans, and analyzing the costs and benefits of collecting and monitoring trend information on commercial loan modifications. The FDIC will complete these actions and deliver its conclusions to the OIG by September 30, 2013.

Finally, the FDIC will continue to reach out to banks and other members of the public that may have concerns about the impact of the SLAs and their impending terminations. This type of communication will provide us with additional information on the potential issues that could arise as the shared-loss coverage period on the SLAs terminate, and enhance our ability to address these concerns in a timely fashion.

Issue 2 -- Losses at Institutions

According to Material Loss Reviews conducted by the OIG in the aftermath of bank failures, losses at community banks during the crisis were most often caused by management strategies of aggressive growth and concentrations in commercial real estate (CRE) loans, including notably, concentrations in acquisition, development and construction loans, coupled with inadequate risk management practices in an environment of falling real estate values that led to impairment losses on delinquent and nonperforming loans. Another common characteristic of failed banks was reliance on volatile brokered deposits as a funding source.

We are not aware of, and the OIG did not identify, any instances where a bank failed due to supervisor required write-downs of current loans – so-called "paper losses." When examiners classified loans considered current by bank management, the examiners did so for safety and soundness reasons in accordance with regulatory guidance on classification of loans.

In addition, the application of fair value accounting was not found to have had a significant effect on most community bank failures. Fair value accounting is most often applied to valuations of securities, and since most community banks classify debt securities as available for sale (AFS), the unrealized gains and losses on AFS securities do not impact regulatory capital under current rules.

OIG Recommendation

The OIG study of the losses that led to the failure of community banks during the financial crisis included no recommendations for the FDIC.

Issue 3 -- Appraisals

Interagency supervisory policy establishes that repayment capacity is the primary driver of examination classification decisions.[4] However, as the crisis unfolded, it became clear that the failure to follow prudent underwriting criteria had contributed to the inability of many borrowers to service their loans. For example, many residential borrowers experienced difficulty in making their payments when their monthly loan payment reset to a higher amount, and many commercial borrowers experienced similar financial difficulties due to diminished cash flows from lower sales or reduced operating income. As primary sources of loan repayment declined, lenders were increasingly forced to rely on the value of real estate collateral as a secondary source of repayment. Amid the real estate market distress triggered by the housing bust and resulting financial crisis, rising levels of nonperforming loans and subsequent foreclosures and distressed sales placed additional downward pressure on real estate prices. As the market value of many commercial and residential properties declined to levels below their original estimated value, the proper valuation of real estate collateral became a critical component of evaluating the condition of troubled banks.

Then, as now, the FDIC reviews the appraisal programs of supervised institutions through the analysis of individual appraisals during loan reviews and through the assessment of a bank's appraisal policies and procedures. Examiners use a risk-focused approach tailored to a lender's real estate lending activities and expand the depth of their review when the examination process identifies any areas of concern. The FDIC uses an exception-based process to document noncompliance with appraisal guidance, regulations, and the institutions' valuation program requirements. When no deficiencies are noted relative to the FDIC's appraisal regulations, current guidance requires that a statement to that effect be included in the examination documentation.[5] While the OIG's report found that examiners documented instances of noncompliance consistent with the FDIC's exception-based process, it also noted that examination documentation did not always include the required positive assurance statement.

OIG Recommendation

The OIG report recommended that the FDIC clarify and remind examiners of the supervisory expectations relative to documenting their review of a bank's appraisal program, including the need to include a positive assurance statement when examiners determine that appraisal practices are satisfactory. The FDIC concurs with these recommendations. In response, the FDIC has clarified its examination expectations relative to examiner review of valuations programs, reminded examiners of the requirement to include a positive assurance statement when appropriate, and compliance with this requirement will be monitored within the FDIC's existing internal review control process.

The OIG also recommended to the FDIC, OCC, and FRB that the agencies strengthen requirements for examiner documentation related to the review of appraisal programs. On February 19, 2013, the FDIC discussed with the OCC and the FRB its strategy to improve documentation by reminding examiners of existing guidance and to monitor compliance as part of our internal control function. The agencies agreed to continue to evaluate whether additional guidance on appraisal review documentation might be warranted going forward.

Supervisory guidance also requires examiners to assess the appropriateness of an institution's Allowance for Loan and Lease Losses (ALLL) within the framework of U.S. generally accepted accounting principles (GAAP). GAAP requires that the ALLL reflect losses which are "probable and estimable;" therefore, bank management must determine an appropriate ALLL level that is supported by reasonable assumptions and objective data. Furthermore, GAAP requires that all credit losses associated with a loan be deducted from the allowance, and that the loss portion of the loan balance be charged off in the period in which the loan is deemed uncollectible. If the ALLL is found to be insufficient during an FDIC examination, we may recommend that management increase the allowance or improve its ALLL calculation methodology to ensure that financial reporting is accurate under GAAP.

The OIG made no recommendations with respect to how examiners follow examination procedures in evaluating an institution's ALLL.

Issue 4 -- Capital

Examiners assess an institution's capital adequacy by considering a number of factors, including: the institution's financial condition; the nature, trend, and volume of problem assets, the adequacy of ALLL; earnings and dividends; management's access to additional capital; prospects and the plans for growth, and past experience in managing growth; access to capital markets and other sources of capital; balance sheet composition and risks associated with nontraditional activities; and risk exposure associated with off-balance-sheet activities.

During the crisis, examiners evaluated capital adequacy in accordance with the criteria outlined in the Uniform Financial Institution Ratings System (UFIRS) and applicable standards under the provisions of Prompt Corrective Action. When an institution was successful in raising external capital, examiners incorporated those capital raises into the analysis of capital adequacy and the overall rating of the institution.

OIG Recommendation

The OIG review made no recommendations with respect to the capital issues identified in the statute.

Issue 5 -- Loan Workouts

During the crisis, diminished cash flows associated with commercial properties contributed to sharp declines in real estate prices and made it difficult for many borrowers to make their payments. In such situations, prudent workout arrangements are often in the best interest of the financial institution and the borrower. In response, the FDIC, working with the other Federal financial institution regulators, issued guidance encouraging lenders to work with borrowers experiencing financial difficulty repaying their real estate loans.[6] The guidance states that renewed or restructured loans to borrowers who have the ability to repay their debts according to reasonable, modified terms will not be subject to adverse classification solely because the value of the underlying collateral has fallen below the loan balance. Financial institutions that implement prudent commercial real estate loan workout arrangements after performing a comprehensive review of a borrower's financial condition are not subject to criticism for engaging in these efforts even if the restructured loans have weaknesses that result in adverse credit classification.

OIG Recommendation

While the OIG determined that examiners had successfully implemented three of the four elements of the interagency guidance – those related to loan-specific workout arrangements, classification of loans, and regulatory reporting and accounting considerations -- the review did note a lack of documentation that examiners had reviewed the institution's implementation of the risk management requirements in cases where no exceptions were noted. The OIG recommended that the FDIC remind examiners of documentation requirements related to the review of loan workout programs.

The FDIC concurs with the OIG recommendations. On February 27, 2013, the FDIC reminded risk management examiners of its examination expectations relative to their review of the risk management elements of loan workout programs at supervised institutions.

Issue 6 -- Supervisory Orders

To promote uniformity of practice and to ensure that banks most in need of corrective action receive the appropriate supervisory attention, the FDIC has adopted a policy that presumes that banks with composite UFIRs ratings of 3, 4, or 5 will be the subject of either a formal or informal enforcement action unless there are specific circumstances that would excuse the institutions from such an action.[7] By definition, banks with composite ratings of 4 or 5 have significant problems that warrant formal action, and banks rated composite 3 have weaknesses that, if not corrected, could worsen to a more severe situation. Accordingly, FDIC policy indicates that at least an informal action, such as a memorandum of understanding, be taken against composite 3 rated institutions.

OIG Recommendation

The OIG determined that the FDIC, OCC, and FRB are each following their respective agency's policy with respect to issuing enforcement actions, but noted that those policies differ somewhat across the agencies. Accordingly, the OIG recommended that the agencies study these differences to determine whether there are certain approaches that have been more successful. The FDIC agrees with this recommendation, and is currently undertaking an internal review of enforcement action trends. We will share the results with the other agencies as part of a joint project to review the effectiveness of enforcement actions the agencies agreed to launch under the Task Force on Supervision, a group of senior supervision officials under the Federal Financial Institutions Examination Council.

The OIG also reviewed whether enforcement actions may have limited credit availability and determined that some enforcement order provisions may have indirectly limited lending. However, the OIG also found that there were important safety and soundness reasons for those provisions and that other factors – such as the weakness in the economy, competition, and a lack of loan demand – impacted lending more. Similarly, the review of whether orders affected the ability to raise capital showed that a bank's ability to raise capital is related more to its condition, earnings, asset quality, and growth prospects than the existence of an enforcement order.

Issue 7 -- Impact of FDIC Policies on Investment

Through various statutes, rules, and policies, and in order to protect the Deposit Insurance Fund, the FDIC is required to consider a number of factors when evaluating applications for entry into banking or expansion of banking activities. The FDIC approved the majority of applications and notices over the review period. In cases where applications were not approved, the FDIC documented its concerns about various aspects of the proposals.

OIG Recommendation

The OIG did not identify instances of the FDIC "steering" potential investors away from failing banks, and made no recommendations for the FDIC with respect to its treatment of potential bank investors.

Issue 8 -- Private Capital Investors

As the financial crisis intensified, the number of problem and failing banks rose rapidly, and these institutions found it increasingly difficult to attract external capital. At the same time, the FDIC found it increasingly difficult to attract bidders to acquire failed institutions. In August 2009, the FDIC Board of Directors adopted the *Final Statement of Policy on*

Qualifications for Failed Bank Acquisitions, a policy statement providing guidance to private capital investors wishing to invest in bank holding companies or insured depository institutions formed for the purpose of acquiring failed institutions.[8] Among other things, the policy requires higher levels of capital – namely, a commitment of Tier 1 common equity to total assets of at least 10 percent for a period of 3 years from the time of acquisition of a failed institution – as well as a commitment for cross-support on the part of institutions making multiple acquisitions, limits on affiliate transactions, and prohibitions on complex, functionally opaque ownership structures.

Overall, private capital investors subject to the statement of policy have played a positive, but relatively small, part in the resolution of failed institutions. As of the date of the OIG's review, a total of 13 private capital investor groups had purchased 36 failed institutions. The FDIC's experience thus far indicates that private capital investors have complied with the statement of policy and have not presented significant supervisory issues.

OIG Recommendation

The OIG had no recommendations with respect to the private capital investment policy.

End Notes

[1] *FDIC Community Banking Study*, December 2012, http://www.fdic.gov/regulations/resources/ cbi/study.html

[2] The 3,238 U.S. counties in 2010 included 694 micropolitan counties centered on an urban core with population between 10,000 and 50,000 people, and 1,376 rural counties with populations less than 10,000 people.

[3] The FDIC has repeatedly communicated its expectations regarding the requirements and approval of portfolio note sales to the acquiring institutions in a variety of settings, including the Annual Risk Sharing Conference held in October 2012 and the Georgia Bankers Roundtable Conference held in November 2012. Formal guidance also was issued to all acquiring institutions in a letter dated October 9, 2012.

[4] See *Interagency Appraisal and Evaluation Guidelines*, December 2, 2010, at http://www. fdic.gov/news/ news/financial/2010/fil10082.html

[5] See Part 323 of the FDIC Rules and Regulations at http://www.fdic.gov/regulations/ laws/rules/2000-4300.html.

[6] See *Policy Statement on Prudent Commercial Real Estate Workouts*, October 2009, at http://www.fdic.gov/ news/news/financialand *Statement on Working with Mortgage Borrowers,* April 2007 at http://www.fdic.gov/news/news/press/2007/ pr07032a.html.

[7] See *FDIC Risk Management Manual of Examination* Policies at http://www.fdic.gov/ regulations/safety/manual/

[8] *Final Statement of Policy on Qualifications for Failed Bank Acquisitions* http://www.fdic. gov/news/board/ Aug26no2.pdf

INDEX

A

B

C

D

E

F

N

O

P

Q

R

Y